Praise for *Changing the Landscape of Eternity*

Whether you are a first-time discoverer of the massive concept of making disciples to fulfill the Great Commission of Jesus Christ, or a lifetime explorer of it, you are in for a challenging treat. It is evident on every page of this insightful book that author John Thompson has bent his energies vocationally to both emulate the model of Jesus and obey His main mandate, to turn people into disciples. Read this book as the author translates a lifetime of learning onto these pages which will be read by many.

HERB HODGES

FOUNDER AND DIRECTOR OF SPIRITUAL LIFE MINISTRIES, GERMANTOWN, TN

John Thompson has done a masterful job of bringing together both a theoretical approach of discipleship and practical application. *Changing the Landscape of Eternity* will help the follower of Jesus Christ gain a deeper understanding of the Great Commission, the discipleship process, and the practical how-tos of selecting a person to disciple. John writes in a manner that gives the reader the feel he is coaching and encouraging them as they disciple others. This book is a must read for anyone who is serious about living a life of irresistible influence and making an eternal impact.

RODNEY M. LARA

PASTOR OF JUDSON BAPTIST CHURCH, OAK PARK, IL

Changing *the* Landscape *of* Eternity

Changing *the* Landscape *of*
ETERNITY

TRANSFORMING
Believers *into* Disciples

John L. Thompson

Published by Deep River Books
Sisters, Oregon
www.deepriverbooks.com

ISBN-13: 9781940269177
ISBN-10: 1940269172

Library of Congress: 2014934976

Printed in the USA

Cover design by Joe Bailen, Contajus Designs

CONTENTS

PART 1
LAYING A FIRM FOUNDATION • 15

PART 2
BUILDING AN EFFECTIVE DISCIPLESHIP MINISTRY • 81

ACKNOWLEDGMENTS

I would like to dedicate this book to my faithful Lord who has guided me and helped me in immeasurable ways from conception to conclusion. He is indeed faithful.

Special thanks go to my loving wife Debbie who embraced our calling into the ministry and faithfully raised our four children to become disciples of Jesus Christ.

Great appreciation goes to Mrs. Dena Owens who tirelessly donated many hours providing editorial assistance. Her labor will always be greatly appreciated.

Also, I owe great thanks to Douglas Knoll for his many hours analyzing my manuscript and giving good advice as well as editorial assistance.

FOREWORD

John Thompson is one of those rare ministers who, thirty-three years ago, followed God out of the suburbs and into the city. With *Changing the Landscape of Eternity: Transforming Believers into Disciples*, John draws from his years of experience working both in small and medium towns as well as the inner city of Chicago, and provides a fresh and evidence-based look at how to fulfill the Great Commission through disciple making. Through his remarkable knowledge, skill, experience, and proven track record, John explains the Great Commission in a doctrinally sound yet accessible way. He explains what real disciple making looks like, and how it's done.

Like Aesop's fable of the Tortoise (disciple making) and the Hare (evangelism), evangelism only appears to be the "fast" way to grow a church and advance God's kingdom on earth. *Changing the Landscape of Eternity* revisits the Great Commission and addresses the key element that has too long been neglected. John points out that the misunderstanding of the Great Commission has led to the drop in membership and attendance, a lessening of spiritual depth and maturity, and the ineffectiveness of American churches positively to affect culture. John covers the requirements for being one who disciples others by carefully outlining what God requires of a disciple maker—perhaps the key to why we have more hares and fewer tortoises.

Recently I witnessed a deacon chairman, in his early fifties, stand before a church congregation. He explained that while he had prayed about the motion the deacons were recommending to the church, and while he thought it was a good idea, he could not say that God had spoken to him on the issue. He went on to say, "The truth is, I don't know how God speaks." The failure to make disciples is the key reason 4,000 churches close their doors in America every year. Churches cannot thrive when leaders have not become disciples and cannot hear God's voice.

Changing the Landscape of Eternity teaches the importance of early discipleship and explains how to overcome problems of disciple making. John details how to lead young converts to a deeper understanding of discipleship while avoiding the obstacles to growth. Believing that programs kill disciple making, John outlines a systematic and relational—and nonprogrammatic— approach. Along with the seven primary principles of disciple making, John shares seven requirements that are necessary for all who want to be disciples.

As you read this book, you'll find yourself evaluating your own relationship with Jesus. You'll come face-to-face with what Jesus requires to be a disciple and learn what's vital in selecting the small group of people you'll disciple. One highlight is John 's explanation of six fundamental qualities needed in those you do disciple. Using the acronym "FATHER" (or "MOTHER" for women) he helps the disciple maker consider fundamental qualities for selecting prospects to disciple.

Changing the Landscape of Eternity is a "must read every page" kind of book, presenting hard realities, frank truth, and challenges to churches that have neglected the command to equip "the saints for the work of service" (Eph. 4:12). As you read this book, you will begin to reevaluate your ministry focus—as well as the ministry of the church. More importantly, *Changing the Landscape of Eternity* will force you to decide if you're willing to be obedient in fulfilling the Great Commission as a disciple maker!

Dr. Eddie G. Grigg
President, New Life Theological Seminary
Charlotte, North Carolina

INTRODUCTION

Why another book on discipleship? Doesn't every evangelical church in the United States—or perhaps I should say, every church around the world—disciple people? And don't we already practice and understand the principles well enough to do a good job fulfilling the Great Commission? The answers to these questions are revealing and perhaps even shocking.

In his book *Growing True Disciples*, George Barna reports the results from a nationwide survey where they interviewed pastors, church leaders, and hundreds of people who regularly attend church services and programs. The respondents were asked to describe their goals in life. The findings of this survey, in which ninety percent described themselves as Christians and four out of ten claimed to be personally committed to Jesus Christ? "Not one of the adults we interviewed said that their goal in life was to be a committed follower of Jesus Christ or to make disciples."[1]

Church congregations around the world are struggling to maintain equilibrium. Attendance has either plateaued or is declining. Giving continues to decrease and the moral problems are an epidemic with no sign of improvement. As we observe the lives of Christians, it is impossible in many instances to distinguish the difference between them and non-believers in how they think and live. What happened to the Great Commission? Does discipleship really work?

Changing the Landscape of Eternity was written to challenge and direct church leaders who desire to create biblical renewal. With God's enablement, I believe this book will help you recapture the zeal and focus the early church had for disciple making. Even without the advantages of technology and a complete copy of God's Word, they "turned the world upside down" (Acts 17:6, ESV).

Barna also took his team and evaluated churches across America to determine how we're doing with the task of making disciples. Based on his findings, he asserts, "Almost every church in our country has some type of discipleship program or set of activities, but stunningly few churches have a church of disciples."[2] Indeed, we have gradually set our eyes on the wrong priorities and the wrong measuring rods. The average church leader concludes that we're doing OK if we can get people to attend our worship services so as to show growing numbers (in order to pay for our buildings and staff salaries), log statistics supporting reports of people being baptized and joining our church, and have an assortment of well-attended programs. But what are the objectives given to us in God's Word? If

Christ is the head of the church, what are his marching orders? I believe that the greatest command of our Lord has been misunderstood, misapplied, or simply ignored by most churches in this modern era.

I am afraid that many pastors and future church leaders will not read this book, in part because it is far easier to maintain the status quo. I believe the natural tendency is to think we're OK, and that all we need to do is to make a few improvements, keep forging ahead, and create better quality in our programs and presentations. However, Jesus commanded us to *make disciples*. My prayer is that this book challenges you to think about what we're really doing to achieve this great challenge and, moreover, to make changes in our structure, goals and procedures in order to accomplish this task.

What we have done in the last hundred years has not worked. If the disciples and the other leaders of the early church had followed our pattern and practices, the church would have ceased to exist by the end of the first century. We need to reinvent ourselves in light of God's Word. Through his grace, we can and must do better.

Part 1
LAYING A FIRM FOUNDATION

Most of us have observed new homes being constructed—and they always have a foundation. If they built the house with no foundation it wouldn't last long. But what if…? The carpenters frame the walls out of two-by-fours. They lay one down at the base of the wall and nail additional boards cut to the appropriate height, with each two-by-four placed every sixteen inches apart to complete the framing. They build the other exterior walls and nail them together. The carpenters and men of various construction skills continue building the ceiling, second floor, roof, and so forth until the house is completed with all its amenities. It may be a million-dollar home; with beautiful skylights, large bay windows, many rooms and a beautiful view. We would love a new home like that, even without a foundation—until the onslaught of a severe thunderstorm collapsed the house.

A foundation is even more critical when we consider something as important as God's plan for mankind, as mapped out by our master carpenter. If we don't take the time to lay the foundation, seeking to understand exactly what he intended, we will fail to finish the project. By the same token, if we lay the wrong kind of foundation, we will fail just as surely as if we'd overlooked the foundation in the first place.

We need to know what our master carpenter assigned us to do, and exactly how he intends for our execution of the plan. In order to understand this, we'll first take a historical view, to see if the former construction workers ever accomplished what the master carpenter instructed. We'll then analyze exactly what the master carpenter said and the cultural context for his command. Finally, we'll look at how his followers proceeded after he departed. Once we understand the plan, we'll evaluate our own lives to see what requirements Jesus placed before us, evaluating if we qualify for such a great construction project—and if needs be, to make the necessary changes.

Without a good understanding of these foundational principles we will not be able to persuade others to join our crew, and we ourselves will become discouraged and fail. This task is eternally important, and the ramifications are great. Let us therefore study carefully, and with God's help be able to proceed with the solid understanding and deep commitment that only a strong foundation can provide. To that, we dedicate the next five chapters.

Chapter 1

Calibrating Our Compass:
Bull's-eye—But Wrong Target

ONE OF THE BEST PISTOL MARKSMEN in the country was traveling from town to town, putting on exhibitions. For many years he heard of a sharpshooter who had become a legend because of his extraordinary skill, and had hoped that one day he would be able to meet this man he had heard so much about. One day he was passing through the small town where his hero lived. Everywhere he looked, he saw posters promoting this man's extraordinary skill. Each poster had a bull's-eye target with a hole exactly in the center.

The young man began to ask the townspeople where this great marksman lived. His home was not hard to locate; everyone knew exactly where he lived. Having followed the directions, the young marksman soon drove into his icon's driveway, walked up to the house, and knocked on the door. Almost immediately, an elderly man greeted him there and, after a brief introduction, the young man said, "All my life I have heard of you and your perfected skill: the man who never missed a perfect bull's-eye no matter how difficult the shot. How did you ever achieve such greatness?"

The old man looked at him with a twinkle in his eye and as he opened the door said, "Follow me." The old man took off across his yard with the screen door snapping behind him and proceeded to walk out behind the barn, where the young man saw a medium-sized target on the side of the building. In the center of the target was a bullet hole, a perfect bull's-eye. "That's what I was talking about," said the young man. After finding out that the old man fired over his shoulder while looking in a mirror he said, "How can you consistently maintain such perfection?"

"Well," the old man said. "It's really quite easy. First I shoot the bullet, and then I draw the circles."

We laugh, but isn't that what we sometimes do in Christian ministry? We shoot first and then decide what the target is. And sometimes we just blast a wide pattern of buckshot; that way we're sure to hit the target. Could it be that one reason the church is failing is because we do not know where the bull's-eye is?

Please think along with me as we consider God's purpose for this age, his plan for the church, and then his procedure for accomplishing his plan. As we "calibrate our compass," it will become clear that many have aimed at the wrong bull's-eye.

God's Purpose for This Age

There are some who quickly respond that God's purpose for this age is to *Christianize the world.* Proponents of this view may cite 2 Peter 3:9 where it says: "The Lord is…not wishing for any to perish but for all to come to repentance." Winning people to Christ is, of course, God's desire, but is it his purpose? Assuming we agree that God is sovereign and that he has never and will never fail in accomplishing his will, we can look at world statistics to see if God has in fact accomplished this purpose.

The history of the church is full of religion but the number of true believers in Jesus Christ is far below the total number of people classified as Christians. In 2005 it was believed that there were two billion adherents to Christianity.[1] This total equals about 30.83 percent of the world's population. It was also reported that eleven percent were evangelicals or Bible-believing Christians.[2] Kenneth Scott Latourette concluded that "the course of Christianity on the planet has only recently begun."[3]

Is God a failure? If God's purpose was to save the world we would have to conclude that He has been a miserable failure, because the vast majority of people in every generation have not become believers. In fact, millions in every age have never seen a Bible and have never heard the plan of salvation. Proverbs 19:21 says, "Many are the plans in a man's heart, but it is the LORD's purpose that prevails" (NIV). It is certain that God will never fail at what he has chosen to accomplish.

If it is not God's purpose to Christianize the world, what *is* God's purpose? There are many who believe that God's purpose is to *evangelize the world*, giving everyone in the world the gospel so that they have the opportunity to believe. Proponents of this view often cite Mark 16:15, in which Jesus says: "Go into all the world and preach the gospel to all creation."

It is true that God has told us to preach the gospel. But is it God's purpose in this age for the church to evangelize the world? Again, since God always accomplishes his purpose, simple research into history will indicate whether or not world evangelization has ever taken place.

Christianity had a great beginning, led by the apostles and their followers around AD 32. This period ended at AD 70 with the destruction of Jerusalem as the Roman General Titus and his soldiers marched into Jerusalem destroying the city and its temple. During this period there was a great expansion of Christianity.

From AD 70 to 313, there continued to be good progress. At the time of the alleged conversion of Constantine, in the beginning of the fourth century, the number of Christians may have reached ten to twelve million—about one-tenth of the total population of the Roman Empire, with some estimates being higher.[4] After 313, when Constantine signed the Edict of Milan, Christianity became legal. Nevertheless, the church accomplished very little after this period to achieve world evangelization.

From 476, when the city of Rome fell, to 1517, the year Martin Luther tacked the Ninety-five Theses on the castle church door in Wittenberg, we have 1,041 very dark years of church history. This period was marked with detestable acts endorsed and perpetuated by the Roman Catholic Church, including the Spanish Inquisition with its many martyrs. Moreover, the Catholic Church sold indulgences, or the selling of grace, so people could graduate out of purgatory sooner. Some were saved, but this period could not be called a time of widespread evangelization.

The year 1700 marked the beginning of the great missions movement, when Christianity slowly began taking hold. However, there has never been a period when world evangelization has taken place or a time when evangelism even came close to being worldwide. Because of the millions of people in every age who never heard the gospel, evangelization—though a necessary part of the process—cannot be God's purpose.

Evangelization of the World

AD 32 – AD 70 – a great beginning

AD 70 – AD 313 – continued progress

AD 476 – AD 1517 – weak evangelization

AD 1700 – Christianity began taking hold

We now consider what I do believe to be God's unwavering purpose for this age, as declared by Jesus in Matthew 16:18: "I will build My church; and the gates of Hades will not overpower it." There are five observations we can make as we analyze this statement:

- Christ is doing the building. Jesus says he will build his church. I am not building the church, I am simply a conduit or channel. Jesus is the builder.
- Second, the building was yet in the future from the moment he made the statement.
- Third, he is building his church. It is not my church; it is his church.
- Fourth, Hades itself (meaning death, perhaps even Jesus' death) will not stop the process.
- Fifth, God's plan, though not begun at the time Jesus spoke the words recorded in Matthew 16:18, is destined to succeed. God will never fail at what he determines to do. God's purpose will be achieved.

God's Plan for the Church

Since we have concluded that it is God's purpose to build his church, let us narrow the focus from *purpose* to *plan*. What is God's plan to accomplish this purpose?

Prior to Jesus' ascension, the disciples gathered on the Mount of Olives where Jesus gave his final instructions, the marching orders for the Church. These parting words form directives from Jesus known as the Great Commission.

In Matthew 28:19–20 Jesus said, "Go therefore and make disciples of all the nations, baptizing them in the name of the Father and the Son and the Holy Spirit, teaching them to observe all that I commanded you; and lo, I am with you always, even to the end of the age." (We will study this passage more thoroughly in chapter three, "The Great Commission Revisited.")

Without going into an exegetical study of this passage, suffice it to say that the command of the Great Commission is to make disciples. For much of our history, however, the church has responded wrongly to this command. Jesus didn't say, "Go therefore, and make church buildings" or "go therefore and make converts." He has commanded us to make *disciples*. Yet the church continues to miss the right target, in part by allocating its time and resources elsewhere.

As I will clarify more fully in the next chapter, I am not minimizing the importance of winning people to Christ. Making converts is part of the process. Likewise, I am not criticizing building churches, which is also part of the process. What I am saying, however, is that when our sole objectives are to win people to Christ and build more churches, we often end up with local churches full of immature believers. That was not Christ's purpose.

What Is Discipleship?

The Greek word for disciple (*mathaytás*) is the general word for a learner or follower, as in the sense of an apprentice, and "always implies the existence of a personal attachment which shapes the whole of life of the one described."[5] Many have emphasized the "learner" part, but as Michael Wilkins, author of *Following the Master: A Biblical Theology of Discipleship*, states, "To say that a disciple is a learner is true, but this overemphasizes one aspect of the term's meaning and misses what the term primarily signified in the New Testament era....Hence, in the Christian sense, a disciple of Jesus is one who has come to Him for eternal life, has claimed Him as Savior and God, and has embarked upon the life of following Him."[6] A disciple was much more than simply a "learner." Culturally, the disciple followed a mentor, who in turn had a profound relationship with his protégé. This relationship fed from the life example, good or bad, that the disciple maker provided.

The word "disciple" occurs 269 times in the New Testament. "Christian" is found three times and the term "believers" only twice. Given such repetition, we can agree with Dallas Willard that "The New Testament is a book about disciples, by disciples, and for disciples of Jesus Christ."[7] This discipleship process starts when a person becomes a believer in Jesus Christ. As a new believer, the young disciple begins his infant stage which Dawson Trotman, founder of the Navigators, referred to as "spiritual pediatrics." The babe in Christ is nurtured from that infant stage to a position of maturity as a follower and servant of his Master, Jesus Christ.

In a larger sense, any ministry that helps a believer grow spiritually is a part of one's lifelong process of discipleship. However, in this book I am seeking to focus on methods that have the deepest and most rapid spiritual impact. I believe these are the methods used by Jesus, his apostles, and other early church leaders.

It would be helpful at this point to establish a working definition of discipleship. Allen Hadidian, in his book *Successful Discipling*, says, "Discipling others is the process by which a Christian, with a life worth emulating, commits himself for an extended period of time to a few individuals who have been won to Christ, the purpose being to aid and guide their growth to maturity and equip them to reproduce themselves in a third spiritual generation."[8]

In the definition above, Hadidian suggests five ingredients of successful discipleship. First, the disciple maker must have a life worth emulating. Often people ask, what are the qualifications for one to be a disciple maker? Paul said in 1 Timothy 4:12, "Let no one look down on your youthfulness, but rather in speech, conduct, love, faith and purity, show yourself an example of those who believe" (see also 2 Thess. 3:9; Heb. 13:7). One of the primary requirements to be a discipler of other people is to have a life others can imitate—especially important today because of the general lack of Christian role models and godly father images in our society. Having a life worth imitating doesn't mean we are sinless, but that we are living a consistent Christian life. When we sin, we are quick to confess it to God and correct our offense with the one we offended. We should neither give the impression of perfection nor should anyone put us on a pedestal, but people should be able to follow our example.

Second, in discipleship we commit ourselves for an extended period of time. We live in a fast-food society, but with discipleship there are no short cuts. There are no crash courses because it is all about transformation, helping the person to grow spiritually. The length of time required to disciple another person depends on the person being discipled, on the spiritual maturity of the disciple, the severity of strongholds that need to be conquered, and the level of commitment and motivation. Most people I have discipled, following the qualifications recorded in chapter six, require about a year and a half of weekly ministry.

Third, for most effective life-on-life discipleship we need to commit ourselves to a few individuals. The temptation is to turn our discipleship into a class, thereby ministering to a larger group. Investing our lives in a few people for life-on-life discipleship seems risky. But as a result, our discipleship deteriorates as we expand the recipients to a larger group, and it continues to deteriorate as class size grows. I am not implying that God can't and won't use us as we teach a group of people, but to have maximum impact in the lives of the individuals we're discipling, it is important that we limit it to a few people. Following this model expands the impact of our relationship on people, making it possible for them to more clearly observe our example. Thus, we are better able to hold a given protégé accountable, as well as provide opportunities to counsel, reproof, and correct our disciple in a far more effective way.

Fourth, the purpose is to guide the disciple to maturity. The mistake many make in an attempt to disciple people is to conduct a short series or study. To repeat what I said before: It takes time to grow. With discipleship, we commit ourselves to helping the person grow to a significant level of maturity, and that is laborious and time-consuming.

Finally, in discipleship we equip disciples to reproduce themselves into a third spiritual generation. Without reproduction, a species will cease to exist; so it is with spiritual reproduction. Fortunately, reproduction has never ceased, otherwise Christianity would have long ago gone out of existence. But imagine if the church would embark on a ministry of discipleship with every new believer who desired to grow. What if we were to help the hungry babe in Christ in the way described above, until that disciple reproduced himself by making another disciple? Imagine the multiplication of mature believers the world would see if this took place. What a revolutionary impact salt and light would have upon society.

To more fully understand discipleship, we need to recognize the difference between discipleship and mentoring. Both mentoring and discipleship seek to impart wisdom to another and unleash the best in that person. However, if we compare mentoring with discipleship, we'll see that we are operating by two different emphases. Discipleship deals especially with helping a person grow to a level of spiritual maturity; it is rooted in biblical wisdom. Mentoring may or may not be so rooted, as it tends to have more to do with skill development. It may be practiced in order to help another believer grow in a specific area of need. For example, one may mentor a person into an occupation or a position. We may mentor a person to be a good father or husband. After I have finished formal discipleship with a person, I often continue with a disciple for a while, mentoring him to be a disciple maker. There is certainly some overlap between discipling and mentoring; however, if spiritual maturity is desired, I am convinced that concentrated disciple making is the best emphasis.

I believe there are three types of disciple making, based on the methods used by Christ and the apostles that may be practiced: remote discipleship, discipleship through small groups, and life-on-life (usually one-on-one) discipleship.

Remote Discipleship. Many may be surprised that I suggest discipleship by correspondence or phone. For sure, this method would be the least effective. However, I believe that when it is used properly, it could nevertheless be a useful form of discipleship. Just as when we share the gospel with another person, the most effective approach in remote discipleship is the method that is the most personal. For example, a personal letter would usually be more effective than a form letter. A phone call may be more effective than a personal letter, and a face-to-face witness would usually be more effective than a phone call. Today, we can send a letter through the postal system in a few days—or better yet, instantly by email or social media. When we lead someone to Christ who does not live a comfortable distance from our home, most of us assume that God, somehow, has let us off the hook and has absolved us of our responsibility. I don't agree with this conclusion.

Remote discipleship was used throughout the New Testament. According to

Herb Hodges, author of an excellent book on discipleship called *Fox Fever,* "77.7 percent of the volume of the New Testament is comprised of personal letters. And every letter recorded in the New Testament conspicuously demonstrates a disciple-making motive.... *Of the twenty-seven books of the New Testament, twenty-one of them are personal letters!* Furthermore, two others bear some resemblance to personal letters and both Luke and Acts were written by one man, a Gentile medical doctor named Luke, and to one man, a Gentile man (apparently a man of rank) named Theophilus."[9] The apostle Paul wrote his letters to encourage and instruct young believers. He wrote two letters to Timothy, a young pastor who he had personally discipled, and those two letters were a continuation of that discipleship process.

In many circumstances, remote discipleship is the *only* way to disciple people. Take, for example. people living far away and often forgotten, such as those in prison, in the military, or away at college. They would benefit greatly by remote discipleship. At the writing of this book it is even possible to disciple a person remotely by phone and computer imagery with programs like Skype, Google Talk, or iPhone FaceTime. With these cell phone and Internet-aided programs, you can talk to and see the person in real time and even transfer documents, videos, and PowerPoint presentations.

One of the men I discipled had the opportunity to disciple his mother and sister-in-law, who he had led to Christ, by using remote discipleship. He understood the principle that as a spiritual father he carried personal responsibility to help them grow and, at the very least, become grounded in the Christian faith. Since he lived several hundred miles away, he challenged them both to enter into a discipleship relationship with him on Saturday mornings over the telephone. He mailed them lesson material for new believers, and they agreed to complete one lesson each week. On Saturday morning, he would call his mother long distance and for about an hour lead a discussion about the basic growth concepts over the phone. He then hung up and called his sister-in-law, and spent another hour with her. He continued this for thirteen weeks, guiding them through the material. One day he shared his joy that his sister-in-law was serving as a leader in Vacation Bible School. She was excited to share that she was memorizing the Scripture verses right along with the children.

But you say, isn't remote discipleship time-consuming? I would answer: *Of course it is!* Isn't it expensive? Again, I would say that there can be some expense involved in remote discipleship. It is not convenient or easy to be a disciple of Jesus Christ, but with privilege comes responsibility. My friend, who did not have free long distance on his phone, was struggling to pay his way through college but he found a way. Can't we trust God with our financial burdens?

I'm afraid the real deterrent, more likely, comes down to priority and commitment. Many followers of Christ who are willing may find themselves positioned by God to have an impact in the lives of people like this. We must not consider lightly such a great opportunity.

Small-group Discipleship. This second type of discipleship was one of the methods Jesus used. Imagine having only a brief time to live with the mission of providing salvation for all mankind, turning the world upside down. The millions who never hear the truth would go into eternity without God. What method would you use? To bring men to a consistent and relatively mature spiritual level, Christ chose to disciple through a small group and by life-on-life discipleship, living with his twelve disciples. We will cover the disciple-making small group more fully in chapter 12 and the smaller groups of three or four in chapter 7.

Life-on-life Discipleship. The third and most effective form of discipleship is the one-on-one or life-on-life approach. The great advantage to this type of discipleship is the impact a relationship can have in helping a person experience transformation in their Christian life. The personal example of the discipler in this relationship becomes a major factor, along with the natural accountability. This approach enables the disciple maker to have an in-depth knowledge of where the disciple is in his growth, which leads to biblical counseling, exhorting, rebuking, correcting, teaching, and guiding. This highly personal form of discipleship enables the leader to pace the process congruent to the needs of the disciple.

To further understand what is meant by disciple making, let me make five additional observations. First, I do not do the discipling; the Holy Spirit is the discipler, using me as a channel and a living example.

Second, they are not *my* disciples; they are being discipled to follow Jesus Christ.

Third, discipleship is a team ministry. Many people will be involved in the process: the pastor of the church, the disciple maker, his Sunday Bible study teacher, etc. God will use each of these people as part of the discipleship process. A wise disciple maker will use the available people and resources to best accomplish the purpose.

Fourth, one person must assume the responsibility. Here is where we have failed through the centuries. If no one assumes the responsibility, we have immediately degenerated to a traditional model of just inviting new converts to our programs. A primary person with whom there can be a significant relationship, along with an accountability structure, must be central to all effective discipleship.

Finally, discipleship is a command, not an option; discipleship is our Great Commission.

Now that we have outlined God's *purpose* for this age, *to build his Church*, and God's *plan* for the church, to *make disciples,* let's look at chapter two, where we will talk about God's *procedure* to accomplish his plan.

Review Questions

1. How involved are you in discipleship currently, either as a disciple or as a discipler (or both)?
2. How have you seen churches or ministries aim at "the wrong targets"? How have these efforts failed to hit the true targets of building God's church and making disciples?
3. How is discipleship more than just "learning"? What else is involved?
4. Review Allen Hadidian's definition of discipling other people. Which of these elements listed are you most comfortable with? Which make you most uncomfortable? In both cases, why?
5. What are the three types of discipleship listed by the author? How can you get more involved with each of these? Come up with examples for each.

Chapter 2

Turn the World Upside-Down: Great Impact Multiplied

THE STORY OF THE FIRST-CENTURY CHURCH is the miracle of how a totally ill-equipped church (by our standards) "turned the world upside down" (Acts 17:6, ESV). They had no television, Internet, computer, cell phone, air or ground transportation faster than walking. They had no printing capabilities, no loud speaker, and none of the Bible-research tools we depend on so heavily as we prepare sermons and lessons. They didn't even have much, if any, of the New Testament available for their use. Why then was their influence so dynamic and so revolutionary? In two thousand years the church has never come close to matching their impact. Simply put, they won people to Christ and discipled them from a committed heart and the power of the Holy Spirit.

In the last chapter we calibrated our compass by adjusting our direction; we discussed God's purpose for this age and God's plan for accomplishing his purpose. Now in this chapter, as we explore the reason for the great success of the early church, let us consider the procedure God wants us to follow.

God's Procedure for Accomplishing His Plan

There is a modern fable in which a father told his two sons that he had a gift for each. To one, he would give a dollar each week for fifty-two weeks. To the other son, his first week's gift would be just a penny, but each week he would double the total amount. The older son quickly chose the dollar a week, because in one year he would have fifty-two dollars. The younger son, having to yield to the older, reluctantly accepted the leftover option. Of course, as the chart below shows, the son receiving the pennies, multiplying each week, passed the older son's dollar-a-week pace after twelve weeks. By the fifty-second week, the younger son had $22,517,998,136,852.50 (more than 22½ trillion dollars). Simple multiplication, as described, begins very slowly but has tremendous exponential power.

Comparing Addition with Multiplication		
Week	Add	Multiply by Two
1	$1.00	$ 0.01
2	2.00	0.02
3	3.00	0.04
4	4.00	0.08
5	5.00	0.16
6	6.00	0.32
7	7.00	0.64
8	8.00	1.28
9	9.00	2.56
10	10.00	5.12
20	20.00	5,242.88
30	30.00	5,368,709.12
40	40.00	5,497,558,138.88
50	50.00	5,629,499,534,213.12
51	51.00	11,258,999,068,426.20
52	$ 52.00	$22,517,998,136,852.50

God's *procedure* to accomplish his *plan* works through the principle of multiplication. Multiplication is a fundamental principle of life. In Genesis 1:28, God said to Adam and Eve, "Be fruitful and multiply, and fill the earth." If God had used the addition method, the population of the earth would have only included Adam, Eve and their children.

The method God uses in the reproduction process of all life is multiplication. The embryo, once fertilized, begins multiplying by two, beginning very slowly and gradually accelerating to an explosive degree. Even after four or five months of pregnancy, a mother shows little visible growth; however, in the last few months of pregnancy one can see major changes because of the unparalleled growth of the child.

We also see multiplication in cancer. It starts out slow but grows by multiplication. One of the reasons that many forms of the disease have been so devastating is because it is discovered after the cancer growth has become exponential and often in the later stages of development.

Multiplication is also God's method of spiritual reproduction, as seen in God's Word. The supreme example is the life of Jesus who came to earth to provide redemption for mankind. He only had three years of ministry available to begin a movement, recruit, and disciple and train his followers through whom he would change the course of history. Jesus chose a multiplication method beginning with twelve men into whom he poured His life. They had the mission to not only win others to Christ (addition) but to make disciples in every nation (multiplication,

Matt. 28:19–20). Jesus clearly desired his disciples to multiply. He not only prayed for his disciples, but in John 17:20–26, he prayed for those his disciples would reach.

By the sixth chapter of Acts, addition changed to multiplication as "the word of God increased; and the number of the disciples multiplied in Jerusalem greatly" (Acts 6:7). One of the followers of Christ we read about in Acts is Philip, who was directed to the Ethiopian eunuch. The eunuch believed in Christ and went back to Ethiopia (Acts 8:26–39). According to tradition, the entire nation and the surrounding country were won to Christ.

Note the four generations of multiplication in the diagram below:

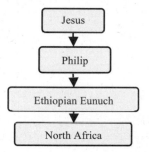

Through the life of Paul, Sylvanus, and Timothy we see their example in reaching the Thessalonians who in turn reached people in Macedonia and Achaia (Acts 16:9-12; 19:22; 20:1,2; Rom. 15:26; 1 Thess. 1:1). Paul told Timothy, "The things which you have heard from me in the presence of many witnesses, entrust these to faithful men who will be able to teach others also" (2 Tim 2:2). In the next two graphics, we see the ministry of Jesus through Paul multiplied to five generations:

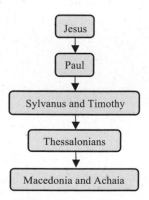

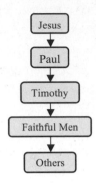

Extending from a few hundred believers, within three decades the Christian community had multiplied four-hundredfold—an annual increase of twenty-two percent. As stated earlier, by the beginning of the fourth century the number of disciples may have reached ten or twelve million.[1] This kind of growth doesn't come by just adding new converts or transfer of membership from one church to another; it comes by multiplication. After the beginning of the fourth century, however, discipleship multiplication as described above was seldom emphasized.

However, centuries later, there would be two men living at the same time in history who had a great impact for God, though they used very different methods. These two contemporaries, George Whitefield and John Wesley, were both men whom God used to awaken revival and touch two continents in the eighteenth century.

Near the end of his life, Whitefield compared his ministry with Wesley's and confessed, "my brother Wesley acted wisely. The souls that were awakened under his ministry he joined in class [small groups], and thus preserved the fruits of his labors. This I neglected, and my people are a rope of sand."[2] Whitefield's ministry spawned many thousands of converts to Christ, but in terms of lasting impact he saw little fruit. His converts were like a "rope of sand" because he didn't make disciples. Wesley, on the other hand, left behind a movement with such increasing momentum that the generations after his death saw more disciples and churches planted than he saw during his life.

Why was John Wesley so successful? He was successful because he set up a system of methods (eventually known as Methodism) allowing ordinary people to do extraordinary things—a system of discipleship.

In Wesley's system small groups of four to six people met weekly. The members had to have a high commitment to the group, which included strong accountability. His system had three types of groups: one for seekers called

Classes, a second designed for Christian growth he called Bands, and a third group called Select Societies designed for personal holiness and discipleship among leaders. It's easy to see why Methodism grew far beyond its founder's life and continues to exist today.

Imagine for a moment we had two modern-day disciples of Christ who developed their own strategies. The first man, having a great passion for the lost, decided that with God's help he would win 1,000 people to Christ each and every day. The second man decided, with God's help, that he would win one person to Christ, but he wouldn't stop there—he would spend a year discipling that person as a follower of Jesus Christ. He would so ingrain in his protégé the importance of discipleship that after one year had passed he and his disciple would split off and they *both* would win one person to Christ and, in turn, disciple that person for one year.

What would happen if both men continued this process? On the chart below we can see the multiplication principle worked out comparing evangelism (addition) and discipleship (multiplication by two):

Comparison of Evangelism by Addition and Discipleship by Multiplication		
Years	Evangelist	Discipler
1	365,000	2
2	730,000	4
10	3,650,000	1,024
17	6,205,000	131,072
23	8,395,000	8,388,608
26	9,490,000	67,108,864
30	10,950,000	1,073,741,824
33	12,045,000	8,589,934,592
184	67,160,000	

By the end of the first year the evangelist would have won 365,000 people to Christ; the disciple maker would have won and discipled only one person (a total of two including himself). It would take more than twenty-three years for the disciple maker to catch up with the evangelist.

But then, notice the exponential growth. To reach the world for Christ, with seven billion people, it would take the evangelist, with an addition approach,

19,178 years, assuming no one was born and no one died. The disciple maker, using a discipleship multiplication model, would not only reach the world for Christ but disciple the world of seven billion people in less than thirty-three years. Of course, everybody will not receive Christ, but the impact on the world would be so much greater following a discipleship multiplication strategy. Jesus Christ and the disciples used a discipleship multiplication strategy and it "turned the world upside down." We are to follow their example.

> **Reaching the World of Seven Billion by Addition Compared to Multiplication**
> One person winning 1,000 people each day (addition) would take 19,178 years.
>
> One person winning and discipling another person for one year, with each discipled person thereafter continuing the process, would take less than 33 years to disciple the entire world.

Walter Henrichson said, "The reason that the Church of Jesus Christ finds it so difficult to stay on top of the Great Commission is that the population of the world is multiplying while the church is merely adding. Addition can never keep pace with multiplication."[3] Imagine what God would do through you if you were to prioritize your time so that you were continually leading people to Christ and discipling them, continuing this through your entire life. Imagine if each qualified church member were doing the same. What a great impact we would have on our city and our world for Christ!

Why Does Multiplication Often Fail in the Modern Church?

Obviously, we will not have a church that produces disciples who continually multiply if we're not adequately making disciples in the first place. The church has failed to produce mature disciples and to promote life-on-life discipleship as the premier ministry of the church. This is foundational. If the church doesn't improve in this area, we will never see effective disciple making—and of course, little multiplication. The reason the church is failing to make disciples is multi-faceted; I will address this more fully in the final chapter of this book. But to discuss it briefly here: What are some of the reasons disciples often fail to multiply?

First, multiplication fails because the church does not instill within new disciples personal ownership for continuing the disciple making ministry. Multiplication must be taught and encouraged all through the discipleship process. The disciple must know that it is his responsibility to be a participant. The Great Commission is *his* commission.

Second, multiplication is stifled because no one in the church effectively trains and guides the prospective disciple maker as he learns to disciple another person. It is very daunting for most new disciple makers to consider carrying the responsibility of directing the discipleship process for another person. Once the mature disciple has completed his discipleship process, the experienced disciple maker should begin mentoring his disciple as he in turn begins to disciple his first protégé. This mentoring isn't as time-intensive as disciple making but is nonetheless vital for the new discipler. The mentor must help the disciple in the selection process, praying with him and guiding him to select the right person. Starting out with a poor selection may discourage the new disciple maker from continuing.

Third, effective multiplication has failed because prayer is not held up as the most vital ingredient. Most churches do not encourage prayer for life-on-life discipleship simply because they do not understand its importance. Since it is difficult for the new believer to select the right person to disciple, the importance of prayer for their selection is obvious. Remind your new disciple maker that Jesus earnestly prayed before he selected the twelve disciples and encourage him to do the same.

Fourth, multiplication has failed because few churches assist future disciple makers in finding prospects. Since many disciplers find selection difficult, it is helpful for the church to keep a prospect list. However, the disciple maker should not overlook any opportunity of leading a person to Christ who he could, in turn, disciple.

Fifth, multiplication has failed because most churches do not have anyone directing an effective disciple-making ministry. When possible, this person should be a full time member of the church staff, with a passion and experience in discipling people life-on-life. This person should continually set the example by his own discipleship ministry, provide training for those who are interested in this ministry, assist people searching for someone to disciple, and promote expansion and multiplication of the process.

Sixth, the multiplication process has failed in the modern church because multiplication is not nurtured. There are a number of things one can do to encourage multiplication of disciplers, including the following:

1. Never allow the discipleship ministry to become a program. It is all about relationships.
2. It is helpful to organize periodic meetings to rally disciple makers together, so they can share with each other and receive motivation and instruction.
3. Emphasize that once a person has completed the discipleship process, the disciple maker should mentor the disciple through his first cycle as a disciple maker. Much of this input and prayer can be conducted over the phone if face-to-face opportunities are limited.
4. Often disciple-making ministries publish quarterly newsletters and hold rallies. Either method may include testimonies of success, continued training, and inspiration.
5. The director, or pastor of discipleship, should never give up. There will be many failures along the way but he should keep sounding the drum of multiplication. Satan will try to discourage, but God will bless the leader's efforts.

I have a dream that someday in eternity there will be a great family tree of people that were discipled because God used me. They didn't all become disciples of Christ through me directly; in fact, there will be many I won't even know. Most will be the spiritual descendants of those whom God used me to impact. What a blessing it will be to see the numbers standing there and to know that they are the fruit of my labors—and of my fellow laborers. This is the personal life vision God has given me, and it is my prayer that God will challenge you in the same way he has challenged me.

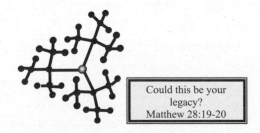

Could this be your legacy?
Matthew 28:19-20

God's *Purpose* for this age is to *build his church*.
God's *Plan* for the church is to *make disciples*.
God's *Procedure* to accomplish His plan is *multiplication*.

Review Questions

1. What's your reaction to the idea that God's procedure is multiplication, rather than addition? How does it differ from what you've experienced as a Christian—or, when have you seen this done successfully?

2. How does the fact that multiplication is a long-term process—that it may be years before you truly see significant "numbers"—affect your response to the idea?

3. How willing are you to make the kind of long-term commitment to one person, then another person, then another, the author describes here? Explain.

4. What did John Wesley do to more effectively achieve multiplication in his ministry? What examples of this do you see in the church today? What examples don't you see—and which therefore might offer some critical ministry opportunities?

5. Review the section "Why Does Multiplication Often Fail in the Modern Church?" Which of the six reasons here resonate most with you? What can you do, in your current situation, to address it (or them)?

THE CONTEXT OF BIBLICAL DISCIPLESHIP: HOW DISCIPLESHIP WAS VIEWED IN THE FIRST CENTURY

IT WAS JUNE 18, 1815 AT THE BATTLE OF WATERLOO, in present day Belgium. The French, under the command of Napoleon, were fighting the Allies (British, Dutch, and Germans) who had the Duke of Wellington at command. The people of England depended on a system of semaphore signals—a type of Morse code, using flags or lights—to find out how the battle was going. One of these signal stations was on the tower of Winchester Cathedral. Late in the day it flashed the signal: "W-E-L-L-I-N-G-T-O-N——D-E-F-E-A-T-E-D-." Just at that moment, a fog cloud suddenly made it impossible for onlookers to read the message. The news of defeat quickly spread throughout the city, and soon the entire population was sad and gloomy, believing that their country had lost the war.

And yet, as suddenly as the fog came, it lifted and the remainder of the message could be read. The complete message had four words, not two, and said: "W-E-L-L-I-N-G-T-O-N——D-E-F-E-A-T-E-D——T-H-E——E-N-E-M-Y!"

It took only a few minutes for the good news to spread. Sorrow turned into joy, and defeat into victory![1]

Most people can relate to this story because we've been misquoted or had our words, whether verbal or written, taken so far out of context that the original statement was misunderstood. Likewise, we can be like the English in the above illustration, not understanding the whole story. Indeed, a written message's context is important if we are to understand its actual meaning.

There is also a cultural context behind written literature. The original biblical text written in Hebrew, Aramaic, and Greek, though totally accurate, is often insufficient for readers of other cultures who seek to understand what the writer meant. To be sure, beyond the meaning of the words themselves, the way discipleship was practiced before, during, and after the time of Christ gives strong evidence to what was in the minds and practices of the disciple makers and of the people being discipled. In short, Scripture must be interpreted in light of its cultural context.

In this chapter we will explore how some of this cultural reality has been clouded by our lack of cultural understanding and buried behind word meanings. We will particularly explore the method of discipleship before and during the New Testament period, in order to see how it was practiced by Christ and the early church.

Long before the New Testament truths were even spoken, the art of discipleship was practiced in Hebrew homes. Parents did not go off to work and leave their children with others to educate and care for them. Instead, fathers took their sons with them to the field or to the family trade, where they mentored and discipled them throughout the day. Daughters likewise worked side by side with their mothers as well. Today, however, the average parent spends little time with his or her children, thereby eliminating opportunities for relational discipleship. We must never undervalue the influence of good example and quality training that devoted godly parents can provide. This was true in Old Testament Hebrew history, and also it is true today. Parents back then didn't organize seminars on character development; they obeyed God's command to teach the precepts of the law through rote memorization along with good child-rearing practices, all of which were supported by close relationships between parent and children (Deut. 6:6–9).

Discipleship in the Hebrew Culture

A thorough study of Scripture, as well as a study of Hebrew culture, unquestionably supports the fact that discipleship was practiced in the Old Testament era. The Hebrew equivalents to the word "disciple," *talmîdh* and *limmûdh*, are rarely found in Scripture; however, other words point to abundant examples of discipleship and, according to Michael Wilkins, "The association between these individuals is a discipleship relationship."[2] Below are just a couple of examples.

Moses and Joshua. Moses spent many years discipling Joshua. When he went up the mountain to meet with God he took Joshua, who was in training and would learn much from the experience while at the same time serve as Moses' aid (Ex. 24:13). From that time until the death of Moses, Joshua served at his side. Joshua became a great leader but he learned it from Moses, primarily by observation and practice. To be a disciple of Moses meant following and obeying the God of Moses and his revelation. Joshua watched as Moses, the man of faith, experienced great and wondrous things from the hand of God. Not only did he watch as God gave Moses great victories but he also watched as Moses failed. Yes, he was there when Moses struck the rock but he was also there as Moses cried out to God for mercy on the Israelites. During these years Joshua became the administrator and learned how to manage up to three million people by the time we total a conservative estimate of men of war (Num. 1:45–46), women, and children. These events must have been great faith-growing experiences, as God daily fed and provided water in the desert for forty years. During those wilderness years Joshua practiced faithfulness and loyalty, even in the face of pressure from Miriam and Aaron in their rebellion when the people demanded meat rather than manna. Joshua's loyalty was also tested when conflicts arose over Moses' new wife. And when all but one other spy warned against going into the Promised Land, Joshua—along with Caleb—remained faithful. Through these years he became a man of faith and courage, with godly character. Finally, the day came when God chose Joshua to replace Moses because he was ready (Deut. 1:38, 31.1–30). Hence, we see that God used a discipling/mentoring relationship to prepare Joshua, thereby enabling him to become a great leader.

The Prophets. Several prophets in the Old Testament are referred to as having mentoring relationships with less experienced prophets. For example, the prophet Isaiah spoke of his ministry of discipleship when he referred to his "disciples" (Isa. 8:16). Samuel also had prophets (1 Sam 10:5), in fact, he is seen as exercising a mentoring authority over them (1 Sam. 19:20–24). This was not a school setting, but rather a "fellowship" of prophets who looked to Samuel as an authority. A similar type relationship is found with the "sons of the prophets" with Elisha as leader (cf. 1 Kings 20:35; 2 Kings 2:3, 5, 7, 15; 4:1, 38; 5:22; 6:1; 9:1). As with Samuel's group, this is not a school setting: it is a master-discipler relationship in mutual commitment of service to God.[3] Finally, we must not forget Elijah, who mentored Elisha for about ten years, preparing him for succession as the lead prophet after he was gone.

Discipleship in the Greco-Roman World

Greece is the birth place of Western civilization and had a profound influence on many aspects of our culture. Discipleship permeated Greek life. We can find the concept of discipleship among each of the great masters of the period who were born from 469–384 BC—Socrates discipling Plato, who in turn discipled Aristotle. Moreover, the first recorded use of the word *mathētēs*, translated "disciple" in English, was by the historian Herodotus in the fifth century BC. He used the word in his writings in a casual way, which indicates that it was in common use at that time.[4] However, Herodotus did not use the word as simply meaning a learner or pupil in an academic setting. He used the word to indicate a person who made a significant and personal life commitment.

As Michael Wilkins has said, "These and other Greek philosophers generally understood that the disciple's life involved apprenticeship, a relationship of submission, and a life of demanding training."[5] A significant and consistent aspect of the use of the word *mathētēs* is that these students in the Greco-Roman World had a serious commitment to their master and his ways. As we look at the Hellenistic period (323–31 BC), we observe that one of the significant characteristics of discipleship had to do with the disciple's imitation of the conduct of his human master. In fact, the master-disciple relationship moved away from "learning" to be characterized more by imitation and conduct. This is also true up through the time of Christ.[6]

Discipleship During the First Century

The historical development of the word *mathētēs* is important because it helps us understand how the word was understood and applied by the culture preceding and during the time of Christ. During this period the pupils in an academic setting continued to be designated *mathētai*—disciples or adherents of their master. The type of relationship was determined by the master with the prominent view being that the person was a committed follower, a "disciple" of a great master or religious figure. This relationship changed the disciple's entire life, and he was known to a large part by the character he developed following the master.

The leaders of the various subgroups in Judaism during the first century had their own followers. For example, the Jewish leaders, according to Josephus and referred to by Matthew and Mark (Matt. 22:15–16; Mark 2:18), mentions the "disciples (*mathētai*) of the Pharisees."[7] Josephus also claimed that another group that appeared during the time of Jesus was the prophetic type.[8] The New Testament focuses on this type of leader, giving special attention to the activity of the forerunner and prophet John the Baptist, and his disciples (Matt. 9:14; 11:2–3; 14:12; Mark 2:18; 6:29). These disciples had considerable commitment, and practiced piety and righteousness toward God like their master. Some even continued as his disciples for years after his death.

Another subgroup were the members of the Qumran community, the group responsible for creating the Dead Sea Scrolls. This group also practiced strong discipleship in their organizational and social structure that could be described as disciple-master relationships.[9]

As we follow Jesus' command to make disciples as recorded in the Great Commission (Matt. 28:19–20), it is important that our understanding is not based solely on the literal meaning of the word "disciple." Again, if we are to understand his command and seek to accomplish his goals we must understand how the word was used and practiced by the people of that day, especially by Christ himself.

Discipleship of Christ

During the precious few years that Jesus spent on earth, his purpose was to provide salvation for mankind and train followers to be his ambassadors. These followers trained others, who in turn trained still others, to continue his mission for several thousand years. With this understanding, one would think that Christ would have selected the most gifted, talented, intelligent, and charismatic people on earth. But when we study the Gospels, we find that Jesus did just the opposite. In fact, not one of the disciples fit what we might believe to be "the mold." It has been said that the only disciple who may have met the world's standards was Judas Iscariot. Most of the disciples were poor and unlearned. None of his men ever held a prominent place in the synagogue; they were common laboring men. According to Robert Coleman, they probably had no formal training except what was necessary for their vocation. They were, for the most part, from poor families; probably the only one who came from a more refined area of Judea was Judas Iscariot. By any standard of sophisticated culture they would be considered a rather ragged group of men.[10]

Simon Peter; Andrew, Peter's brother; and James and John, the sons of Zebedee were poor uneducated fishermen. Matthew was a Jewish turncoat, working for the Roman government as a tax collector, an occupation that at that time was tainted by corruption and self-centeredness. These men routinely made their money by gouging the residents, increasing the amount of taxes required of the common folk in order to keep the excess for themselves.

Another group of men were political revolutionaries. This included James son of Alphaeus, Judas Iscariot, Thaddaeus (aka "Judas, not Iscariot"), and Simeon who was called a Zealot because of his identification with a violent political party that was extremely patriotic and rebellious against the occupying Roman government. Under different circumstances Simeon the Zealot would have killed Matthew the Roman government tax collector in a heartbeat. These are not the kind of people one would expect to recruit as the prime ambassadors and leaders of the world-changing early church. In fact, Herb Hodges believes that Christ's greatest miracle was not the feeding of the five thousand, healing the sick, or even raising the dead. Instead, his greatest miracle was "the construction out of 'impossible' material of a band of twelve men who would send the shock waves of spiritual reproduction to the ends of the earth of that day!"[11]

As to the selection process, it was not elaborate. There were no applications, reference contacts, or assessment testing. Jesus did not even conduct a formal interview. His selection of twelve disciples to carry on and expand his revolutionary movement was only bathed in prayer and divine guidance. Some of the disciples took personal initiative to follow Jesus, while he personally approached and called others to be his followers. For example, Jesus stopped at the seashore and challenged two sets of brothers who were already familiar with Jesus because they were disciples of John the Baptist at the time (John 1:35ff)—Peter and Andrew (Matt. 4:18–22; Mark 1:16–20), and James and John the sons of Zebedee. The call to follow Jesus was also true of Philip (John 1:43) and Matthew (Mark 2:14). The selection process of the Twelve was never based by a volunteer system; Jesus specifically chose his twelve disciples.

There were also women who were called disciples. Some were among the Seventy and some were even involved to some degree with the ministry of the Twelve, as seen at the crucifixion and after the resurrection (Luke 23:49, 55; 24:9). Several women traveled with the disciples. Among them were Mary Magdalene, out of whom Jesus had cast seven demons; Joanna, who may have had some financial means because her husband, Cuza, was a manager in Herod's household; Susanna, and many others (Luke 8:1–3). It is not clear what responsibilities these women had; the passage just cited says they supported the work of Christ out of their personal means. However, it should not be concluded that all they did was cook, do the laundry, and provide financial support. In Luke 8:1 the use of the phrase "with Him" is significant. It is a technical phrase meaning much more than just traveling with Jesus (see also Luke 8:38; 9:18; 22:56). It indicates that these women were themselves disciples of Jesus.[12]

Moreover, Jesus chose many from the multitudes who witnessed miracles and heard his teachings. In fact, Jesus' primary objective in ministering to the multitudes was to call them to be his disciples. To become his disciple specifically required that they respond positively to a call to believe in him, becoming children of God by repenting of their sins. Once a small percentage of the multitudes believed and followed him as Lord, the young disciples were included in a smaller group of people called "the seventy" (Luke 10:1, 17). And it was from the seventy disciples that Jesus selected twelve men he called apostles (Luke 6:13).

As we look at these disciples, we can only conclude that Jesus didn't choose his disciples because of their abilities or connections. He chose them for who they could become through his discipling impact. In 1 Corinthians 1:27–28, the apostle Paul declares that "God has chosen the foolish things of the world to shame the wise, and God has chosen the weak things of the world to shame the things which are strong, and the base things of the world and the despised God has chosen, the things that are not, so that He may nullify the things that are." Truly, the history of the early church is a perfect example of the impact of God's transforming power to change a weak, motley crew of men into a mighty force who led the early church. Christ himself set the example of what a committed, effective discipler can do when filled with the infinite power of the Holy Spirit.

The new followers found quickly that it was not easy to be a disciple of Jesus. He expected much, and imposed serious requirements upon them. (See chapter 5, "Jesus' Requirements.") These expectations demanded great commitment, requiring them to first "count the cost" (Luke 14:28–33). However, the discipleship of Jesus was also filled with examples and illustrations of how to live and how to minister. One of the benefits in studying the ministry of Christ is that he provides many principles that we can practice as we attempt to follow his methods in making disciples. We will look at seven of those principles now.

One of Jesus' primary principles is that we must practice and teach that *a disciple must be obedient to the commands of Christ.*

PRINCIPLE NUMBER ONE:
A disciple must be obedient to the commands of Christ.

The cultural understanding of the traditional method of discipleship would imply that the disciples of Jesus would eventually have their own personal disciples. But now, during Christ's earthly ministry, the discipleship process changed for the first time. In the Christian realm, no one any longer was authorized to make a disciple to follow himself. As the disciples implemented Christ's Great Commission, they were only to make disciples of Jesus. The disciple will emulate the life of the discipler but they never become *his* disciples—only Christ's disciples. He is the one the disciples must obey whether it is by clear command or by a principal being taught.

Another principle Christ demonstrated is that *the smaller the group of concentration, the greater the impact.* Jesus ministered to the multitudes and a smaller group called "the Seventy," but his ministry with the twelve disciples allowed Christ to be more personal and direct in his approach. Notably, Jesus did more than meet with his disciples once a week for a Bible study. He lived and traveled with them for about two and a half years. This allowed him to spend extensive time with his disciples individually—especially Peter, James, and John—as well as in a group. Herb Hodges estimates that Jesus spent eighty-five percent of his public ministry with his twelve disciples.[13] According to John 21:25, he taught the disciples much more than what is recorded in the Gospels, but it is clear that his living example had profound impact on their lives. The disciples were forever changed by the concentrated, intensive discipleship relationship that Christ had with them, as they lived and traveled with him.

> PRINCIPLE NUMBER TWO:
> The smaller the group of concentration,
> the greater the impact.

Once Jesus selected the Twelve, he spent most of his life on earth with this small band of disciples. With the warnings and announcement of John the Baptist, the Son of God could have had thousands of followers but he did not capitalize on this golden opportunity to build a mammoth ministry. Instead he chose to spend the limited time he had on earth with a few select men. Why?

I believe Jesus' objective was not to lead a multitude to salvation, as wonderful as that would have been. Instead, he purposed to train a band of followers to carry on his ministry after he left. In fact, on the night of his arrest, Jesus told his disciples that they, and those who followed them, would accomplish greater things than he had done (John 14:12). Therefore, he sacrificed what could have been, in terms of size of ministry, in order to train a few who through multiplication would lead and disciple millions to Christ.

Jesus did not conduct a formal school or regular Bible study. He did not follow a written curriculum, or any outlined course of study. Instead, all Jesus did was spend time with his disciples. As we look at the ministry of Jesus we have to conclude that he was his own curriculum—and being so, he became the primary example by which we develop young believers into mature, godly servants.

In order to optimize growth, every serous *young believer should have a person assigned as his personal discipler*. This person answers questions, clarifies truth, encourages, guides, and exhorts the young disciple. According to Coleman, about half of those who make professions of faith and join the church eventually fall away or lose the joy and excitement of their Christian life. He says that fewer still grow in sufficient knowledge and grace to be of real service to the kingdom.[14]

Why are we failing, and what did Jesus do to prevent such a high percentage of failure? Simply put, he spent time with the disciples. *This* is what is missing in most churches in the twenty-first century.

> **PRINCIPLE NUMBER THREE:**
> Every young believer must have a person assigned as his personal discipler.

One can never underestimate the impact of life example on another person. The example of our Lord, for instance, demonstrated to his disciples how to live and serve. First, this is clearly illustrated in his prayer life. He prayed daily, many times for hours at a time, even praying all night on at least one occasion (Luke 6:12). He prayed separately and with the disciples. Yes, Jesus gave them instruction on how to pray (Matt. 6:9–13; Luke 11:1–4) but he primarily taught by example.

Second, Jesus used the Word of God often in ministry, as he discussed truths and he fought temptation. According to Herman Horne in his book *Jesus the Master Teacher,* Jesus made reference to Old Testament Scripture at least sixty-six times in the Gospels, and ninety allusions to Scripture as he spoke to others.[15]

Third, Jesus talked often and throughout his ministry about believing in him. He exhorted people to believe almost daily and sent out the disciples to do the same. This idea of winning people to Christ was the heartbeat of Jesus and should be emulated by every disciple of Christ. Even the Great Commission requires leading a person to Christ in order to make a disciple. The rest of the commission is about helping the new Christian grow through discipleship.

This aspect of his life highlights another important principle to follow, *we need to disciple people by life example*. If we merely instruct without living what we teach, our protégés will not wholeheartedly receive that instruction—and often, never learn it.

> **PRINCIPLE NUMBER FOUR:**
> We need to disciple people by life example.

Ministry therefore serves as an important aspect of discipleship as it provides opportunities for both discipler and disciple to exemplify Christlikeness.

Interestingly, the disciples did little service for their master until they had observed him for the first year. They were there to watch and learn. As Coleman points out, even after Christ formally ordained them into the ministry (Matt. 4:19; Mark 1:17; Luke 5:10), there is little evidence that they practiced evangelism.[16]

Eventually Jesus put the disciples in situations where they would have to share their faith. He gathered them together and sent them out two by two (Matt. 10:5; Mark 6:7; Luke 9:1–2). This illustrates another important principle we can glean from Christ's ministry: *We must send the disciple on ministry assignments.*

A few months after he sent the disciples on their mission, he sent out the Seventy on a similar training mission (Luke 10:1:1–16). It appears that the disciples were sent out with this second group as well. There were other ministry experiences the disciples took part in as discussed below. Overall, as Coleman points out, the disciples were told on at least four occasions after the Lord's resurrection to go out and do his work (Luke 24:38–43, 47; John 20:21; 21:15–17; Matt. 28:16; Acts 1:8).[17]

PRINCIPLE NUMBER FIVE:
We must send the disciple on ministry assignments.

When a young disciple experiences the Holy Spirit working through her life, service becomes a tremendous encouragement and motivator as she continues to grow in her relationship with Christ. The experience also helps her improve the skills used in the ministry, and when her disciple maker both praises and critiques her work it becomes even more of a motivator for perseverance and growth. In the case of being sent out by Jesus, the disciples also grew in faith after being instructed not to take food or money (Matt. 10:9; Luke 10:4). They were forced to live totally by faith while they were away, which allowed them to see God providing for their needs and thereby increasing their faith.

After a disciple participates in a ministry experience, a good disciple maker will attempt to hold the disciple accountable. A principle we can glean from the discipleship of Christ is that we must recognize that *accountability and instruction are important aspects of training.* Holding the disciple accountable by having him report back is an indispensable training tool. Jesus did that after the Twelve came back from their mission (Mark 6:30; Luke 9:10), and again when the seventy-two returned (Luke 10:17). They had a debriefing meeting in which the members of the mission had a chance to share with Jesus what took place and the blessings they experienced. Consider also Jesus' reaction when the disciples failed to heal the demon-possessed boy (Mark 9:17–29; Matt. 17:14–20; Luke 9:37–43). Using the opportunity to impart additional instruction, he emphasized the importance of prayer and fasting in dealing with such cases. In general, Jesus used their ministry as an opportunity to further train his disciples.

> PRINCIPLE NUMBER SIX:
> Accountability and instruction are important aspects of training.

Finally, Christ's ministry reveals to us that *discipleship must include multiplication.* The entire movement of Jesus was based on this principle. If the disciples only reproduced themselves, Christianity would have ceased in the first century. If every generation would have practiced this principal of discipleship with multiplication as their prime objective, every generation would have won their receptive world to Christ. Our failure to effectively make disciples throughout most of history does not stem from having disavowed Christ's plan, but from having consistently ignored it.

> PRINCIPAL NUMBER SEVEN:
> Discipleship must include multiplication.

The Discipleship of the Early Church

Before Jesus left earth he left a set of instructions called the Great Commission. All men, women, and children who were old enough to understand were to be won to Christ and then discipled.

Peter's primary disciple was John Mark, whom he called "my son Mark" (1 Peter 5:13). The description "my son" is the exact affectionate designation Paul gave to his primary disciple Timothy. This is the same Mark who wrote the second gospel in the New Testament. Peter had such an influence in Mark's gospel that Justin Martyr, a half-century later, called the book the "Memoirs of Peter."[18]

Many have debated who discipled Saul before he became the apostle Paul. Many believe that Barnabas had a profound impact on his life and even became a discipling influence. After Saul became a believer on the road to Damascus there was a lapse of time before he entered into his missionary ministry. There were a number of years between his conversion and Barnabas' recruitment of him in Tarsus in order to bring him back to Antioch to assist him in the ministry (Acts 25–26). During this time Barnabas became Saul's prime spiritual influence. Their relationship spurred Barnabas to vouch for Saul when the apostles were skeptical of his reliability and afraid of him (Acts 9:26–27). During their time ministering at the church in Antioch they were always referred to as Barnabas and Saul, indicating that the primary leader at that time was Barnabas. It wasn't until they were well into the first missionary journey that it was no longer "Barnabas and Saul" but "Paul and Barnabas," with Paul assuming the primary leadership position (Acts 13:42).

Paul was strategic as he practiced relational discipleship. Yes, he had a preaching ministry to the unsaved, but his discipleship was done primarily in small groups, via house churches and life-on-life discipleship.

Paul was very conscious of the need to develop leaders; therefore, since he spent much of his time traveling, he always took these growing disciples with him. For example, Paul had a close friendship with Priscilla and Aquila and lived with them for a time (Acts 18:2–3) and likely spent many hours in a discipleship relationship. Paul then took them with him to Ephesus, where they had great impact in the life of a misguided preacher and teacher, Apollos (Acts 18:19–26).

Paul also had a discipleship ministry with Titus and wrote an epistle to instruct him as he shepherded his church. Paul also had a ministry to Luke and Silas and took them with him as he traveled on ministry expeditions. But that wasn't all. Paul referred to more than sixty people by name in his epistles. These were people he loved and appreciated. They were co-workers who Paul had impacted at various times during his discipleship ministry.

During Paul's ministry to the cosmopolitan city of Ephesus, where he spent three years, he met a man by the name of Epaphras who became a faithful "minister" of Christ (Col. 1:7). After Epaphras was sufficiently prepared, he went to Colossae where he led many to Christ and established a new church in that city. In Colossians 1:6b–7, Paul further acknowledges Epaphras' evangelistic activity as he addresses the Colossian church: "Since the day you heard of it and understood the grace of God in truth; just as you learned it from Epaphras, our beloved fellow bond-servant, who is a faithful servant of Christ on our behalf." To further clarify the meaning of this verse, I would like to note that the word "learned" is translated from the Greek verb *manthano*, which means "to learn" or "to disciple." And as Herb Hodges points out, the word "you" in the Greek is the plural form and can be translated "all of you," suggesting that Epaphras led many of them to Christ and invested his time discipling them. Therefore, verse seven literally says "you were discipled by Epaphras."[19] Thus, Epaphras obeyed the Great Commission just as his discipler, Paul, had done.

Normally when we think of Paul we automatically link him with his primary disciple, Timothy (Phil. 2:19–24). This young man, who was initially discipled by his mother and grandmother, was further discipled and mentored by Paul. The way in which Paul instructs and speaks about Timothy reflects their close association. For example, Paul opens the book of Colossians with the sentence, "Paul, an apostle of Jesus Christ by the will of God, and Timothy our brother" (Col. 1:1). This opening greeting mirrors five other letters in which Paul includes Timothy; in fact, in four of the books, Paul only mentions Timothy in his greetings. As part of the discipleship process Paul took Timothy on several missionary trips and wrote two epistles to him, giving him instruction as he pastored his church at Ephesus. It is believed that Paul's ministry to Timothy lasted for at least twenty years.

It was Timothy whom Paul exhorted, "The things which you have heard from me in the presence of many witnesses, entrust these to faithful men who will be able to teach others also" (2 Tim. 2:2). In this verse Paul emphasizes multiplication as part of the discipleship process. It is true that Paul refers to "many witnesses," and I will not dispute that part of the discipleship input came through the small-group Bible studies in which Timothy took part. But I would like to also consider several verses from 2 Timothy that shed light on the other methods Paul used in his discipleship ministry. The first verse is 2 Timothy 3:14 where Paul told Timothy, "You, however, continue in the things you have learned and become convinced of, knowing from whom you have learned them." The word "knowing" used here is a form of the Greek word *oida*, which means "know by seeing," indicating that Timothy had received up-close and personal discipleship.

Second Timothy 1:13 constitutes the second instructive verse on Paul's discipleship method. Here he instructs Timothy, "Retain the standard of sound words which you have heard from me, in the faith and love which are in Christ Jesus." Here I would like to focus on the phrase, "from me," which in Greek is *para*, which also serves as the root for words such as "parallel" and "parable." *Para* refers to something nearby, expressing a relationship of immediate vicinity or proximity. It literally means "by the side of" or "alongside." Such Scripture allows us to conclude that the major part of Paul's discipleship of Timothy did not take place essentially in a crowd, from a pulpit, or from a teacher's podium. On the contrary, it took place "along the way" as Paul and Timothy lived and moved near each other, moving "side by side."[20]

Along with Paul's emphasis of an up-close and personal approach, which mirrors that of Christ, another important aspect of relational discipleship has to do with the disciple maker's example. Three times Paul exhorted disciples to imitate the faith of their leaders (2 Thess. 3:9; 1 Tim. 4:12; Heb. 13:7). Identification and imitation only truly takes place in a discipleship relationship when a discipler imitates Christ in such a way worthy of the disciple's imitation. Due to lacking an intimate enough setting, a small-group Bible study, for instance, makes having this kind of discipleship relationship very difficult.

Just as Jesus sent his disciples out on ministry assignments, Paul also sent Timothy on a number of assignments as his personal representative. In Acts 17:14–15 Paul left Timothy behind with the more seasoned leader, Silas, to finish the work he had started. Several other times Paul sent Timothy as his substitute, such as when he was in prison and sent Timothy to the Philippians (Phil. 2:19).

It seems clear to me that Paul did not disciple Timothy or his other protégés through his preaching ministry since this ministry was primarily, if not entirely, evangelistic. For sure, some of his discipleship came from his teaching ministry with small groups. Even the school of Tyrannus in Ephesus (Acts 19:19) was apparently a discussion group held in a room he was able to reserve for teaching. Paul's practice of discipleship, as was true of other first-century leaders, was based on a relational form of instruction—which is most effective with one or two disciples because it is here that encouragement, reproof, instruction, and accountability can best take place.

The Early Church Fathers

It is believed that the Christian community multiplied four-hundredfold in the first three decades after Pentecost. The growth rate continued remarkably high for three hundred years.[21] This growth would have never continued if the church only evangelized. For this growth to continue for three centuries, multiplication had to have been the emphasis. After that period the progress of effective discipleship began to deteriorate.

Some of the early church fathers who had a direct connection to the apostles continued to practice a relational approach to discipleship just as their mentors had practiced. Two of these key people were Ignatius, who was a bishop at the church of Antioch in Syria from AD50– 117; and Polycarp, bishop of Smyrna. Both men were discipled by the apostle John. Ignatius, for his part, used discipleship terminology more than any of the other apostolic fathers, revealing the most about the practice of discipleship after the death of the apostles.[22] Demonstrating a practice of multiplication discipleship, Irenaeus, the bishop of Lyons, considered himself a disciple of Ignatius.[23] According to Virginia Corwin, "The Ignatian letters have more references to imitation and discipleship than all the other Apostolic Fathers together."[24]

The only known writings of Ignatius were written a few weeks before his martyrdom as he anticipated his death. He used the same terminology for discipleship as found in the New Testament fourteen times in the six letters he wrote during this period. For example, according to Michael Wilkins, he used the same verb, *I make a disciple* or *I become a disciple* (*mathēteuō*), which is the same verb used in Matthew 28:19 when Jesus gave the Great Commission. He also used the noun form of disciple (*mathētēs*) which means "a learner." Finally, Ignatius uses the term to designate a mentor relationship between a Christian leader and an immature believer.[25]

I believe an in-depth and unbiased study of the early church, especially the life of the apostle Paul, shows that the discipleship we must practice emphasizes an interpersonal methodology that can only effectively take place in a life-on-life relationship—and for most people this will be a one-on-one relationship.

How about Today?

When Jesus told the apostles to "make disciples," they would have naturally defined the process in terms of how disciples were made by the rabbis and especially by the process Jesus used to disciple them. Bill Hull suggests five characteristics of first-century discipleship:

1. *Deciding to follow a teacher.* All of these men knew that a disciple always makes a serious commitment to follow the leader. This was especially true as it pertains to their experience, because the disciples of Jesus were held at a very high standard. The disciples of first-century Judaism learned everything from their teacher. They learned the teacher's stories, life habits, and interpretation of the Old Testament. The goal was to learn everything that the teacher knew. (Of course, it was not possible to learn all that Jesus knew.) The bond that developed between the teacher and disciple was so powerful that it was similar and sometimes stronger than the bond between father and son.

2. *Memorizing the teacher's words.* Because their culture and technology made it impractical to take notes, the disciple memorized much of what the teacher said. Without memorization, the disciple would not be able to

pass on his discipler's teachings when needed. This fact illustrates one reason why Jesus chose to disciple his men twenty-four hours a day, seven days a week, for two and a half years.

3. *Learning the teacher's way of ministry.* The disciple learned how his master kept God's commands and principles. They learned not only by what he said; much of what they learned was from observation. They learned how to fast, pray, and keep the Sabbath. They learned much about humility and how to confront dissenters. They learned about faith and love and how a leader demonstrates it. And lastly, they learned how to lead and how to teach.

4 *Imitating the teacher's life and character.* Most of all, their learning was not primarily academic. As they continued to learn, their lives were transforming as they became more like their master daily. In Luke 6:40 Jesus said, "A pupil is not above his teacher; but everyone, after he has been fully trained, will be like his teacher." Paul called on Timothy to be like him (2 Tim. 3:10–14). He also encouraged other followers to do the same (1 Cor. 4:14–16; 11:1; 2 Thess. 3:9; 1 Tim. 4:12; Heb. 13:7).

5. *Raising up their own disciples.* When a disciple finished the training he was expected to teach what he had learned to his own disciple. This was the standard practice in the rabbinical world, and Christ expected the same. However, there exists one caveat, and this was a major change: No disciple will ever raise disciples of themselves. They will all be disciples of Jesus Christ, and they must follow their discipler as they followed Christ (1 Cor. 11:1).[26]

I agree with Bill Hull that these five characteristics describe what it means to make disciples in the first century. If this is so, I think believers in our churches should make disciples in the same way. Perhaps this is why the kingdom of God is not advancing as it should. Perhaps this is why the first 300 years after Christ's death, with all its limitations and lack of technology, dwarf our results in making disciples today.

Which of these five characteristics does your ministry practice? Many solid ministries practice numbers 2–4. Their results may not be perfect but they make a real effort to do their best to practice these three characteristics. They encourage people to memorize Jesus' words, to learn his way of ministry, and to imitate his life and character. These three characteristics are the things we learn about Jesus through instruction and as we spend time reading and studying the Bible.

However, few ministries practice characteristics 1 and 5, which are critical in bringing real transformation. These two characteristics of first-century discipleship are made possible only through a disciple maker who trains a protégé to be a disciple of Christ. Most people are never discipled in this New Testament sense. There is no one who consistently and regularly guides, rebukes, exhorts, corrects, teaches, provides an example, and holds the believer accountable. No wonder churches have so few true disciples of Christ. We will continue to fail at achieving the Great Commission as our greatest purpose as long as we do not emphasize the importance of relationship in the transformational discipleship process.

Review Questions

1. What were some of the qualities of Moses' discipleship of Joshua? Which of these do you see in the church today? Which of these would you like to see more? Explain.

2. If Jesus didn't choose his disciples based on their talent, knowledge, connections, or wealth, what was the basis for their selection? What does that say about whom we should pursue in our disciple making relationship? For that matter, what does this say about us?

3. Review the seven principles Jesus demonstrated, in the section "Discipleship of Christ." Which of these two principles are the most important in making disciples and why? Which of these resonate the most with you personally, and which need work in your own discipleship? In each case, why?

4. Read 2 Thessalonians 3:9; 1 Timothy 4:12; 2 Timothy 1:13 and 3:14; and Hebrews 13:7. How do each of these verses demonstrate the value of life-on-life discipleship?

5. Review Bill Hull's five characteristics of discipleship in the section "How about Today?" Why are characteristics one and five so critical in bringing transformation within the disciple and fulfilling the Great Commission? What steps can you take to integrate them into your own discipling relationships?

Chapter 4

THE GREAT COMMISSION REVISITED: THE GREAT OMISSION OF THE GREAT COMMISSION

IN THE CLASSIC LEWIS CARROLL NOVEL *Alice's Adventures in Wonderland*, Alice finds herself in a strange world. Seeking direction, she engages in conversation with the Cheshire cat:

> "Would you tell me, please, which way I ought to go from here?"
> "That depends a good deal on where you want to get to," said the cat.
> "I don't much care where—" said Alice.
> "Then it doesn't matter which way you go," said the cat.
> "—so long as I get SOMEWHERE," Alice added as an explanation.
> "Oh, you're sure to do that," said the cat, "if you only walk long enough."[1]

As Alice says here, just going *somewhere* is not good enough. Doing good and even accomplishing what may seem to be noble and right is not necessarily God's direction. As we look at the history of the church, we must consider where the church has been trying to go for the last 1,900 or so years. Surely, we have gone *somewhere*, yet I believe that we have been heading in the wrong direction. A close examination of God's directive demonstrates that we have either misunderstood or misapplied God's greatest command to the church; this is what Dallas Willard referred to as *The Great Omission*.[2]

We read in Matthew 28:16–20 that Jesus scheduled an appointment with his disciples since they went "to the mountain which Jesus had designated" (Matt. 28:16). In fact, this passage serves as the only record of Jesus ever setting an appointment with his disciples, accentuating the importance of this single event. As Scripture records, their meeting was on the Mount of Olives, and after having seen the resurrected Lord, the disciples fell down on their faces and worshipped him. Moments later, Jesus gave his final instructions. Granted, during the forty days between his resurrection and ascension, Christ met with the disciples numerous times. However, this meeting was profoundly different. One would expect that the final words spoken on earth by the divine Son of God before his ascension to the Father would be profoundly important. And so, as we study his famous command, we must wholeheartedly receive these sacred words as defining his will for the entire church age. Christ's final words are the cornerstone of the church's mission.

Jesus further illustrates the importance of this command by placing two bookends around his Great Commission. Before stating the command Jesus reminded his disciples, "All authority has been given to Me in heaven and on earth" (verse 18), emphasizing his sovereignty in delivering such an imperative. After giving the command, he ended with another bookend, by stating his unconditional commitment in ensuring their success. As they obeyed, he promised to be with them "always, even to the end of the age" (verse 20).

For two thousand years, the Christian community has consistently called Christ's words in Matthew 28:19–20 the Great Commission. They are *our* standing orders and, therefore, foundational for purposeful living and in forming the directions for our lifelong service for Jesus Christ. Indeed, the Great Commission should be the ruling principle of Christian service for every believer, and I believe each of us will give an account to Christ for how we labored to see his command accomplished.

The Authority behind the Commission

A story is told of two battleships assigned to a training squadron that had been at sea on maneuvers in heavy weather for several days. Shortly after dark, the lookout on the wing reported:

> Light, bearing on the starboard bow. "Is it steady or moving astern?" the captain called out. The lookout replied, "Steady, Captain," which meant we were on a dangerous collision course.
>
> The captain then called to the signalman, "Signal that ship: 'We are on a collision course, advise you change course twenty degrees.'" Back came the signal, "Advisable for you to change course twenty degrees."
>
> The captain said, "Send: 'I'm a captain, change course twenty degrees.'" "I'm a seaman second-class," came the reply. "You had better change course twenty degrees."
>
> By that time the captain was furious. He spat out, "Send: 'I'm a battleship. Change course twenty degrees.'"
>
> Back came the flashing light, "I'm a lighthouse." The battleship changed course.[3]

Like the lighthouse, Jesus has steadfast and unmovable authority. In Matthew 28:18, Jesus began his final words by saying, "All authority has been given to Me in heaven and on earth." The Father gave the Son all celestial authority in heaven and all terrestrial authority on earth. There exists no higher power and authority. Thus, Christ speaks with all authority when he commissions the disciples, "Go therefore."

Indeed, he who wields absolute, full authority entrusted his disciples with the most important command of this age. And yet, Christ did not direct his last words solely to the eleven remaining disciples present at his ascension. He issued the command to the disciples with the clear intent that all future disciples of the church age obey it. We easily minimize our responsibilities by thinking of the Great Commission as marching orders for the church, which it is. However, we err in that we often mistake the church for what it's not, whether a building or organization. It is a body of called-out ones, believers who have placed their faith in Jesus Christ as savior and Lord. If you are a believer, you are the church. The Great Commission is *your* commission.

The Commission Explained

Matthew 28:16–20 has been misunderstood and misinterpreted by many. To better understand what Jesus is saying in this passage, let's first talk about what he is *not* commanding us to do.

Almost every sermon I have ever heard preached on the Great Commission treats Christ's words as a command to share one's faith or to become a missionary. Yet these interpretations water down Christ's original purpose for the Great Commission. The command here is not to make converts. I like the way Christopher Adsit put it: "In a spiritual sense, we have a tendency to think that the greatest thing we Christians can do is beget babies. Consequently, what we have here in America today is the largest spiritual nursery in history."[4]

Jesus' command was not solely an injunction to win the lost to a saving faith in him. Likewise the Great Commission does not serve as a directive to be a missionary though being a missionary can certainly be an application of accomplishing his commission. On the contrary, Jesus commands us to make disciples of all people of the earth. So, what *does* this command entail?

Let's come back to Jesus' original words, in Matthew 28:19–20: *"Go therefore and make disciples of all the nations, baptizing them in the name of the Father and the Son and the Holy Spirit, teaching them to observe all that I commanded you; and lo, I am with you always, even to the end of the age."*

Many preachers have taught that Christ commanded every follower to *"go!"* After all, the command starts with the words *"Go therefore."* However, Christ's actual command becomes clearer when we consider the Greek grammar in the passage. The imperative here is to "make disciples." Furthermore, the words "go," "baptizing," and "teaching" are adverbial participles which modify the command "make disciples." Thus, the words "go," "baptize," and "teach" tell us *how* we are to follow Christ's command. In the Greek grammar, the word "go" is an aorist passive participle—which means that the correct translation of the command is "going," "in your going," or "having gone," to "make disciples." In other words: *You're already going. So as you go, make disciples.*

Prior to Christ's proclamation of the Great Commission, the disciples had just fallen on their faces in worship (Matt. 28:17). Peter didn't get up from worshipping the resurrected Christ and say, "It's been good knowing you Jesus. Hey John, want to stop for coffee on the way back to the boat?" Since the natural response of true heartfelt worship is service, telling the disciples to "go" was unnecessary; they had just finished worshipping the resurrected Messiah. Jesus knew they were going to go; all that the disciples needed was direction. Therefore, he gave the command, "In your going, make disciples." This command of Jesus to make disciples is every bit as important and in every way as serious a command as any of the Ten Commandments. Jesus Christ fully expects you and me in fact, commands us to make disciples and to help young disciples grow and mature. Truly, disciple making is Jesus' top priority.

Discipleship in no way devalues the importance of evangelism. No one can disciple a person for Christ unless he has first been won to Christ. However, many people can be won to Christ without ever being discipled. I am convinced that the church would win far more people to Christ, and create many more leaders, if we were effectively discipling people. True disciples are always active in sharing their faith with nonbelievers. Sadly, Christians across the United States, and worldwide, tend to misapply the Great Commission. We win people to Christ and they "sit, soak, and sour." I am appalled at the great number of believers who have never grown up. Many supposedly receive Christ as Savior and yet never faithfully attend a Bible-believing church; many do attend church and yet take years before they grow to a moderate level of maturity.

Since most missionaries have come from the United States, this fact may in part explain why the modern church in general has been so ineffective in accomplishing Christ's command. Indeed, the church as a whole has perpetuated this error in its interpretation of Matthew 28:16–20, which in turn has drastically changed the primary purpose of the modern church and led to deterioration in attendance and spiritual maturity.

The lack of effectiveness in the American church is evident. According to Robert Coleman, the church as a whole in North America is barely keeping pace with the increase in population, whereas in Western Europe there is a steady decline.[5] In reference to the church Chuck Colson, president of Prison Fellowship, told a journalist, "If this were a business, you'd be contemplating chapter 11 (bankruptcy)."[6] Studies demonstrate that few churches are doing effective discipleship. Christian researcher George Barna, after completing a two-year research project across America, concluded, "Almost every church in our country has some type of discipleship program or set of activities; but stunningly few churches have a church of disciples."[7] Elsewhere he says, "the twenty-first century church has many 'followers' of Christ in the sense that I follow the Yankees: We dabble in Christianity. That's not what Jesus had in mind when He called us to be His disciples....Discipleship is not a program. It is not a ministry. It is a lifelong commitment to a lifestyle."[8]

I am convinced that this lack of mature disciples in America stems from our ongoing avoidance of the most effective approach God has given us to change lives: life-on-life discipleship. It is through life-on-life discipleship that the Holy Spirit most effectively enacts biblically driven life change, through the relationship between a hungry young believer and a mature discipler. Our deviation from effective discipleship is our Great Omission of the Great Commission.

Those We Are to Disciple

Once we decide to follow Christ's command to make disciples, we need to consider who to engage in the process. In Matthew 28:19 Jesus didn't say to go to every nation. The English word for "nation" in the Greek language is *ethnos*, from which we get our word "ethnicities." The early church believers (and all believers in every generation) were told to go to all the world, to every ethnic group, to make disciples. In Acts 1:8 Jesus commanded us to be "witnesses *both* in Jerusalem, *and* in all Judea *and* Samaria, *and* even to the remotest part of the earth" (emphasis mine). The insertion of the word *both*, followed by the word *and* between each location, indicates that we are to go to all of these people groups. With God bringing the world to our doorsteps through urban migration, especially in large cities, we have the opportunity to go to these ethnic groups without even leaving our country.

Just giving to a missions program, though important, is not enough. *We are* to go. All men, women, and children, old enough to understand, are to be won to Christ and then made to become mature disciples.

The early church began to follow these commands as Philip, followed by Peter and John, went to Samaria (Acts 8:4–16). Then Christ sent Philip to the Ethiopian eunuch (Acts 8:26–40) who believed, was baptized, and then went back to his homeland. Peter was sent to evangelize a house full of Gentiles at the home of Cornelius (Acts 10:24–48). Soon the great persecutor of Christians, Saul, was gloriously converted while on a mission of persecution (Acts 9:1–19). Later, Paul (previously Saul), after some time of personal growth, along with other disciples began the great missionary journeys (Acts 13 21). The church moved quickly to begin making disciples of people from all ethnic groups in the known world.

Our God desires all people to be his children. Not only does his love extend to all ethnicities, but it is multicultural as well, since there are many cultural groups within each ethnic group. God does not favor any ethnic group, culture, or subculture. And Jesus' command requires that we make disciples of each of these people groups.

The Scope of the Discipleship Process

Regarding the discipleship process, Jesus commands us to "baptize them in the name of the Father and the Son and the Holy Spirit." Additionally, he says we are to "teach them to observe all that I commanded you." To *observe* means the disciple maker must emphasize obedience to the total teachings of Jesus, not just the teachings one finds convenient. Of course, for any follower of Christ, this process of growth fueled daily by reading and studying the Word of God spans a lifetime. The emphasis never centers upon simply transmitting knowledge. Instead, as disciple makers, we continually help others grow toward consistent obedience and practice of biblical principles. And as we train them to serve the Lord, they will win others to Christ, by God's grace, and begin discipling these new converts. In this way we perpetuate Christ's primary purpose of the church: to win people to Christ, baptize them, and grow them to a level of maturity so that they can continually reproduce themselves.

Other Passages on the Great Commission

Even though Matthew 28:19–20 remains the most thorough and descriptive version of the Great Commission, I would be in error if I ignored the other Scriptural accounts. In Mark 16:15, Jesus tells his disciples, "Go into all the world and preach the gospel to all creation." In Luke 24:46–47 Jesus says, "that repentance for for-giveness of sins would be proclaimed in His name to all the nations, beginning from Jerusalem." The starting point of the Great Commission is to lead people to a saving belief in Jesus Christ. Matthew 28 states this also, then goes on to com-mand us to baptize these new believers and to help them grow to maturity.

Also, in the book of Acts, Jesus commands believers to go to ever-increasing regions extending to the uttermost parts of the earth. I agree when Herb Hodges states, "Each Christian is to have *equal and simultaneous impact in each of the geo-graphical areas specified in the statement* Acts 1:8…I am *commanded* individually to impact the whole wide world, and I believe this is true for every believer."[9]

Let me explain it this way: In this country, as well as in many other places, we place money in the offering plate and depend on the church to disperse some of it upon those who feel "called" to be the missionaries. In doing so, we subcon-sciously absolve ourselves of the responsibilities of the Acts 1:8 command. Hodge argues, "We practice a brand of 'world missions' that sends a few highly motivated people to distant lands while the others stay home and 'pay the way' of those who go. What a convenient side-stepping of the clear mandate given to each Christian to have simultaneous impact in his Jerusalem, and in his Judea, and in his Samaria, and *unto the uttermost parts of the earth*" (Acts 1:8).[10] While it is important that we financially support our church ministry and the worldwide missionary effort, we must understand that our giving does not erase the command that *we* go and make disciples.

It's my belief that most Christians don't even seriously pray for the individual needs and problems facing their church missionaries. Jesus, in this imperative, puts the command for going on the backs of every disciple. That doesn't mean God wants every Christian to be a foreign missionary—and I believe many are incorrectly waiting on some sort of "Macedonian call." To the contrary, we have already been called. Thus, the question every disciple of Christ must come to grips with is, "Where does he want me to serve?" It may or may not include mis-sionary support or a salary coming from a ministry, but we are called just the same. Our calling is not just a hobby. It is a serious lifetime calling, and we should treat discipling others as a major part of our life's purpose.

One other point is worthy of mention here: The command is to go into all the world, to every people group (Matthew 28:19 *ethnos,* as noted earlier). Making it easier for us to obey this command, God has brought every ethnic group to the doorsteps of believers in every city of the world. If God directs us, we should go to other parts of the world; however, let us not overlook the masses of every ethnic group present in the cities. We can reach every people group right here at home. These immigrants come with weakening cultural stigma and restrictions present in their homeland. By moving to a new place they are freer and more receptive to the gospel than they were in their place of origin. We need to send people to the cities, and to support effective ministries that are fulfilling this commission in urban areas.

The Most Effective Form of Discipleship

Many claim that discipleship includes most everything we do in church. I would agree that this statement is true in many evangelical churches; anything that helps believers grow to become like Christ is part of the discipleship process. That being said, what would Jesus' disciples have concluded to be the method they should use in obeying his command?

I am sure this wasn't even a question to them, because there was only one common method in that day for making disciples. But if there had been other methods, there still would have been only one answer. Without question, they would have said that Jesus meant for them to make disciples of others just as he had made disciples of them. Jesus' method is the only method they would have considered.

Secondly, let us question what modern-day method and procedure most effectively accomplishes the task of making disciples. When we make a financial investment, we undoubtedly want the mechanism that will give us the best return on an investment. We should evaluate our eternal impact in a similar way if we desire to have the greatest impact on people's lives. We should actively be "redeeming the time" (Col. 4:5, KJV), "making the most of the opportunity," practicing the method that will produce the greatest yield in discipleship.

Based on my thirty-five years of experience and the opinion of countless number of Christian experts, life-on-life discipleship remains the primary method used in our modern age that incorporates the discipleship methods of Jesus Christ. This discipleship method, when followed correctly, will more deeply develop a person's spiritual transformation and growth in the shortest amount of time than any method known to man.

Granted, those who argue that the best method we can use in our ministry is small-group discipleship correctly state that Jesus had a small group of twelve men. But we must remember that Jesus spent twenty-four hours a day, seven days a week for about two-and-one-half years with those men. Conversely, the average small group usually lasts for one to two hours, once a week. Obviously, because of the enormous amount of time it would take and because of our transient society, we cannot disciple people with the great thoroughness and intensity in small groups that Jesus accomplished living with his disciples.

Small groups can be an effective disciple-making tool (see chapter 12 for how to make them even *more* effective), but it does not have the great impact life-on-life discipleship has. Though many churches may choose to do both, it is important that we emphasize the high-yield impact only life-on-life discipleship can produce.

In addition to small-group proponents, others correctly note that Jesus also spent some of his time practicing one-on-three discipleship with Peter, James, and John. Again, meeting once or twice a week can hardly achieve the depth that the Son of God invested in his one-on-three discipleship with these men, twenty-four hours a day, seven days a week. We must recognize that we have limited time to spend discipling people; therefore, we need to put weight on the method that will return the greatest result with the least investment—which I believe is, clearly, life-on-life discipleship.

By espousing a life-on-life discipleship emphasis am I blasting most traditional methods of church ministry? Absolutely not! Many churches are filled with impressive ministries, large services, conferences, programs, and elaborate events that advance the kingdom. Nevertheless, we are responsible for constantly evaluating whether these activities best accomplish our mandate of making disciples.

Any good investment counselor will tell you that you must diversify your investments. Simply speaking, they mean for you to place your money into different types of investments sources. Some methods are low yield, some are medium yield, and others are high yield investments. Jesus ministered to people in a similar manner: He diversified his time into different concentration levels. As I will elaborate on in chapter 7, Jesus cared for and preached to the masses, to the seventy followers, to the twelve disciples, and to Peter, James, and John. Each level had a different objective, but each aspect of Jesus' ministry was necessary and accomplished his intended purpose.

Like Christ, we need to diversify, clearly determining the purpose each ministry plays in accomplishing the Great Commission. Acknowledging that various types of ministries will have different yields of impact, we must make sure that God's kingdom benefits from the Spirit's work through high-yield ministries. While it may take a person ten years to get to a mature level using traditional church programs, it may take one year to grow to the same level through life-on-life discipleship.

The traditional church around the world continues to lose ground. We cannot keep pace with population growth, and our record of discipleship is dismal at best. We can't continue judging success based on attendance size and the breadth and number of programs, for the Lord desires that his disciples strive for biblical transformation and spiritual maturity. This type of discipleship translates itself into a multiplying ministry of souls saved and discipled. It's time to admit our failure and begin capitalizing on the methods that Jesus and the disciples modeled.

As we obediently labor to obey and achieve Christ's greatest command, our Lord gives us a glorious promise: "And surely I am with you always, to the very end of the age" (Matt. 28:20). I am struck how the Amplified Bible's attempts to catch every nuance of the original text: "*I am with you all the days (perpetually, uniformly and on every occasion), to the [very] close and consummation of the age.*" Here, words and phrases such as "perpetually," "uniformly," and "on every occasion" declare that we are not alone as we work to make disciples. When you share the gospel or disciple someone, you are not alone. The God of the universe remains with you in a very personal and productive way, as he transforms others through you.

Postscript

In proclaiming the Great Commission, Jesus assumes that every disciple of Christ will go; he commands each of us to devote our lives to the process of making mature disciples of every ethnic group all around the world. Yet, somehow, we have relegated this responsibility to others, especially to missionaries and full-time ministers.

One day each believer will stand before Jesus Christ and answer the greatest accountability question one could ask: How faithfully did we obey his greatest command for our lifetime of service, to "make disciples?" How many have you guided to become mature disciples of Jesus?

If we understand the methods that Jesus and the disciples followed, we will know the best spiritual investment ingredients to incorporate. These methods will be discussed in the remainder of this book.

Review Questions

1. What's your reaction to the Great Commission? Do you take it personally, or do you believe it applies more to full-time ministers, missionaries, or other "professional" disciples? Explain your answer.

2. Who are we commanded to disciple? What are the implications of this for you personally?

3. What is included in the discipleship process? Where has your church succeeded, or failed, in these areas? Where have you succeeded, or failed, in these areas?

4. What are the benefits of life-on-life discipleship? What advantages does it have over small-group ministry, or other discipleship models?

5. What is the commitment Jesus makes to every disciple maker? How does—or should—this affect your own discipleship efforts?

Chapter 5

JESUS' REQUIREMENTS: ARE YOU A TRUE DISCIPLE?

THE AVERAGE EVANGELICAL CHRISTIAN in America is weak when it comes to their personal, active commitment to Jesus Christ. In a nationwide survey including interviews with pastors and other church leaders as well as hundreds of adults who regularly attend church services and programs, four out of ten said they had a saving and committed faith in Jesus Christ. But not one of the adults and leaders interviewed had a goal to be a committed follower of Jesus Christ or to make disciples.[1] The average believer in our nation is sadly uncommitted. Most of those who faithfully attend church would call themselves followers of Jesus Christ. However, many are unaware they don't make the cut—not on Jesus' roster. I am not suggesting that large numbers of church attenders are nonbelievers, nor am I referring to their eternal destiny. But as we will unpack shortly, Jesus put heavy requirements on his followers—and sadly, many believers fail to meet these requirements.

One would expect the lack of commitment among believers to provide a tremendous incentive for churches to intentionally make changes in their approach and emphasis. Why is the church so reluctant to promote the terms that Jesus Christ required? As Greg Ogden says, "We are afraid that if we ask too much, people will stop coming to our churches. Our operating assumption is that people will flee to the nearby entertainment church if we ask them to give too much of themselves. So we start with a low bar and try to entice people by increments of commitment, hoping that we can raise the bar imperceptibly to the ultimate destination of discipleship."[2] Jesus was not apologetic, nor reluctant, to make strong requirements of his disciples. He had no fear of losing people or their offerings. He laid out serious requirements and allowed the chips to fall where they may. It's time we followed his example, trusting the Holy Spirit for the outcome.

For those who want to raise the bar, for those who are serious about following the command of Jesus to make disciples, it is necessary that we clearly understand just what his requirements are. In the Gospels of Luke, John, and Matthew Jesus states seven absolute requirements, or conditions, of being his disciple. We will look at each of these in depth.

John L. Thompson

To Be a Disciple of Jesus, We Must Deny Self

We will begin our exploration in Luke 9. Jesus had recently multiplied seven loaves of bread and a couple small fishes to feed 4,000 people. But now, as he ministered near Caesarea Philippi, the crowds gathered once again. Many had brought family members to be healed; some expected to be fed; others came to satisfy their curiosity. Of course, Jesus knew that their desires were primarily self-seeking. The Lord didn't mind healing and feeding them, but his purposes were infinitely greater than lovingly meeting the crowd's physical needs; his aspirations for them were eternal in nature. Jesus did not come to institute a welfare program; he came to give eternal life and to call believers to follow him. Therefore, as Jesus spoke to the self-seeking crowd he began putting requirements upon those who desired to be his followers. In Luke 9:23 he gives the first condition for those who would desire to be his disciples: "If anyone wishes to come after Me, he must deny himself, and take up his cross daily and follow Me."

In case there is any question, may I remind the reader that Jesus is not making requirements for sonship, but rather requirements for being his disciple. Further-more, the audience to which Jesus is conveying his requirements is to *anyone* who wants to be his follower—not only the people who could hear his voice at the time, but also those who read his words today.

As we examine Jesus' words, we see there are three parts to this condition. First, one must deny one's self. The Greek word *aparneomai*, translated "deny," means to renounce a claim. It is a choice I make in life. Jesus is not telling us to deny personal desires, as in asceticism. Jesus is not telling us to move to Tibet and live in a monastery. The attitude Jesus is most concerned with is not toward what we have. Jesus is most concerned with *what has us*.

In discussion about money Jesus told the Pharisees, "No servant can serve two masters; for either he will hate the one and love the other, or else he will be devoted to one and despise the other. You cannot serve God and wealth" (Luke 16:13). Some might mistakenly assume that Christ's main issue here is with what we own; however, the primary teaching here is that our God refuses to share ado-ration. He must be the Lord of our lives, which means we must turn from such idols as self-centeredness and selfish ambition that we often feed by pursuing material wealth. God will not share the place of supremacy and worship in our lives. He will not allow us to follow him on our own terms. In Matthew 8:21–22 a man asked permission "first to go and bury [his] father." Yet Jesus told him, "Follow Me, and allow the dead to bury their own dead." In other words, the dead are physically gone and have little importance or impact as far as one's future and calling. We have opportunities in the realm of the living to make great impact fulfilling our purpose, having lasting eternal value.

Albert Barnes observes, "For one to deny self means to let him surrender to God his will, his affections, his body, and his soul. Let him not seek his own happiness as the supreme object, but be willing to renounce all, and lay down his life also, if required."[3] We must decide who or what will be God in our lives, and this is most clearly demonstrated by where we put our money, time, and desires. All other things must become subservient to the affections, aspirations, and service that we dedicate to the only worthy and true God, Jesus Christ.

Second, denying self means taking up the cross. By this phrase, Jesus did not command us to take up his cross. His cross was one of death, a death necessary for our salvation. He likewise did not command us to suffer as he did or be crucified as he was. Certainly, we must acknowledge that the "cross" of many non-Western believers around the world has indeed been a martyr's death. With this cross, there have been more people executed for their faith in the last hundred years than during any other period in world history. And yet, Jesus was not discussing a piece of wood fashioned with a cross beam.

Some also mistakenly interpret Christ's words in Luke 9:23 "take up his cross" to mean that we must bear life's burdens. One woman said, "If you were in my shoes, if you had to live with my husband you would understand. I guess it's the cross I have to bear!" Living with one's selfish, self-centered spouse is not the cross Jesus is referring to. The cross Christ commands us to take up is a cross of self-sacrifice and self-denial. He intends for us to relinquish our personal goals, desires, and dreams in conformity to God's will to build his kingdom.

In the days that Christ walked on earth, cross-bearing brought to mind the sight of a condemned man who was forced to demonstrate his submission to Rome by carrying part of his cross through the city to his place of execution. Thus, to "take up one's cross" was to demonstrate publicly one's submission or obedience to the authority he had rebelled against. For believers today, this means to be obedient to God's will as revealed in his Word, accepting the consequences without reservation for Jesus' sake.

The apostle Paul illustrates death to self, or self-denial, in another way. In Romans 12:1 he says, "Therefore I urge you, brethren, by the mercies of God, to present your bodies a living and holy sacrifice, acceptable to God, which is your spiritual service of worship." In this case, he clearly illustrates that the kind of sacrifice we are to present is not dead but living. Our sacrifice is a continual act, a self-denial offered to God on a regular basis. According to Paul, this cross is our spiritual service of worship.

Self-denial takes many forms. It may mean setting aside a personal dream, such as buying a home, in favor of a missionary calling; or it may be as simple as setting pride aside in a personal dispute and resolving it, as in the following illustration:

Karen had been angry. She struck out at her dad with biting words, and then ran to her room. After a flood of tears she felt better. But she knew that following Jesus would now mean going to her father to apologize. How she fought against taking that step! She believed that the conflict had been his fault and in some ways it was. She also told herself she couldn't go and say "I'm sorry," not when he should, by rights, apologize to her first! Everything in her struggled against the self-humiliation that an apology would bring. And for a long time she stayed in her room, as the tension within her grew. Finally, Karen got up off her bed and, denying the fears and pride of her old nature, went to do what she knew Jesus wanted of her.

Karen's story illustrates the kind of living self-denial we all must exercise. Commitment to Jesus Christ demands the often brutal setting-aside of pride and fear, and all the rights that the old self demands as its due, to instead live a Jesus-centered life.

Third, the act of taking up one's cross is a daily requirement. We must understand that practicing self-denial and self-sacrifice involves daily, often repeated choices that help keep our sinful natures in check. Jesus recognizes that our pride and self-centeredness wars within our being to do just the opposite. Paul faced this war of the flesh (Rom. 7:14–15), and concluded that victory is only in Jesus Christ (Rom. 7:24–25), which is why he stresses that we must deny ourselves daily.

The first requirement Jesus gives all who desire to be his disciples is to deny self, taking up our cross daily and following him.

To Be a Disciple of Jesus, Jesus Must Take First Place

In tandem with daily practicing self-denial, Jesus requires his followers to place him first in their hearts and lives. In Luke 14:26–27, Jesus said, "If anyone comes to Me, and does not hate his own father and mother and wife and children and brothers and sisters, yes, and even his own life, he cannot be My disciple. Whoever does not carry his own cross and come after Me cannot be My disciple." At first glance it seems as though Jesus has made an impossible requirement. Even today, this passages remains one of the most exacting and piercing thoughts that ever came from the lips of Jesus. How exactly can he require anyone to "hate" the people they love the most?

God never contradicts himself. Jesus does not advocate "hatred"—in fact, he even commanded his followers to love their enemies (Luke 6:27, 35). Likewise, he was not going against his command to "love your neighbor as yourself" (Matt. 22:39) or the fifth commandment to "honor your father and your mother" (Ex. 20:12).

Instead, when Christ commanded potential followers to "hate" their parents in Luke 14, he employed what is called a Semitic hyperbole—an obvious exaggeration designed to emphasize a point. We use hyperbole in our communication all the time. For example, in exasperation I once heard a mother crassly say, "Billy, if you don't do as I tell you I'm going to knock you into the next block." Likewise, I heard a father angrily tell his son, "Get over here or I'm going to knock your head off!" Whether we agree with the parental threat as a means of control or not, neither parent literally meant what they were saying. They were warning their children that if they didn't do what they were being commanded to do, there would be unpleasant consequences.

This literary device of hyperbole is found in other passages of scripture besides Luke 14. One example is in Mark 1:33, after Jesus healed Peter's mother-in-law: "And the whole city had gathered at the door." It seems very unlikely that the every person in the city had gathered at Peter's mother-in-law's house. The text is simply saying that her healing had such an impact on the city of Capernaum that it seemed like everyone showed up at her door.

On another occasion Jesus said, "If your right eye makes you stumble, tear it out" and "If your right hand makes you stumble, cut it off" (Matt. 5:29–30). He is not telling us to gouge out our eyes and cut off our hands. If he was, our churches would have an auditorium full of blind, crippled people on Sunday mornings! Likewise, when Jesus said one must "hate his father and mother," he meant that he wants our love for him to be so complete and wholehearted that, in comparison, the love for our family members and life itself pales in comparison. Our sovereign God will not compete; he must be first in our life above everything.

In the same chapter, Luke 14:33, Jesus said, "So then, none of you can be My disciple who does not give up all his own possessions." Does this mean we can't own anything? No, what Christ means is that your possessions cannot own *you*! Anything that owns the believer prevents him from being a disciple of Christ.

It could be a beautiful car, home, career, reputation, or some luxury. Again, Jesus will not take second place.

Our love for materialism persists as one of the worst sins and greatest idols we have in the United States. There is nothing wrong with owning things, but as soon as things begin to own us we cannot be a disciple of Christ. A.W. Tozer said, "There can be no doubt that this possessive clinging to things is one of the most harmful habits in the life. Because it is so natural it is rarely recognized for the evil that it is; but its outworkings are tragic. We are often hindered from giving up our treasures to the Lord out of fear for their safety; this is especially true when those treasures are loved relatives and friends. But we need have no such fears. Our Lord came not to destroy but to save. Everything is safe which we commit to Him, and nothing is really safe which is not so committed."[4]

How has the world's cares impacted your efforts to put Christ first? It's not hard to see through the emptiness and superficiality of materialism. The idea that the meaning of life is to be found in the things acquired, the trophies accumulated, and the amount of money made loses its credibility in the emergency room and the funeral parlor. In the final analysis, what is really important in life is our consistency in putting Christ first in our life above all other things.

My "Tale of Two Cities"

One of my major tests in life came from my desire for materialism and comfort thirty years ago. I had decided that God was leading me to leave my second full-time ministry as education pastor in Baraboo, Wisconsin. As I went through the search process, one opportunity stuck out. As I corresponded and talked to the staff at the church I was considering, I was asked to visit for a Friday night and Saturday. This ministry was in Joliet, Illinois, an affluent and growing area in one of the suburbs of Chicago. It would represent a major increase in income, improved living conditions, and would probably be the nicest place we had ever lived. On the way to Joliet I decided to make a quick stop to see a ministry, whose director I had also corresponded with, about serving in a position as program director. This ministry was located in the inner city of Chicago, in one of its worst neighborhoods. In fact, a professor at the University of Chicago at that time was quoted as saying that the neighborhood of Humboldt Park had the greatest concentration of gangs of any city in the nation. One requirement, if we were to choose the Chicago ministry, would be to live in the neighborhood where I served. On top of it all, I would have to raise my own support as a missionary.

I never wanted to live or serve in Chicago, and only gave this ministry a passing look. But when I drove into the city, took the tour, and talked to the staff, God began to work. In fact, he so captivated my heart with conviction that I went to the suburban church, turned down the lucrative position and, along with my wife, began the process of raising missionary support. My friends in Baraboo pleaded with me not to move to Chicago, especially that area of the city. "It is a terrible place to raise children," they said. It was true that the gang violence was heavy, drug trafficking was intense, and the environment would be just the opposite of what I had gotten used to in the little town of Baraboo. When warned, God led me to make a statement that I have repeated a hundred times since: "The safest place in all the world is in the center of God's will, and the most dangerous place is outside of his will."

With God's help, I passed the test. I am so thankful that I decided to choose God's will over my fleshly desires. God directed me into one of the biggest life-changing decisions I have ever made to move into the inner city of Chicago, where my wife and I have lived now for thirty-three years. Contrary to the warnings and urging of many friends, God has been faithful, enabling us to raise our four children in a hostile urban environment. My children are all married adults now, and along with their spouses are raising their children in the inner city. All four are active in their service to God.

Materialism is not just the problem of the rich. We all struggle with its elusive enticement and powerful grip. A true disciple, however, has the Lord as his top priority by loving himself last and keeping possessions in the proper perspective. I found that life is like a coin; you can spend it any way you want to but you can only spend it once. How are you spending your life?

The requirements of Christ are extremely rigid. One may ask why this is the case. I believe that Christ's requirements are rigid because the stakes are so high. The eternal destiny of billions hangs in the balance. The requirements are also stiff because he is God and he will allow no one before him. To meet these stiff requirements, we must take up our cross daily to follow him by relinquishing the throne of self to him so that our Lord remains, first and foremost, King of our lives.

To Be a Disciple of Jesus Requires Commitment and Sacrifice

This third requirement for those who would be Jesus' followers is found in Luke 14:28–33. Using two illustrations, Jesus taught that discipleship must include commitment and sacrifice.

Christ first illustrates one of his requirements through the building of a tower. Before a person begins to build, he should be sure he will be able to pay the full cost of the project. "For which one of you, when he wants to build a tower, does not first sit down and calculate the cost to see if he has enough to complete it?" (Luke 14:28).

The second illustration is about a king considering going out to battle; he should be willing to sacrifice a desired victory and agree to a peace treaty if he senses he is unable to win. Once again, Jesus is saying that we need to evaluate our commitment and count the cost, because we must be willing to give up everything for Jesus if we want to follow him. Many people who would follow Jesus throughout the Roman Empire would do just that. They would give up possessions, employment, and sometimes their very lives, knowing that the task of following him was the most important assignment on earth. We must ask if we are willing to pay the full price of discipleship.

In counting the cost of being a disciple of Jesus, we must first count what it will cost if we choose *not* to be his disciple. It may be said that the greatest sin a believer can commit is the sin of unrealized potential. Our Lord commanded us to make disciples in Matthew 28:19–20, and then followed the commission with a lifelong promise of blessing on that activity. Therefore, we can conclude that those who obey have great potential for impacting many lives for eternity. Each one who chooses not to make disciples has chosen not to impact countless numbers of people through disciple making, and I believe they will suffer the loss of rewards at the judgment seat of Christ (1 Cor. 3:12-15).

Secondly when we choose to follow Christ, we deny self, choosing to follow his purpose for our lives. This may result in one experiencing a smaller salary or inferior living conditions. Life may include suffering of one sort or another. However, our God is not an ogre looking for an opportunity to blight us with some catastrophe. He is the sovereign Lord, and though our obedience can result in suffering we will always experience his enablement, provision, and blessing, and we will carry the joy he instills in those who are faithful to his calling.

Jesus climaxes his teaching on discipleship in Luke: "Therefore, salt is good; but if even salt has become tasteless, with what will it be seasoned? It is useless either for the soil or for the manure pile; it is thrown out. He who has ears to hear, let him hear" (Luke 34–35). He begins with the word *therefore*, indicating that he is linking this passage to our prior passage in Luke. By way of this linkage, Jesus directly relates saltiness to personal sacrifice. Salt is good only as long as it contains the characteristics of saltiness. If it loses its saltiness, it has no value at all and is thrown out. Since the context of this passage addresses the disciple's commitment and sacrifice, we must conclude that a disciple needs to retain this seasoned character, the character demonstrated when one is fully committed to Jesus Christ and lives a life of sacrifice. As I ponder this passage, I cannot help but believe that contemporary Christianity's loss of saltiness has in part perpetuated the United States' sad condition in the twenty-first century.

Without this life practice of commitment and sacrifice, I have no value to Jesus. In fact, he compares me to flavorless salt that is utterly useless. If you allow all of life's cares to supersede the importance of Jesus Christ in your life, you have little value of service to God. Commitment and sacrifice allows your service for Christ to have the lasting impact Christ desires, impact that is preserved just as meat is preserved by salt. It also makes your service pleasant to the Lord, just as well-seasoned food is pleasant to us. Therefore, commitment and sacrifice are necessary ingredients for those who would deny self and place Christ first in their lives.

In the gospel of John, Jesus gives three more requirements for being his disciple. Let's look at the first of those now.

To Be a Disciple of Jesus Requires a Commitment to His Teachings

In John 8:31 Jesus said, "If you continue in My word, then you are truly disciples of Mine" (see also Matt. 28:20; John 14:21). Of course, continuing in his word entails more than merely reading—it requires obedience to those teachings (John 14:15, 21; 15:9–10). The reference to "My word" includes all the word of God. The study of God's Word gives us authority as a basis of all we believe in, forming the content for a Christian world-and life-view. We must search God's Word for answers to problems and principles by which to live. In John 15:7 Jesus said, "If you abide in Me, and My words abide in you, ask whatever you wish, and it will be done for you" (see also John 15:9). To abide in Christ means to maintain an unbroken relationship with him. Thus, we must always be quick to restore our relationship with Christ whenever we sin. We do this first by both confessing the sin to God and forsaking its practice (Prov. 28:13). Secondly, we must restore our relationship with our fellow man when needed.

Therefore, the disciple of Jesus lives his life in obedience to God's Word. This is a growing and lifelong process which includes forsaking both sins of commission and omission. Sins of commission include sins God's Word tell us to avoid or cease. Sins of omission include sins one commits when he chooses not to obey or is careless in the obedience of the directives and principles found in God's Word. This study and practice of his Word, then, is a mark of a true disciple. If we are committed to Jesus' teachings, we will demonstrate the fifth requirement he places on those who desire to be his disciples.

To Be a Disciple of Jesus Requires Fruit-bearing

In John 15:16 Jesus said, "You did not choose Me but I chose you, and appointed you that you would go and bear fruit, and that your fruit would remain." Fruit-bearing is the natural byproduct of an obedient response to the teachings of Christ. As we grow spiritually, our fruit production will increase as John seems to indicate referring to fruit (verse 2a), more fruit (verse 2b), and much fruit (verse 5). This increase in fruit production comes not only from our being nourished by knowing and practicing the Word of God but also by the pruning process (verse 2). Sometimes he removes the parts of our life we don't need, such as our wasteful use of time as we engage in excessive unproductive recreation or hobbies. Often, pruning becomes painful as God introduces trials into our lives in order to make us more productive. Regardless of how much fruit we possess, the presence of fruit in a believer's life enables other believers to recognize him as a child of God. Jesus said, "For each tree is known by its own fruit" (Luke 6: 44). He then concluded his explanation of fruit-bearing in verse 45, saying that we can discern the maturity level of a believer by the type of fruit he possesses.

A true disciple of Jesus Christ does not live a hypocritical life; he lives what he believes, demonstrated by his fruit. One clear manifestation of fruit is demonstrated in the sixth requirement to be his disciple.

To Be a Disciple Jesus Requires Love for the Brethren

In John 13:34–35 Jesus said, "A new commandment I give to you, that you love one another, even as I have loved you, that you also love one another. By this all men will know that you are My disciples, if you have love for one another" (see also John 15:12, 17). These references use the highest form of love in the Greek language, *agápē* love—which is not a fluffy feeling or emotion but an action, a love demonstrated. That's how the world can know we are disciples, because we show our love for our brothers and sisters in Christ through our actions.

Finally, the seventh requirement of anyone desiring to be his disciple is to obey his final command, the marching orders for every believer living in the church age.

To Be a Disciple, Jesus Requires Commitment to Fulfilling the Great Commission—Making Disciples

One begins the process by first making a disciple. This takes place when one is led to a true saving faith in Jesus Christ. In Matthew 9:37–38, Jesus demonstrates his commitment to world evangelism, "The harvest is plentiful, but the workers are few. Therefore beseech the Lord of the harvest to send out workers into His harvest." Given that Christ emphasizes that "the workers are few," we must teach every disciple to become proficient in sharing his or her faith and leading people to salvation in Jesus Christ. Also in Mark 16:15 Jesus said, "Go into all the world and preach the gospel to all creation" (see also Luke 24:46–47; Acts 2:8). As important as it is, evangelism is not the Great Commission; it is only the first step.

Secondly, once the person becomes a new disciple we must begin the process of discipleship which entails leading him to be baptized in the name of the Father, Son, and Holy Spirit; then we are to teach him to observe (practice) all that Jesus commanded. This is a lifetime process, but our responsibility is to directly help the new disciple grow to the place where he can take responsibility for his own growth, make disciples by winning others to Christ, and with the Holy Spirit's help, make mature multiplying disciples out of them (Matt. 28:19–20). Everyone who calls themselves disciples of Christ and does not actively practice these two responsibilities misses the great purpose for every believer in this age. God's plan for the church today necessitates that we step out into his harvest and make mature disciples.

Therefore in summary, Luke, John, and Matthew record seven requirements Jesus gives that are necessary for all who would desire to be His disciples:

1. Jesus requires that a disciple deny himself, take up his cross daily and follow him.
2. Jesus requires that he take first place in the disciple's life.
3. Jesus requires his disciples to be committed and sacrificial.
4. Jesus requires that his disciples commit to his teachings.
5. Jesus requires that his disciples bear fruit.
6. Jesus requires that his disciples love the brethren.
7. Jesus requires his disciples to commit to both aspects of the Great Commission: to make disciples (world evangelism) and to discipleship (teaching them to observe all that he commanded). This is intended to be a continuing multiplying process until he comes again.

If we incorporate these seven requirements we will find our lives exceedingly productive as God blesses and multiplies our ministry's impact. So where are you, and where are those under your care, in meeting the requirements Jesus placed on those aspiring to be his disciples? It's all about priorities. As one wise old man put it, "I've never heard anyone on his deathbed say, 'I sure wish I'd spent more time in the office.'" Perhaps it is best stated from a quote of an unknown author, "Only one life, 'twill soon be past, only what's done for Christ will last."

As a reader, you may be at the crossroads between something really significant happening in your life, or the terrible mediocrity that characterizes so many of God's people. Because this may be the case, I would like to end this chapter by sharing an anonymous letter written by a young African pastor. It is said that they found this letter in the author's home after he was martyred in Sudan:

I'm a part of the fellowship of the unashamed. I have Holy Spirit power: The die has been cast. I have stepped over the line. The decision has been made. I'm a disciple of His. I won't look back, let up, slow down, back away or be still.

My past is redeemed. My present makes sense. My future is secure. I'm finished and done with low living, sight walking, small planning, smooth knees, colorless dreams, tame visions, mundane talking, cheap living, and dwarfed goals.

I no longer need preeminence, prosperity, position, promotions, plaudits, or popularity. I don't have to be right, first, tops, recognized, praised, regarded, or rewarded. I now live by faith, lean on His presence, walk by patience, lifted by prayer, and labor by power.

My face is set, my gait is fast, my goal is heaven, my road is narrow, my way rough, my companions are few, my Guide is reliable, my mission is clear. I cannot be bought, compromised, detoured, lured away, turned back, deluded or delayed. I will not flinch in the face of sacrifice, hesitate in the presence of the adversary, negotiate at the table of the enemy, ponder at the pool of popularity, or meander in the maze of mediocrity.

I won't give up, shut up, let up, until I stayed up, stored up, prayed up, paid up, and preached up for the cause of Christ. I am a disciple of Jesus. I must go till He comes, give till I drop, preach till all know, and work till He stops me. And when He comes for His own, He will have no problem recognizing me my banner will be clear.

May it be so with you.

Review Questions

1. One requirement Jesus makes for anyone to be his disciple is to deny self and take up his cross. What does Jesus mean? What does this mean for you, personally?

2. In Luke 14:33 Jesus said, "So then, none of you can be My disciple who does not give up all his own possessions." How would you explain this verse? Again, what are the ramifications of it for you personally?

3. Where do you need to count the cost right now, in order to follow Jesus more closely?

4. In John 8:31 Jesus gave another requirement for his disciples: "If you continue in My word, then you are truly disciples of Mine." How does one continue in Jesus' word? What would that look like for you?

5. When have you seen Christians truly loving one another? How did that change them (and you, if you were a part of it)? Either way: How *would* loving your fellow Christians as Jesus loved us transform your life?

6. Review the two primary aspects of the Great Commission. Why is each aspect important? How will you respond to that call?

Part 2

BUILDING AN EFFECTIVE DISCIPLESHIP MINISTRY

Now that we've talked about laying a firm foundation, we can begin building our structure. Let's start with the required materials. First we will have to choose what's needed to build a strong disciple-making structure. The people we build upon must be carefully selected. What are their qualifications, and what selection principles can we learn from the master carpenter? Then, what are the ingredients from which we need to build a ministry that will become strong and multiply?

As we begin this important project we are endeavoring to accomplish, we will encounter many obstacles. Our construction manual will provide answers to most of our questions. Then, for our structure to be transformed into a beautiful edifice, we will learn about the makeover of believers and how we can be a part of this miraculous transformation. One of the building methods we will explore is how to use small groups of future builders who will continue the progress. We will also learn how to make new structures beginning at the early stages, constructing disciples at home, and how the church can equip its parental carpenters. Since our God who is an infinite general contractor has laid out a perfect plan, we must ask why we have failed throughout the centuries to fulfill his plan.

Perhaps it is not too late to reinvent our process in line with the plan that the great contractor designed. And with his direction, let us embark on the greatest mission ever conceived—a project to *Change the Landscape of Eternity*.

Chapter 6

The Right Choice:
Selecting a Disciple Who Will Flourish

Every election season, candidates barrage voters with claims they hope will convince the electorate that they're the best qualified people; a candidate may spend many millions of dollars to secure that office. Unfortunately, the candidate elected is not always the best suited to hold the office. By the same token, we must also exercise caution during the "election" process of selecting who to disciple. Choosing the wrong person could result in scores of hours spent with little solid growth. There are a number of cautions to consider as you prayerfully look for a person to disciple.

First, God does not necessarily direct you to disciple every person who approaches you. Most young believers have not learned how to determine God's will. They are often more idealistic, and often prove to be insincere when asked for a solid commitment to being discipled. It is up to us, as disciplers, to determine if these people are indeed ones who God is directing us to disciple.

Second, the person may approach you with improper motives. I once had a man ask me to disciple him primarily because of his drive to feed his ego—to be able to tell others that the pastor discipled him. We must consider proper motivation—both ours and that of our potential disciple—when deciding in whom to invest in effective long-term discipleship.

Third, prayer is essential as we select the person God wants us to disciple. None of us want to disappoint and discourage another person. How does one say "no" when asked to disciple a person? We must remember that one's desire to grow does not necessarily mean that God is directing *you* to be her discipler. Therefore, we need to rely on prayer in our decision process.

We only have one life to live and to spend in service to Christ, so there are only a limited number of people we can minister to in this way. Since we are going to devote a significant amount of time to a few individuals, we need to use discretion. Perhaps that's why Jesus told the disciples, as they went from town to town, to concentrate their time on individuals who carried the most potential (Matt. 10:11; Mark 6:10; Luke 9:4). As we ponder who to disciple, let us consider the following principles.

Selection Principles

Less is better! For most laypeople, the maximum number you'll be able to handle at one time is one or two. If a person is fortunate as I have been, as a pastor, to include discipleship in one's daily schedule, he may be able to handle more. However, it is still better to concentrate on a few individuals. As discussed earlier, effective discipleship includes more than just meeting once a week for a Bible study. One should always look for opportunities to spend time with the protégé beyond the regular meeting. I often take men with me to visit at the jail, hospital, nursing home, and on home visitation. I also look for opportunities for social interaction, like going with them to lunch or having them over to my home. These activities provide an opportunity to minister through relationship and through one's example. Therefore, a disciple maker should choose a smaller number of individuals, and allow for relational opportunities beyond the weekly meeting.

Should be God-given. Many people may appear needful and desirous of discipleship, nevertheless, God has prepared certain people for you to disciple. Jesus referred to his followers in John 17:6 as men God gave him to disciple. He taught them and spent considerable time praying for them (John 17:6–10). God wants to give men or women to us for the same purpose. Thus, we must make it a serious matter of prayer by asking God to reveal those God-given people to us.

Don't choose hastily. Jesus took one-and-a-half years to choose his twelve disciples. He didn't rush; he knew what was at stake. I'm not suggesting that it will take a year and a half to choose someone to disciple, but we should not be hasty. Get acquainted with the prospect, observe the person's character, and evaluate if he or she meets the "FATHER" or "MOTHER" criteria (I'll explain this in a few pages). If you believe the person qualifies, meet with him or her and explain the commitment required. The disciple needs to understand the importance of the discipleship process. Once he or she does, the true disciple will be eager to agree to the commitment.

The necessity of prayer. Jesus spent an entire night in prayer before he selected twelve men to be his disciples (Luke 6:12–13). If selection was so critically important to the Son of God, how much more important would it be for finite man? Because of the limited number of people we can disciple, the importance of selecting the right person cannot be emphasized enough. We should look for people who we can pass the torch to—people who will become true followers of Christ who will in turn make the most of their lives in dedication to him. Jesus said, "apart from Me you can do nothing" (John 15:5). Without God's direction and help in the selection and discipleship process we will fail; therefore, prayer is the key from beginning to end.

The true value of the prospect's visible qualities. One would think that when a movement founder recruits key individuals to be leaders in a worldwide movement—armed with the vision to bring transformation to billions in the years to come—abilities would play an important role in the selection process. In my study of Scripture I do not see any of the twelve disciples bringing any assets to Christ, whether finances, personal abilities, or social connections that would enhance the embryonic movement to make disciples. Ironically, Judas Iscariot may have had the most going for him as far as assets are concerned. And the repeated performances of the disciples revealed that their character lacked something to be desired. This was Peter's own evaluation as he attested to his sinful condition: "Go away from me Lord, for I am a sinful man" (Luke 5:8).

Writing about the selection process of Jesus, Gordon MacDonald says, "It seems instructive that Jesus did little talking about His disciples' past. You would think we'd have heard a lot about Matthew's way of life as a tax collector or about Simon the Zealot's association with a political movement known for violence. But we don't. Jesus never exploits their 'testimonies.' If dark moments existed in the background of the Twelve (and there had to be), Jesus downplayed them, buried them in redemption. The Lord simply didn't deal with the past of people in public."[1] Just as in an election, a candidate's visible qualities often have little to do with his or her true character. It's the inner qualities, developed in us by the Spirit of God, that really influence success when one is knee-deep in the pressures and temptations of life.

Christ's selection of his men was not based on what they were outwardly but on what they would become through his discipling of their lives. We must be careful not to pick a disciple because of his talent, intelligence, gifts, pleasing personality, or outgoing nature. If we were going to select disciples for Jesus, understanding their background and training, we probably would not have selected any of the Twelve. Concerning these men Robert Coleman noted, "They do not impress us as being key men. None of them occupied prominent places in the synagogue nor did any of them belong to the Levitical Priesthood. For the most part they were common laboring men, probably having no professional training beyond the rudiments of knowledge necessary for their vocation."[2] Does this not give you, as it does me, great hope as men and women who, through the power of the Holy Spirit, have the ability to see great things accomplished for Christ?

Praise God for his unsurpassable greatness! Since we also want to select people based on what they could become, it is critical that we not allow ourselves to be biased because of the prospect's outward characteristics. We must follow God's direction for the selection of the people of his choosing.

The gender required. Even though it may be obvious, the importance of discipling someone of the same gender is a principle that many have unwisely violated. Discipling another person is a long-term process that becomes both intensive and intimate. Therefore, attempting to disciple someone of the opposite sex is both ineffective and dangerous. The discipleship process involves informal counseling that includes personal and gender-sensitive issues. A wise disciple maker does not enter this type of relationship with one of the opposite sex.

I am often asked if it is okay to disciple one's spouse. Of course, the intimate and sensitive aspects would not necessarily cause a problem in such a case. However, because of the accountability and authority the disciple maker has over his disciple, it is best that one other than a spouse conduct the discipleship. A person of the same gender can more fully comprehend the problems and needs of another, and can address these needs with more complete understanding. I am not implying that one person should not have spiritual input and responsibility regarding his or her spouse, but rather, that the nature of discipleship is better suited with another of the same sex.

Character qualities needed. As we pray and consider disciple prospects, the right person must have certain fundamental qualities before we enter into a deep relationship with them. Granted, a young believer will not be advanced in all or any of these traits, but I believe we should see a degree of these qualities in him, assuring us that spending the kind of time necessary to disciple that person will be well spent. The person who enters an in-depth process of discipleship with another person becomes a "spiritual father" (or mother) to him. Therefore, I suggest we look and pray for the six qualities enumerated by the acronym FATHER (for women I use the acronym MOTHER):

Faithful (Maternal faithfulness, for women)—God looks for men and women who are committed to him. In 2 Chronicles 16:9, we read that "the eyes of the LORD move to and fro throughout the earth that He may strongly support those whose heart is completely His." So many believers have a half-hearted commitment, often diluted by the influence of worldly desires. God sees right through our half-hearted efforts, and requires that we daily demonstrate our commitment throughout the Christian life by faithfulness. Paul exhorted the young pastor Timothy by saying: "The things which you have heard from me in the presence of many witnesses, entrust these to faithful men who will be able to teach others also" (2 Tim. 2:2). Notice he didn't say *slothful* men, nor does he give approval for him to choose *disloyal* men. Paul is concerned that the time Timothy spends in discipleship is not squandered away in a discipleship relationship characterized by unfaithfulness.

When selecting someone to disciple look for wheat, not chaff. I have made the mistake of selecting disciples who were characterized by chaff. This kind of person will do nothing but drain the discipler physically, emotionally, and spiritually. The disciples of Christ were called *followers* of Christ—he never chased them. Yes, thankfully his grace compels our Good Shepherd to go after his wayward strays, but once one becomes his disciple, he has no need to chase them because they are his followers. I'm not saying we should never chase down a stumbling disciple, but I am saying that we need to be careful in the selection process so there will be little need to go after lost sheep.

How do we know if the prospective disciple is "faithful"? I would suggest that the disciple maker begin observing the prospect. Is he coming to church with some consistency? Has the person demonstrated some faithfulness in the new believers' class? When asked to lend a helping hand in minor ways for setup or tear-down at church events, is he joyfully willing to help? When he makes a commitment, does he show up? Is he on time? What do other discerning people say about the person? In every instance, pray that God will reveal whether or not this person has a significant level of faithfulness.

During the first meeting, I always explain what I expect from my disciple. I share my confidence that God will do great things to develop him spiritually. I explain that if we enter into this kind of relationship God will be giving me spiritual oversight and authority over him; therefore, I will enforce certain requirements in order for him to receive the kind of growth God wants to impart. Then I list my expectations, which include faithful attendance in the regular services of the church, never missing scheduled meetings with me unless excused, and being on time. I tell him that he must call me in the event that he will not be able to make a meeting or if he is running late. I also require that he complete all assignments on time. I put these requirements in a written form I call the Disciple's Covenant, which I have him sign after emphasizing the seriousness of the commitment. (See a sample Disciple's Covenant in Appendix III.) I find a disciple's covenant to be a very good communication and commitment tool and I rarely proceed discipling a person unless the prospective disciple agrees to this commitment.

Faithfulness is a primary characteristic and is foundational to all others. A disciple who does not demonstrate faithfulness will waste many hours of effective discipleship. Until he becomes faithful, he will never be a fruitful disciple of Christ.

Available (Obtainable, for women)—The disciple may have all the other qualities desired, but if she doesn't have a time available that fits with the discipler's schedule, obviously she cannot be discipled effectively. For many, their commitment to the cares and desires of this world are an obstacle, even when legitimate. For instance, his responsibility on the baseball team or bowling league, the need or desire to work a second job, or perhaps college responsibility, may prevent him from meeting.

Often a potential disciple's commitment is not the issue at all. Sometimes the discipler's schedule and the schedule of the prospective disciple simply conflict. And so the answer may be that you help find someone else to disciple this person, whose schedule will harmonize more fully.

Teachable—Does the person have a genuine desire to learn? Is there a willingness to submit to being taught? Does the disciple ask questions, or just want to debate issues?

A potential disciple will display eagerness as he attends learning opportunities such as Bible studies or other church services. During these ministries, the prospect will be alert and engaged, sometimes taking notes and often asking questions. The discipler will quickly conclude that this person has a keen desire to learn about God and effectively live the Christian life.

I met with a man once who was constantly trying to teach me. When I tried to instruct him, he would change the subject because he was not interested in being taught. He just wanted to display his knowledge. The amazing truth is that when we use the Word of God in a life-on-life relationship with a person who has a teachable spirit, almost any barrier can be overcome.

It is a great pleasure discipling another when the protégé displays an eagerness to learn and continually applies the truth of God's Word. It seems like he can't get enough and has come to the discipler to help him grow. The disciple's teachability then serves as a necessary quality that can bring about transformation in his life.

Heart for God—If a disciple wishes to grow into a true servant of God, it is absolutely necessary that he or she has a heart for God. Does the disciple have a desire to know God? In Matthew 22:37–38 Jesus said, "You shall love the Lord your God with all your heart, and with all your soul, and with all your mind." Of course we all fall short of this command, but if a person desires to be a disciple of Jesus Christ, he or she must have a desire to love and obey him. Jesus also said, "If anyone wishes to come after Me, he must deny himself, and take up his cross daily and follow Me" (Luke 9:23) This command will only be followed by one who has a heart for God.

You will recognize if a disciple has a heart for God because *you* have a heart for God, and this yearning has become your primary motivation. Consider these questions: Does the disciple have questions about God? Does he or she share testimony of what God is doing in his life? Does the prospect seem to want to be around other brothers and sisters? Does he or she love to worship God and seem to relish the opportunity to sit under the preaching of the Word? Ask God to show you if the prospective disciple has a heart for God, and it will soon become evident.

Eager to Serve—I don't know of anything outside of God's Word and the active work of the Holy Spirit in one's life that more fully motivates us than our involvement in service to the Lord. We experience a great sense of gratification when we understand that we're doing something significant and of eternal value. The sense that the Holy Spirit is using us to impact another person's life is thrilling indeed.

Jimmy was a nineteen-year-old homeless young man and a new believer in Jesus Christ. He came to our city to move in with his brother, who lived at a nearby military base. When I found he would not be allowed to live on the base we took him into our home, and what I thought would be a few days lasted a year. During that time, I became his surrogate father and at the same time began to disciple him.

Jimmy had developed a high level of proficiency in the martial art of kung fu, which we used in several programs as a tool to draw kids. That summer we took Jimmy with us on a youth mission trip to Casa Grande Arizona to work with the children of Mexican migrant workers. One day we encouraged the kids to bring their friends the next day to see the kung fu master. The word spread rapidly, drawing a large number of children and visitors. Jimmy put on an exhibition, breaking pieces of wood and a stack of cement capping stones. The demonstration was then followed by his testimony of how he received Jesus Christ as his personal Savior and how God had changed his life. His witness had a great impact on the children that day, and a number of kids received Christ.

When I noticed that there were six teenagers in the crowd, I asked Jimmy to take them to a back room while we continued the children's program. I asked him to share more about how he got into this sport and about his workout regimen, as well as to explain more about how God helps him each day and what Jesus means to him. Since we had not planned for this additional meeting, Jimmy was afraid that he wouldn't know what to say. I told him that God would give him the words. And so, as requested, Jimmy took the boys and shared about his sport and his relationship with Jesus Christ.

After the meeting, Jimmy eagerly told me how God worked through him and as he talked to the boys he saw tears in their eyes. I asked Jimmy if God helped him as I said he would. He told me it was amazing and that he thought of things he forgot he knew and he shared verses he didn't know he remembered. Jimmy said he felt like he grew six inches spiritually that day. This experience was the highlight of the trip for this young man and probably the high point in his Christian life since his salvation.

Serving God has a profound impact on our motivation and love for him. If the prospective disciple has no eagerness to serve God, it will greatly impede his growth. Therefore, look for a person to disciple who sincerely wants to serve God.

Respect for Authority—Evaluate if the prospective disciple has respect for the authorities around him; this would include leaders at church as well as the police and elected officials. People tend to perpetuate a common disrespect for government officials, especially the police. Some go so far as to openly resist anyone who exercises authority and holds them accountable for their actions. However, as Romans 13:1–2 tells us, "Every person is to be in subjection to the governing authorities . . . Therefore whoever resists authority has opposed the ordinance of God, and they who have opposed will receive condemnation upon themselves." If the individual doesn't respect the civil authorities, he or she will likely disrespect the discipler's authority as a leader, and it will be difficult to disciple him or her. A general disrespect for authority will result in disrespect for God's authority as well. If the prospective disciple doesn't have these qualities, at least to a degree, it may not be wise to invest massive time beyond new-Christian classes.

F – FAITHFUL
A – AVAILABLE
T – TEACHABLE
H – HEART FOR GOD
E – EAGER TO SERVE
R – RESPECT FOR AUTHORITY

M – MATERNAL FAITHFULNESS
O – OBTAINABLE
T – TEACHABLE
H – HEART FOR GOD
E – EAGER TO SERVE
R – RESPECT FOR AUTHORITY

Considering these FATHER (or MOTHER) qualifications, we must discern whether the prospect meets the above requirements through prayer and simple observation. If the person is a new believer, for instance, he or she should begin attending a new-Christian class either in a small group or with another person one-on-one. We can then assess if the individual has been faithfully attending and finishing assignments such as memorizing Scripture. If there are no organized new-believer classes, we can begin taking the person through the new-Christian materials one-on-one with no commitment beyond this stage. Once the prospect completes the series, you'll be ready to judge if he or she meets the criteria. As you spend time praying, ask God to reveal the God-given person he has prepared for you.

Now that we've discussed these criteria, you might feel concerned that *you* don't have the FATHER or MOTHER qualities discussed above. Indeed, to be an effective spiritual father or mother, we need these qualities in our lives. If we're lacking in one or more of these qualities, we must ask God to develop us in these areas and to help us make an aggressive effort to add these qualities to our Christian walk. Equally important to assessing one's qualifications, we must determine whether we live a life worth emulating—whether we live a life others could follow. If the answer is no, we will do much damage to the prospective disciple. Nonetheless, we cannot be derailed from the great calling to make disciples. We must do whatever it takes to make ourselves ready, then by God's grace forge ahead to an effective, God-blessed discipleship ministry.

You Can Change the Landscape of Eternity!

Discipling others is one of the most rewarding ministries one can undertake. Every person we lead to Christ and every person we disciple changes eternity. As each one grows and serves God, he will in turn contribute to the change because the new convert or new discipler will now spend his life in service to God, impacting others by helping them grow closer to salvation, leading many to Christ, and by earning eternal rewards through their service to God, thus magnifying the changes to the landscape of eternity. Some may object by saying that believers will throw their crowns at the feet of Jesus. Literally, it is true that the twenty-four elders, who many believe represent believers, will throw their crowns or trophies at his feet, acknowledging that it is all because of him (Rev. 4:10). However, regardless of whether we throw our crowns at his feet, he certainly deserves all adoration we can give him. I believe, nonetheless, that we will enjoy the benefits of our rewards all through eternity. One of the rewards is the crown of life (James 1:12; Rev. 2:10). Believers may throw this crown at the feet of Jesus but they will not throw eternal life at his feet; they will enjoy the fruit of this reward and I believe the fruit of all rewards throughout eternity. Truly, this will change our eternity forever.

We also experience a tremendous joy in this life, when we see a person's light of understanding turn on as he develops a desire for growth and a hunger for God. It is always a great joy to watch the young believer live a consistent Christian life and to one day begin discipling other people.

As a discipler, you demonstrate obedience to the most important command Christ ever gave his followers—the command to make disciples. And it is by this same obedience that God weaves our legacy, one that will continue after we are gone from this earth—a legacy we will enjoy forever. What a joy it is to be used of God for something far bigger than ourselves!

"Now may the God of peace Himself sanctify you entirely; and may your spirit and soul and body be preserved complete, without blame at the coming of our Lord Jesus Christ. Faithful is He who calls you, and He also will bring it to pass" (1 Thess. 5:23–24).

Review Questions

1. Given your current circumstances, how many people can you truly disciple at this time? Why would you say that?
2. How did Jesus demonstrate that prayer is the key in selecting one to disciple? How have you implemented prayer into your own disciple-making (or disciple-making decision) process?
3. How can one sense that the disciple has a "heart for God"? Explain.
4. Review the FATHER (MOTHER) criteria above. Who do you know that fits these criteria right now? Describe that person.
5. How well do you fit these criteria right now? Where can you honestly say "follow my example"—and where do you not feel qualified to say that? Explain. How can you address the areas where you feel you're lacking?

Chapter 7

BASICS OF A DISCIPLESHIP MINISTRY: FOLLOWING THE EXPERT

IN A DISCUSSION ABOUT THE WEATHER Mark Twain said, "Thunder is good; thunder is impressive; but it is lightning that does the work."[1] Many churches across the United States fill their schedules with impressive ministries, large services, conferences, highly organized Bible-study programs, and elaborate events. Granted, many of these activities have discipleship potential, but we must continually ask ourselves what activities will bring about the greatest eternal impact.

There exists no greater task than working to achieve the primary mission for one's life. As discussed earlier, the Great Commission serves as Christ's marching orders for the church and, thus, the primary objective of each member of the body of Christ. Members may function in different capacities; however, their ultimate directive to make disciples constitutes the most important task.

If we truly desire to achieve our responsibility of the task spelled out in the Great Commission, we need to redeem the time. And if we are to use the most effective method to grow people to become mature, multiplying disciples of Christ, we must follow principles used by our divine expert, Jesus Christ.

Necessary Ingredients of the Life-on-Life Disciple Making Process

To effectively carry out the mission of making disciples, we need to explore the ingredients that make life-changing impact effective. I would liken it to a triangle with its three sides. For illustration purposes let's call it the Triangle of Discipleship. One side of the triangle would be the relationship component of disciple making, emphasizing the importance of the strong relationship between the disciple maker and the disciple. The second side of the triangle is the content used in the disciple-making process. The third side of the triangle is prayer, the source of power. As we pray, God guides the disciple maker to use the content in a relational setting to transform a life.

One does not have to study the life and methods of Jesus very long before he sees these three ingredients being central to his method of disciple making.

The Triangle of Discipleship

All three sides of the triangle are necessary for disciple making to be effective and complete. If relationship is missing, disciple making deteriorates into a classroom. A classroom has value but misses all the important elements relationship brings to the transformational process. If content is missing, there are no principles or precepts learned and applied that can bring transformation. Of course, if prayer is missing, all we have is self-empowered effort, with no ability to bring growth or change a life. It is God who transforms, and this foundational ingredient of prayer should never be missing. Let's now look at each ingredient in more detail.

Relationship

The basis for effective discipleship is the foundational ingredient of relationship between the disciple maker and his protégé. As Greg Ogden puts it, "If the mantra regarding the value of real estate is 'location, location, location,' then the core ingredient in making disciples is 'relationship, relationship, relationship'."[2] I cannot overemphasize the importance of relationship in the discipleship process if transformation is to take place. Many so-called discipleship ministries emphasize using a course or study series. While their content may be strong, and may depend on presentation which includes discussion or other methods, the series will not have relationship as its core ingredient unless the relational process is set up between two people.

There are five relationship tools I would like to note. Second Timothy 3:16–17 refers to several of these tools used in conjunction with the Word of God and are necessary to help men to become "adequate, equipped for every good work."

Reproof and correction. Because of discipleship's intimate and respected nature, the discipler represents the most effective conveyer of reproof and correction with the highest level of acceptance, especially once the relationship has been established. Paul told Timothy, "All Scripture is inspired by God and profitable for teaching, for reproof, for correction, for training in righteousness; so that the man of God may be adequate, equipped for every good work" (2 Tim 3:16–17). The most effective implementation of this verse is through relational discipleship. In applying this verse, I have found that a good disciple maker can be lovingly direct when reproving the disciple for sin, and find it well received. Moreover, the discipler then has the opportunity to instruct the disciple in how to respond to the reproof as he receives correction from God's Word. Gordon McDonald, in his book *Restoring Your Spiritual Passion,* said that "one solid and loving rebuke is worth a hundred affirmations."[3] As the Holy Spirit applies the reproof to the soul, the disciple experiences true life change.

Let me say at this point that reproof is not the same as criticism. Criticism is the act of passing judgment on a person or his activity. Reproof means to rebuke, and its purpose is to call attention to a sin; when coupled with correction, especially from the Word of God, it gives direction. Criticism beats down and takes away all hope, whereas reproof and correction help the person get on the right track.

The ministry of Jesus was filled with reproof and correction. When Jesus publicly rebuked sin and hypocritical practices it was to condemn a lifestyle of members of sects like the scribes and Pharisees, who he referred to as whitewashed tombs (Matt. 23:27). His rebuke challenged them that their life practices needed to be based on the inward character coming from obedience to the Word of God and not legalistic practices used to support man's prideful appetite. Jesus rarely rebuked an individual publically unless the particular sin was public. Jesus rebuked Peter, apparently in the hearing of the disciples, for being a spokesman for Satan (Mark 8:22–23). In this case Jesus had a very intimate relationship with the disciples since they traveled and lived with them. When we rebuke an individual in front of his peers, it usually has a disastrous effect. Tools of reproof and correction are rarely applied effectively to an individual from the pulpit, in the classroom, or even in a small-group setting. They are effectively administered only in private, and by a respected and loving mentor who has developed a close relationship with the person being corrected.

Accountability. This is one of the greatest tools for "training in righteousness." It is often said that "People will do what you *inspect*, not necessarily what you *expect*." Our sinful human nature follows the path of least resistance, and thus we often find ourselves choosing the path of sinful desire. As Christians, then, accountability between disciple maker and disciple is essential. Our sinful nature wars with our ultimate goal to be conformed to the image of Jesus Christ.

That being said, it is important to note that the disciple's commitment to honesty and transparency enables success in the accountability process. Not surprisingly, people tend to admit to only what will not embarrass them. Because of this tendency, we must ask the protégé for absolute honesty, while at the same time assuring total confidence. When they hesitate, we must also guarantee that we will not condemn. And when they are dishonest, we must rebuke and encourage a return to an honest relationship. Surely, accountability is a powerful tool of discipleship. It helps the disciple to make changes in his life by providing opportunities to remove practices that hinder his growth and to develop disciplines encouraging the adoption of new habits.

Accountability is one of the strengths of relational discipleship, far superior to discipleship based on programs that insufficiently stress personal accountability. As Ogden again explains, "Discipling relationships focus accountability around life change, whereas programs focus accountability around content."[4] Knowing content and even the application of that content has minor value. However, when a disciple maker can help his protégé make decisions, add practices, and passions that will change his entire life and service for the Lord, we are now talking about a truly eternal return on our investment.

Counsel. The value of relationship in the discipleship process also makes effective counseling possible. The disciple may not realize that the advice given by the discipler is an act of counseling, but that often is essentially what is being experienced in the relationship. The biblical counseling approach is by far the most effective for discipleship. The Word of God is all sufficient and is the most powerful tool to help the offender overcome every stronghold and struggle with sin one can face. When the Word of God is explained and the disciple begins to apply its truth, amazing decisions are made; this helps the person develop strong spiritual character as he learns to follow biblical principles and practices. I often recommend that those who are interested in discipling others enroll in courses on biblical counseling or at least read some of the many books on the subject.

Encouragement. Along with the Word of God, one of the strongest counseling tools and resources the Holy Spirit uses to motivate the disciple in the transformation process is the relational tool of encouragement. This is one of the great needs each disciple has. Encouragement coexists very well with biblical reproof, because reproof comes from the Word of God as the Holy Spirit convicts of wrongdoing and encouragement comes from the disciple maker as the Holy Spirit uses him to give hope.

We are encouraged when someone acknowledges our success or achievement; when we feel appreciated we sense that we are on the right track. All humans need encouragement. The quickest way to defeat and discourage the disciple is to criticize him. We need to avoid criticism and look for ways to affirm the person we are discipling. We need to follow what the apostle Paul said to the church at Colossae, "So, as those who have been chosen of God, holy and beloved, put on a heart of compassion, kindness, humility, gentleness and patience; bearing with one another, and forgiving each other, whoever has a complaint against anyone; just as the Lord forgave you, so also should you. Beyond all these things put on love, which is the perfect bond of unity" (Col. 3:12–14). Paul is telling us to be men and women of encouragement. He wants our lives to exhibit patience, graciousness, and kind expressions of appreciation always seasoned with love. This is the attitude we should display with those we are discipling.

Life example. Other than the Word of God applied by the Holy Spirit, life example is perhaps the strongest component of relational disciple making. The disciple will not remember much of what you said, but he will always remember how you lived and reflect on how you responded when faced with difficult circumstances. Relationship is critical because the disciple will learn far more from how we live than what we say. The old adage "more is caught than taught" is repeated throughout life. A disciple needs to see the Christian life lived out, and he needs someone to follow. The whole disciple-making ministry of Jesus was led by example. From the very beginning Jesus told Peter and Andrew, "Follow Me, and I will make you fishers of men" (Matt. 4:19). The discipleship relationship goes beyond a weekly instructional meeting. The more the disciple maker spends time with the disciple, whether recreationally or in ministry opportunities, the more impact the disciple maker's example will have on the disciple's development.

In summary, relationship provides dynamic opportunities to reprove, correct, and train in righteousness, holding the disciple accountable in ways that no other method can. Secondly, counseling is most effective in the context of a mentor relationship, helping the disciple gain victory over sin and direction for life's decisions. Third, through relationship, the disciple receives much encouragement as he moves forward toward Christlikeness. Finally, relationship makes it possible to see and experience the power that the discipler's life example has as the disciple seeks to emulate the former's life. Relationship truly remains the key to effective discipleship, as used by our Lord and the disciples. This foundational tool allows us, with the power of the Holy Spirit, to forge a life-changing, Christ-driven movement that will continue to save and change millions for eternity.

Content

If we have relationship without informational content, we have nothing more than a "friendship circle" that will do little to help the new believer's spiritual growth. Remember that in Matthew 28:20 Jesus said that the Great Commission involves "teaching them to observe all that I commanded you." In other words, he stresses that the disciple "observe," or practice, what the Word of God teaches. Therefore, information must never be given the disciple for the sake of knowledge alone, but instead for transforming their minds and lives just as we continue to be transformed as well.

There are many discipleship materials that are biblically based. As we select material, we should remember that Paul teaches we must start with the milk (1 Pet. 2:2) of the Word first. One reason many new believers never grow is they don't understand the basics and are thrown into more advanced material before they are ready. Once they are ready they can move into topics that are more meaty (Heb. 5:14). In other words, there are basics or foundational topics that should be discussed in the discipleship meeting or in a new believer's class and practiced before we address the deeper things of God's Word. For solid growth, we need to follow this systematic order from God's Word.

I remember meeting with a man who was totally discouraged after an assignment. He was supposed to look up a particular verse and answer the prescribed question. After the first week he came to me in frustration and said, "The Bible is too hard to understand, I just am not able to comprehend it." I said, "Bill, show me the verse you are trying to understand." We discovered then that he had looked up the *gospel* of John 1:9, though I had assigned the *epistle* of 1 John 1:9. And so of course, the reference he'd looked up had nothing to do with the question. He simply didn't recognize at the time that there are four books titled John in the Bible: the gospel of John, 1 John, 2 John, and 3 John. When I explained this, the light came on; he was able to continue and found that the Word of God was not so difficult to understand after all.

We mature Christians usually take such basic understanding for granted, but a new believer absolutely needs foundational instruction as well as basic truth if he is to continue moving forward. Therefore, content based on God's Word is absolutely necessary. Without it, there is no information with which the Holy Spirit can produce growth.

Prayer

Even though we have relationship and content, our discipleship will be ineffective without prayer. Jesus prayed regularly for his disciples. In John 17 we find Jesus' "high priestly prayer," in which he prayed for himself (verses 1–5), then for the twelve disciples (verses 6–19), and in the final verses (verses 20–23), for all future disciples which includes you and me. Notably, Jesus prayed for his disciples forty-six times in these twenty-three verses. Yes, we are the result of the twelve disciples' prayerful multiplication ministry. Therefore, the examples of our Lord and his disciples illustrate the importance for the disciple maker to continually pray for the disciple.

We are helpless to change lives without God's power. James said, "The effective prayer of a righteous man can accomplish much" (James 5:16b). Discipleship requires transformation, and only the Holy Spirit can accomplish that as he works through us. We are totally dependent on him which illustrates the importance of prayer. In John 15:5b Jesus said, "for apart from Me you can do nothing." Yes, perhaps I can humanly conduct a good lesson, but without God's illumination and power the lesson will have little if any transforming impact.

When we are in the search process for one to disciple, it is important to bathe the selection process in prayer. Once we begin discipling we need to pray on a regular basis for the protégé's growth and victory over sin. When we have finished the discipleship process, we need to continue praying that God would use the mature disciple to disciple others. Prayer is the integral foundation of everything we do, if we desire eternal impact.

Most discipleship ministries are lacking one of the sides of the triangle of discipleship. Yet we must remember and be resolute to the fact that each element of discipleship *relationship*, *content*, and *prayer* is necessary if we are to have effective and biblical discipleship ministries.

Six Characteristics of the Discipleship Ministry of Jesus

One cannot think about the life of Christ without being intrigued by the era in history in which he chose to come. He had no modern conveniences such as a cell phone, automobile, or airplane. He had no publishing capabilities, computer, Internet, television program, radio broadcast, amplifiers, or microphones. He had no church building or modern curriculum—not even the New Testament. He came in an era where the new movement would have to adjust from the Jewish economy of Old Testament law with all its ceremonial requirements to a New Testament age of grace based on the death of Christ apart from the law.

And yet, Christ came during this era and changed the world forever. After following Jesus for just a few years, these disciples turned the world upside down (Acts 17:6). And they didn't do it using mass media or mass evangelism. Jesus himself had only a thousand days to save all mankind, and he chose to invest his limited time with only twelve men.

As we observe the life of Jesus recorded in the gospels, I would like to note six qualities of his discipleship ministry that need to be incorporated in our own lives as disciple makers:

1. *Jesus had an intimate relationship with those he discipled.* Much has already been said about the importance of relationship, but it is significant to note that Jesus too placed a major emphasis on it. Herb Hodges estimates that Jesus spent eighty-five percent of his time of public ministry with twelve men! "Only one valid conclusion can be reached, and that is that Jesus' primary strategy was *not* ministry to the masses, though he did that wonderfully. It was not social influence, though His influence has been vast and permanent. It was not mere soul-winning, though He was the master soul-winner." Hodges goes on, "A common adage in our society is that 'the main thing is to keep the main thing the main thing.' Jesus did this, though it is obvious today that *our* 'main thing' and His are not in alignment."[5] Mark 3:14 says, "He appointed twelve, so that they would be with Him." Jesus not only lived with his disciples twenty-four hours a day, but was a perfect model of how to live. The disciples of Jesus were gradually transformed as they interacted with him, learned at his feet, and observed his life.

Notice what Paul said about the importance of relationship to those he ministered: "Having so fond an affection for you, we were well-pleased to impart to you not only the gospel of God but also our own lives, because you had become very dear to us" (1 Thess. 2:8). This loving relationship between Paul and his protégés is especially evident when we read Paul's letters to key disciples such as Timothy and Titus. He laboriously and yet joyfully spent a lot of time with these two young men in instruction and encouragement, and Paul's life example had a profound impact on both of them. Clearly, Paul maintained a dynamic relationship with those he taught.

Discipleship through relationships is especially effective in the urban setting because the value system of many urban people places much importance on associations. In fact, relational discipleship is well received by poor people and people of many ethnic groups throughout the world. Relationship is also critical because of the high percentage of people who were not raised with good role models, as well as the large number of children who were brought up in single-parent homes.

2.   *Jesus practiced perfect guardianship.* A guardian is responsible for another person. His duties include providing protection, rescuing those who stray, praying, counseling, teaching, warning, and rebuking when necessary. In the New Testament, the shepherd who watches over his sheep represents guardianship. Jesus, of course, is the Good Shepherd and the believers are his sheep. When he went to heaven, he sent the Holy Spirit to continue this ministry.

As the spiritual guardian, the disciple maker oversees the spiritual walk of the disciple. In Hebrews 13:17, we read that we must "obey" and "submit" to our church leaders, who "keep watch over your souls as those who will give an account." Here the writer is specifically speaking of pastors and church leaders, but I believe that the disciple maker likewise acts as guardian, or overseer, of the souls of those whom he or she disciples.

3.   *His duration continued until completion.* It would be ridiculous for a farmer to cram farm work like many students cram for a final exam. It would be absurd to procrastinate, planting in the spring while playing all summer, and then cramming in the fall to bring in the harvest. The farmer knows the price one must pay and the process that needs to be followed. In farming, we always reap what we sow and there are no shortcuts.

So it is with discipleship. Spiritual growth takes time. Jesus Christ only had three years, but he chose to invest the bulk of his time in a few chosen men. Paul began his discipleship ministry with Timothy around 53 AD; fourteen years later, he was still discipling—or at this stage, mentoring—Timothy the bishop, as we see in 2 Timothy. I am not suggesting that one should necessarily continue discipling a person for fourteen years. My point is: There are no shortcuts. We cannot conduct a six-week course and then expect that we have adequately discipled people.

Many in modern society have experienced an unstable life. One may not have known his father growing up, or his mother may have had a temporary boyfriend and may have moved from one apartment to the next. His entire experience may have been unstable; therefore, he desperately needs consistency and stability from a discipler if there is to be solid growth in his life.

A disciple maker should persist with discipleship until he has completed the process or until someone else takes over. The length of time will vary from person to person, depending on the motivation, background, and growth level of the one being discipled. Generally speaking, it will take a minimum of one year to bring a motivated adult to a significant level of maturity. If he was raised in a dysfunctional home, it may take many more years. I know of one man raised without a father in a dysfunctional family who was discipled for six years; he still has quite a ways to go before he is ready to disciple another person.

It has been said that it takes a hundred years to make a great oak tree, but only three months to grow a squash. Our priority must be to develop people, with the aid of the Holy Spirit, into spiritually mature disciples of Jesus Christ.

4. *Jesus prepared his disciples through teaching and training.* Much has been written about Jesus, the master teacher. He continually taught through instruction, parable, and example. Jesus was a perfect model for the disciples to follow. As Robert Coleman put it: When it comes to discipleship, Jesus was his own method.[6] "It is good to tell people what we mean, but it is infinitely better to show them. People are looking for a demonstration not just an explanation."[7]

Jesus also trained his disciples by giving them tasks to achieve. He sent the Twelve out two by two (Mark 6:7–13; Luke 9:1–6) and sent the seventy disciples on a similar mission (Luke 10:1–11). He assigned numerous tasks to various disciples, such as securing the colt for his triumphal entry into Jerusalem (Matt. 26:17–18), and sending Peter and John to secure and prepare a room for the Last Supper (Luke 22:7–13). These assignments are important steps in the training process. As the disciple serves, she experiences the Holy Spirit working through her and is sometimes placed in situations in which she must choose to trust in God for the results as well as for her needs. The service opportunity gives the disciple experience and confidence in her service but it also motivates the disciple in her daily walk. Therefore, service is one of the best tools to spur the disciple on in her spiritual growth.

5. *Jesus created the perfect environment for discipleship.* When growing a tender plant, one must choose the right environment. If you planted a garden in the Mohave Desert you wouldn't expect it to grow—unless you erected a hothouse where you could control the amount of sun, water, and heat. The environment for the new believer is just as important. Jesus created and controlled the environment of his disciples by actually living with them. He required that they leave home and follow him. He continually critiqued and commented on his discussions with various types of people, warning his disciples of the dangers they would face. Moreover, in 1 Corinthians 15:33, Paul warns us, "Bad company corrupts good morals" (see also Ps. 1:1–3; Prov. 13:20). In other words, if the new believer continues to hang out with unsaved friends, they will choke out his

growth until they are weeded from his life.

After thirty-six years of discipling others, I can't think of anything that more regularly prevents a new believer from becoming spiritually established than a sinfully wicked environment. Through God's direction, we can help the disciple create a new environment by planting him or her in the church, within the soft soil of Christian friendships—God's people who love the Lord. In this environment, and with effective discipleship, rapid and healthy growth will follow.

What about maintaining friendships with unsaved people for the purpose of witnessing? Of course, one cannot divorce himself from the world. We are in the world but we must not be of the world. We should look for opportunities to be witnesses to our unsaved friends and relatives. In fact, we should pray for them daily and look for opportunities where we can share our faith; however, the immature believer must not make the nonbeliever his source of fellowship or spiritual development will be hindered. Environment is critical for healthy development, and the discipler should do all he can to encourage the proper balance.

6. *Jesus provided focus through purposeful concentration.* Our modern obsession to minister to as many at a time as possible continues to be one of the reasons we as the church fail to effectively achieve our portion of Christ's Great Commission. The value of relationship diminishes as group size increases. Concentration on a few is vitally important for effective discipleship. Jesus had various groups of greater or less concentration. The smaller the group, the more time he spent with them.

The masses came and went; some believed, most did not. They came for various reasons; some to be healed, others for food, and many to see what the commotion was all about. As with any large gathering, Christ's purpose was very limited. Some of the masses believed and became followers of Jesus Christ and likely were among those known in Scripture as the Seventy. Undoubtedly, many of these were among the 120 present in the upper room on the Day of Pentecost. They were taught and, to some degree, trained as we can see when they were sent out two-by-two to preach the gospel (Luke 10:1–11).

Christ's ministry to the Seventy was much more concentrated than his ministry to the masses. His ministry to the Twelve was even much more concentrated. He lived with and had an intimate relationship with the Twelve day and night. They not only heard his teaching but also asked many questions, most of which were never recorded in the Gospels. By far, Jesus' greatest teaching tool in discipling the Twelve was his living example.

Finally, there was one-on-three with Peter, James, and John. He took them with him to the sick room of Jairus' daughter (Matt. 9:23–26; Mark 5:35–43; Luke 8:49–56). They went with him to the Mount of Transfiguration (Matt. 17:1; Mark 9:2; Luke 9:28). Peter, James, and John also went on ahead with Jesus when he asked them to watch and pray while he prayed alone at Gethsemane just before his betrayal (Matt. 26:36–46; Mark 14:32–42; Luke 22:39–46). We can read of the many instances that Christ spoke to these three men giving them instruction, encouragement, and sometimes a rebuke.

So, why one-on-one discipleship? Why not emphasize small group or even one on three? First, there were many instances Jesus spent time individually with his disciples. Secondly, if we are going to completely pattern our discipleship after our Lord, we need to remember that he lived with his disciples twenty-four hours a day, seven days a week, for two-and-a-half years. The customary meeting frequency for most modern discipleship sessions is once a week for one to one-and-a-half hours. We cannot even begin to compare our discipleship to Jesus' example.

Greg Ogden, in his book *Transforming Discipleship*, suggests that discipleship is more effective through what he calls "triads," which consist of one leader with two disciples.[8] I believe there are several weaknesses a discipler must overcome in using this method. First, the members are often at varying degrees of maturity and knowledge level. I believe it is best if the discipler selects two members who are near the same level, so the more knowledgeable person doesn't monopolize the meeting and the person with less knowledge feels intimidated and afraid to speak. Second, many leaders using this approach rely on a topical, extemporaneous approach, allowing members to suggest the topics of study as prompted by their personal questions and problems. This approach requires the discipler to be well-learned and seasoned, which is not the case of most lay disciplers. It is important to use good progressive curriculum, beginning with milk and progressing into solid food. The discussion of questions and problems can be interjected, but the discipler must always return back to the material. Without the curriculum the recipients will end up with many holes in their understanding because of overlooked content. As stated before, many disciples will be unable to emulate this approach as he begins to disciple another person.

Third, invariably one or more of the participants will come unprepared. It is difficult to grow together unless each person is prepared. Of course, signing a covenant agreeing to complete each assignment will help but will not totally eliminate the problem. Fourth, I believe there is less likelihood of producing multiplying disciples. Most lay people feel hesitant to lead group discipleship. By having a curriculum as a guide, more members will be comfortable to begin their own group once their initial group has ended. When questions or needs come up, the unprepared disciple maker can plan on talking about those subjects the coming week(s) after he has had a chance to prepare for the discussion.

I personally believe that the potential of producing a multiplying disciple is greater in one-on-one discipleship. The accountability is more private and better received coming from a respected mentor rather than through the peer accountability approach sometimes used by groups. Also when there is a need, rebuking or correction is more palatable in a private setting. Because of these hindrances, one-on-two discipleship is not the best method for most people. However, if a discipler can use this method effectively, it has advantages such as peer fellowship, peer pressure, helpful group discussion, and horizontal accountability that can be established between the disciples.

Living with his disciples provided Jesus with many opportunities for life-on-life, even one-on-one discipleship. There are many references of Jesus talking to an individual disciple, such as with Peter (Matt. 14:28–29; 16: 22–23; et al.).

Concentration on small units of people is critical to any effective discipleship ministry. Waylan Moore, in *New Testament Follow-up*, states, "A decision that our ministry will be intensive, rather than extensive will change our whole life. Quality begets quantity. It takes vision to train one man to reach the masses."[9] A wise decision for any servant of God is to spend his life concentrating on a few individuals at a time. Following this methodology over the long haul will produce many solid disciples who are equipped to win people to Christ and to continue the discipleship process.

Jesus gave us the perfect example of how to disciple people. As we consider specific principles from his discipleship ministry as outlined in this chapter, we have an excellent framework with which to develop our own effective disciple making ministry.

Review Questions

1. According to the author, what is the most effective method of growing a person to become a mature disciple of Christ? Do you agree? Why or why not? What objections, or difficulties, do you still have with this approach?

2. Reflect again on the Triangle of Discipleship. Which of the three elements—relationship, content, and prayer—are you strongest in? Weakest? What can you do to strengthen all three sides in your disciple making process?

3. In your own words, why is relationship so necessary to life-on-life discipleship?
4. The author states: "I can't think of anything that more regularly prevents
   a new believer from becoming spiritually established than environment."
   How have you seen this to be true?
5. How can you create an environment in which a disciple can thrive? Be
   specific.

Chapter 8

GOING TO THE NEXT LEVEL:
A DEEPER UNDERSTANDING OF DISCIPLESHIP

IMAGINE FINDING A FIVE-MONTH-OLD BABY buckled in a car seat, placed in a baby crib, and left for eight days. This is what happened to Benjamin Sargent. His diaper wasn't changed for at least five days and possibly up to a week. According to the *Peoria Journal Star*, his last meal was given to him three or four days before he was found lifeless. Prolonged exposure to the unchanged diaper caused his skin to be eaten away and allowed bacteria to seep into his body, ultimately causing his death. The 2008 incident left his father James Sargent convicted of first-degree murder and sentenced to one hundred years in prison. The baby's mother, Tracy Hermann, was also convicted of first-degree murder and sentenced to fifty years. The charges stated that the parents' actions, or lack thereof, were "brutal and heinous...indicative of wanton cruelty."[1]

The above story is shocking and unbelievable, and the parents of the child were cruel to say the least. But how often have we been guilty of ignoring the spiritual malnutrition of many of our babes in Christ?

An infant clearly does not have the ability to pick out the appropriate food, prepare it, or even feed himself when he is hungry. Yet we often abandon new believers whom we've led to Christ. I have heard report after report from individuals who led a person to a saving knowledge of Christ but then failed to provide next-step information, invite them to a new-believer class at church (if one existed), or even wrote down the convert's address and phone number for someone else to follow up. According to Wayland Moore, "99 percent (of believers) never spend time following-up the souls they have won to the Lord."[2] No wonder the church has done such a dismal job in fulfilling the Great Commission. We have neglected Christ's greatest directive.

Unfortunately, when we do invite these spiritual infants to church, they often receive food unsuitable for their undeveloped spiritual palate. We contently allow them to sit under the preaching or teaching of the Word better suited for more spiritually mature Christians, thereby leaving new believers to assume that the church and the Bible are incomprehensible or at best impractical for them.

We often use flawed or incomplete methods of evangelism. That is, we give a poor explanation of how one is saved and lead him in a prayer, without the understanding necessary for a heart belief. It was only an intellectual decision. What's worse, we often tell the nonbeliever that he has eternal life and that the angels are rejoicing in his newfound faith while the seeker goes through life believing the lie that he is a believer.

When a spiritual babe is neglected, he becomes sick and dwarfed spiritually. When we go without food for several days, perhaps through fasting, our hunger subsides. The same thing happens to the new believer. When first saved he is starved for spiritual truth, but if he is not fed appropriate food, his hunger eventually subsides. Left alone he "sits, soaks, and sours," often becoming stagnated. I have known many people who have been saved for fifteen or twenty years who never grew past the spiritual-infant stage. They were never fed spiritual food they could digest, and as a result they became spiritually malnourished.

The Importance of Early Discipleship

Jesus demonstrated by personal example the importance of following-up with new believers. He went home with Zacchaeus after his conversion on the streets of Jericho (Luke 19:7). Likewise, after the conversion of the woman at the well in Samaria, Jesus stayed two extra days in Sychar to instruct the people who believed (John 4:40). Often the new believer was allowed to join the precession, to learn more from the Master (Mark 10:52). There are a number of reasons why it is so important to follow-up with new believers, so that they can benefit from early discipleship.

First, early discipleship is essential because of the weakness of new Christians. New Christians are more helpless and at risk in their fight against temptation and spiritual discouragement than at any other time in their lives. As Herb Hodges states, "Satan knows better than most of us that spiritual ministries are most easily prevented or twisted at their beginning. He fears acceleration and momentum in a true and productive spiritual ministry, so he acts quickly when he sees a threat from such a ministry."[3]

The new believer knows little about the Word of God, and therefore is defenseless. He will easily accept thoughts whether from within, by Satan, or even his unsaved friends. Trials become stumbling blocks to the new believer, especially if well-meaning friends tell him that life will be wonderful now that he is saved. Sadly, we often neglect to point out that Jesus is not the "bridge over troubled waters," but instead the One who takes us through these hard times. When facing trials a new Christian often comes to the wrong conclusion that his newfound faith just doesn't work. If we teach basic principles to the new believer, he will quickly learn that God's Word has answers for his every concern, and he will find that Christ came to give us life "more abundantly" but not life free of pain (John 10:10).

Secondly, the early stage of discipleship is essential because the new believer is spiritually hungry and has tremendous potential for growth. The potential for spiritual growth could be likened to the growth rate of an infant. By four years old the child has doubled in height and weighs five times her birth weight. It is similar with the baby Christian. The early stages of growth are the most foundational and pivotal point in his life. He can become spiritually malnourished and sickly, continuing that way for a lifetime, or he can grow to spiritual health and strength through basic discipleship.

When a person is truly saved, he gains a hunger for God. Leading the new believer through basic Christian life principles thus greatly increases his probability for transformation. The author of Hebrews 5:12 says, "For though by this time you ought to be teachers, you have need again for someone to teach you the elementary principles of the oracles of God, and you have come to need milk and not solid food." Apparently the people to whom he is writing should have grown faster but did not learn the "elementary principles," also referred to as "milk." Therefore, the new believer needs an early diet of spiritual milk, followed by deeper teaching of "solid food" as he is able to process it.

New Believer Follow-up Process

The new believer is a spiritual baby requiring every measure possible to help him or her upon the path of spiritual growth. Since the new believer is spiritually weak and vulnerable, we must begin new believer follow-up as soon as possible, preferably making contact in person or by phone within twenty-four hours. Satan will attack the new Christian in those early days, so contact by the new believer's spiritual parent—the one who led him or her to Christ—is often best received. During the initial contact, focus on encouragement, guiding him or her in dealing with recent sin, answering questions, and sharing the importance of and information about the new-believer class. If no class is available, someone—perhaps even the person who led him or her to Christ—should lead the person individually through the new-Christian material.

Later in the week the spiritual parent should make a second follow-up contact, repeating the basic discussion topics from the first contact. In addition, be sure he or she has transportation to the new believer class, and make arrangements if needed. If the class is held at church it is wise to meet the young believer outside the building at the specified time, escorting him or her to the class with an introduction to the class leader. Imagine how foreboding it is for the new believer, especially if he or she has never attended a class at your church, to wander through an unfamiliar building alone, searching for a class taught by a stranger, and after class meandering his or her way, trying to find the worship service. We should make the experience "user friendly," escorting him or her to the class with an introduction to the new class leader, picking the new student up after the session and escorting him or her to the worship service. We never want our lack of thoughtfulness to be the reason a new believer became fearful or frustrated, leaving the church without completing the initial instruction.

Every new believer should have the opportunity to go through a new-believer study, learning to practice foundational principles needed to launch the growth process. This class, whether a small group or one-on-one, should begin within a week of conversion and continue weekly, focusing on basic "milk" topics such as those suggested in Appendix II ("Discipleship Topics"), with curriculum listed in Appendix I ("Bibliography").

Unfortunately, most churches do not have new-believer classes available. However, when one is available, don't make the common mistake of merely inviting the new convert to attend. Follow the steps suggested and love him into the study. I encourage churches to organize a repeating new-Christian series, going continually without a break. In a repeating format a new believer can begin right away, even if the next lesson is not at the beginning of the series. He can finish the current series then continue on to the new series until he has completed all the sessions he has missed. If the church cannot sustain an ongoing new-Christian class, several people should be recruited to lead new believers through the material individually at the location and on the day that works best. These early months provide great opportunities for growth in the life of the new believer. Conversely, when we don't seize this precious opportunity, many new believers will stagnate or simply stop coming altogether.

New Believer Follow-up Steps

1. Phone call from spiritual parent within 24 hours of conversion
   - Encourage the new convert, rejoicing about his/her salvation
   - Ask how the new life is going, dealing with immediate sin issues
   - Answer questions he/she may have
   - Share its importance and invite him/her to the new-believer's class
2. Call the new believer again toward the end of the week
   - Ask how the new life is going, dealing with immediate sin issues
   - Answer questions he/she may have
   - Remind him/her about the new-believer's class.
   - Make sure he/she has transportation and make arrangements if needed.
   - Tell the new believer that you will meet him in front of the church to take him to the new-believer's class
3. On the day of the class meet the new believer at the specified location
   - Walk the new believer to the classroom and introduce him/her to the class leader
   - If he/she is new at the church escort him/her to the worship service
4. Once the new believer has attended the class, future follow-up should be handled by the new-believer class leader
   - The class leader should contact the new believer if he/she is absent from class.
   - The class leader should contact the student before the next series and let him/her know when his missed lessons will be repeated.
   - Each new believer who demonstrates recommended qualities should be linked with a disciple maker to continue the process.

Understanding the Disciple Making Process

People often think that discipleship is all about teaching content or completing prescribed material. Discipling another person consists of *much* more than dumping information. It's not sufficient for one to back up his Mack truck, unloading all his knowledge. That reminds me of a poem from an unknown author I once learned:

"Ram it in, cram it in, students' heads are hollow;
Slam it in, jam it in, still there is more to follow."

Discipling others is more than dumping information from the teacher's jug into the student's mug. The discipler imparts his very life into another. The apostle

Paul, for instance, emphasized his love and commitment for the people he was ministering to when he told them, "Having so fond an affection for you, we were well-pleased to impart to you not only the gospel of God but also our own lives, because you had become very dear to us" (1 Thess. 2:8). Disciple making involves the discipler caring for the needs and especially growth of the disciple.

Given the importance of the relationship between the discipler and disciple, the serious disciple maker should consider the following seven principles:

PRINCIPLE 1:
THE DISCIPLE MAKER MUST BE SOLD ON THE ETERNAL VALUE OF DISCIPLE MAKING

As discussed earlier, Christ's command to disciple others constitutes the greatest and final directive he gave his followers, which includes you and I today (Matt. 28:19–20). It is the only way to make real change in people's lives, changes that impact eternity. In other words, the work of discipleship is much bigger than any one of us, so we must let the importance of this mission grab our hearts and lives. If you and I don't believe that Christ's call to disciple others is important, our efforts will fizzle out through the stress and complexities of life. Moreover, if we don't fully devote ourselves to life-on-life discipleship, then the disciple will soon become infected by our disingenuous attitude and ultimately fall by the way-side—or, even if he does complete the process, will never multiply his life through another.

The most important ministry we can ever have is to fully disciple another person. It is so important that Christ made it his greatest command. We must therefore let this truth grab us and demonstrate our belief in its importance by how we live our lives.

PRINCIPLE 1:

The Disciple Maker Must be Sold on the Eternal Value of Disciple Making.

PRINCIPLE 2:
GOD IS THE ONE WHO TRANSFORMS A LIFE

Our ministry, by itself, is useless. It will only change the disciple and produce growth when our Lord takes it, impresses the truths taught on the disciple, and uses them to bring transformation. Understanding our inability to produce the needed results, we must spend time in regular prayer for the disciple, praying that God will guide and work through us producing a disciple that will multiply his life into the life of another as a new disciple of Jesus Christ.

> **PRINCIPLE 2:**
> God is the One Who Transforms a Life.

PRINCIPLE 3:
THE DISCIPLE MAKER MUST BE REAL WITH THE DISCIPLE

To be real means that we allow ourselves to be human and to be ourselves, admitting when we are wrong or when we have sinned. We should never succumb to the pressure of putting on a front. Likely the disciple will see through the facade and recognize his disciple maker as a phony. If the discipler successfully conveys a false veneer, he would give the disciple unreal expectations of what a mature Christian life should look like, thereby giving him a sense of hopelessness and a cynical attitude as he concludes that he could never measure up to the perfection displayed by his mentor. Instead, the disciple maker must biblically deal with sin so that the disciple will in turn learn and grow, seeing the proper way to respond to sin. As the discipler becomes involved, the disciple will learn that he can trust his mentor, and that his mentor cares for him and desires to help him grow. With an accepting, loving example, the disciple will usually respond by becoming transparent and open about his own problems and struggles.

> **PRINCIPLE 3:**
> The Disciple Maker Must Be Real With the Disciple.

PRINCIPLE 4:
THE DISCIPLE MAKER MUST CARE FOR HIS OWN SPIRITUAL DEVELOPMENT

Personal discipleship is a lifelong process. Therefore, the disciple maker must maintain a consistent relationship with Christ, continuing to grow as he applies biblical truth to his own life. Once he ceases abiding in Christ he sets himself up for sin and spiritual failure. In other words, the person who thinks he "has arrived" and settles into a plateau of complacency in his Christian life will become totally ineffective in leading others spiritually.

Because of the impact of our example in the disciple-making process, one of the key ingredients in our Christian life is having the character worth emulating. In Luke 6:40 Jesus said, "A pupil is not above his teacher; but everyone, after he has been fully trained, will be like his teacher." Because the one we disciple will in many ways become like us, we must strive to maintain a pure and close relationship with our master disciple maker, Jesus Christ. The protégé must follow our life, as we follow Christ. Of course, unlike Christ we are not sinless models; therefore, throughout the discipleship process we as disciplers must display a level of consistency and biblically deal with our sin as it arises.

> PRINCIPLE 4:
>
> The Disciple Maker Must Care for
> *His Own Spiritual Development.*

PRINCIPLE 5:
THE DISCIPLER MUST HAVE AN ATTITUDE OF PERSEVERANCE

Perseverance is an attribute we must all develop in our Christian walk, in everyday life, and in our discipleship ministry. One would think that Christ's twelve disciples would have experienced quick growth with no failure on their part. However, Scripture paints a different picture. Perseverance was greatly needed by the disciples, as it is in our own lives. Jesus certainly practiced perseverance in his disciple making ministry.

According to Gordon MacDonald, "An overview of how many times the original disciples fell short of reasonable expectations will quickly remind any would-be disciple that the process of apostolic development includes disappointment. Failure was all over the menu of the original Twelve, but rejection wasn't."[4] As we look at the ministry of Christ, we are astounded at the patience of Jesus with the motley crew that he discipled. If there was ever a need for perseverance, it was with these twelve men. Assuredly, Christ demonstrates perseverance and enables us through the Holy Spirit to do the same.

Because of man's sinful nature, the disciple will often seek the route of least resistance. We always want an easier life, tend to take shortcuts, and are often satisfied with mediocrity. Disciple making, on the other hand, requires work and takes time. Disciples commonly become discouraged and threaten to give up, especially after they stumble. A good shepherd, however, goes after his sheep, picks him up, knocks off the dirt, and encourages him to keep going.

Indeed, when the disciple fails, the disciple maker must not take it personally and must not become discouraged. The fact that the disciple stumbles is not a reflection of the discipler's effectiveness or lack thereof. The disciple maker must pray for the protégé when needed, and help him renew his relationship to Christ and continue to grow.

> PRINCIPLE 5:
>
> The Discipler Must Have an Attitude of Perseverance.

PRINCIPLE 6:

DISCIPLE MAKING MUST INCLUDE QUALITY TIME

Again, relationship constitutes a key ingredient of discipleship. It has been said that the protégé will learn ninety percent of what the mentor does and ten percent of what he says. Don't conclude that your regular meeting each week is sufficient. Spend as much time with the disciple as your schedules will allow.

Since it is difficult to find time to spend with another busy adult, the wise disciple maker should look for activities he is already involved in which he can involve the young Christian. Besides inviting the disciple to be part of family and personal activities, it is great to have him take part in your ministry opportunities.

As a pastor I try to take my disciple with me on ministry activities. As he is available, I take him with me to visit people in the hospital, at the county jail, on home visitation, on speaking engagements, and to seminars where I'm teaching. I recently took a young man I was discipling to a funeral I conducted. Since he was preparing for the ministry I told him to follow me everywhere I go, sticking with me like a shadow. One cannot overestimate the value of these experiences, especially when you realize that the value is far more than the event itself. In fact, the travel time may be the most beneficial element. On some of these occasions the disciple becomes my personal assistant, thereby providing a training component. There is no substitute for quality time spent with the disciple, and it will have a profound impact when he begins to emulate the disciple maker's life.

> PRINCIPLE 6:
>
> Disciple Making Must Include Quality Time.

PRINCIPLE 7:
THE DISCIPLER MUST BE A LEADER

The disciple maker or the disciple should never form a discipleship relationship with someone with whom he hopes to be best friends. Discipleship is a mentor-protégé relationship. They must not hang out purely for the sake of recreation, because discipleship is a purposeful relationship in which the discipler needs to remain the disciple's leader and spiritual guide.

The serious disciple maker will hold the disciple accountable and even confront when necessary. There are times when he will have to rebuke, correct, as well as instruct him. Becoming best friends will get in the way of these necessary encounters.

> PRINCIPLE #7
> The Discipler Must Be a Leader.

Elements of Discipleship

There are three main elements used in the life-on-life disciple making process: teaching, counseling, and encouragement.

Teaching is an obvious ingredient in the discipling relationship; however, most teaching will not occur in a formal manner or setting. Truly, the most effective teaching opportunity comes when the disciple maker seizes a teachable moment, such as when the disciple is going through a trial or has a friend or relative experiencing the consequences of sin. These experiences, though difficult, lend themselves to teachable moments.

Furthermore, all teaching and training does not have to come from the disciple maker. The wise leader uses his available resources. For example, if the church is offering a class on spiritual gifts, the wise discipler encourages his protégé to take the class. The same is true when it comes to training opportunities. An evangelism class combined with practical experience in witnessing is an excellent opportunity for training, and a wise disciple maker will encourage his protégé to enroll. Using these resources makes discipleship a team ministry. Nevertheless, while many people are involved in the disciple's development, the disciple maker must retain responsibility for guiding the process.

Part of the teaching process is the gentle rebuke but we must rebuke sparingly and keep the admonishment biblically grounded. The disciple should be rebuked when he has sinned and has not dealt with it through confession and repentance.

Correction, in turn, helps the disciple see the God-honoring way by which to judge his life. The discipler instructs his protégé regarding how he ought to act and speak before the world and his God, without making an issue of non-sinful mistakes. In most cases, the disciple maker should place his emphasis on correcting that which relates to the disciple's Christ-honoring testimony and pursuit of godly living.

Along with teaching, *counseling* is a regular part of life-on-life discipleship, even though the protégé may not think of his time with the discipler as counseling since it occurs during informal discipleship meetings. Discipleship counseling should be biblically based, involve all areas of life, and be conducted out of an attitude of love. (See Appendix IV for Topical Scripture Passages to use in biblical counseling.) Counseling will help the disciple learn to have victory over all types of sin, provide guidance for life's issues, and—when used correctly—be a tool of affirmation. Our use of God's Word as the source of authority allows our counseling to be a dynamic life-changing ingredient in the discipleship process.

Encouragement is possible because of the dynamic respect/love relationship, usually a common part of the mentor-protégé bond. The encouragement from the disciple maker comes through affirmation, rebuke, and correction. In general, affirmation does not come often enough for most people. We tend to be much more negative in close relationships. The disciple maker therefore needs to look for ways to affirm his disciple. Compliments, praise, a gesture or look of approval, and even public recognition all work together to help the one being discipled have a positive and motivated attitude.

Another type of encouragement comes from accountability. This is perhaps one of the strengths of life-on-life discipleship. Helping the disciple to follow through with his commitments, whether it has to do with lifestyle changes or just becoming more consistent in his Christian walk, will become a major aid in his development.

As you can see, each of these three elements are vital to the discipleship process. Whether teaching, counseling, or encouraging the disciple in his Christian walk, the benefit experienced by the disciple of Christ will be life-changing.

Major Milestones of Growth

I have found that the disciple-making process presents six general milestones of growth that need to be followed up on and completed before the basic discipleship process can come to an end:

1. *Assurance of salvation* is an early milestone the disciple must realize before

he can grow and progress. One of the men who I discipled struggled for months with this. I went over numerous verses and passages of Scripture that very clearly taught his position in Christ, and yet after every service I would see him sitting with another brother, asking questions pertaining to his assurance. Finally after three months of perseverance and prayer, he got it; from that point on his growth began to soar. When a person lacks assurance of his salvation in his life he becomes consumed with this burden. He cannot give complete attention to the growth process until he understands and trusts his eternal position in Christ. If he does not pass this milestone, it will hinder solid spiritual growth.

2. *Consistency in basic disciplines* is the next milestone the disciple needs to complete. As a disciple maker, we must do our best to teach and exemplify basic biblical practices that will help the disciple to maintain a consistent relationship with Jesus Christ.

First, the discipler needs to guide the disciple in understanding the importance of a disciplined devotional life, helping him to become proficient in conducting his own inductive Bible study and prayer. Once trained, the disciple maker can hold him accountable to integrate the practice into his daily life. Until the disciple incorporates a consistent devotional time into his schedule, he will not experience consistent growth in his Christian life.

Second, the practice of fasting is usually combined with prayer. In many cases, despite the example and admonition of Christ, the modern church has neglected the practice of fasting. The objective, of course, is not weight loss but an act of devotion, in which we abstain from food in order to devote ourselves to a time of concentrated prayer. Many serious requests, along with guidance for major decisions, are often granted by God both during and after seasons of prayer and fasting. There may be personal health restrictions that need to be observed, but when followed correctly fasting is a practice that is both physically and spiritually healthy.

Third, the important fundamental is Bible memorization and meditation, which is a necessary discipline for victory over sin. David says, "How can a young man keep his way pure? By keeping it according to Your word....Your word I have treasured in my heart, that I may not sin against You" (Ps. 119:9, 11). Here he is telling us that God's Word is a key tool in helping us obtain victory over the temptations of sin. In addition to David's example in Psalm 119, the life of our Lord Jesus Christ gives us a wonderful illustration of the Word of God being used to secure victory over sin. Following Jesus' baptism, for example, he used scripture to combat Satan's attempts to tempt him in the wilderness. Through Jesus' example, we learn that quoting a verse when tempted helps us to resist temptation.

Also, without verse memorization, one's ministry to others will be greatly hindered, because his ministry will lack the authoritative transforming power of the Word of God. Without Bible memorization, the disciple will not be "ready to make a defense to everyone who asks you to give an account for the hope that is in you" (1 Peter 3:15b). When a disciple is armed with the Word of God, he becomes much more effective in his ministry to others.

Fourth, guide the disciple to become involved in a good Bible-believing church. For accountability purposes, it is best if the disciple attends the same church as his disciple maker. Also, if he has never followed through with biblical baptism, have him take this step of obedience. As he becomes involved, he will become friends with other brothers and sisters and enjoy good Christian fellowship. God designed the church to provide the environment necessary for his growth. If we as disciple makers do not stress the importance of the church to disciples, they will be lacking in the importance of this positive, God-initiated environment and will not grow to the depth God desires.

Finally, the disciple must begin serving the Lord as often as he can. Some ministries and opportunities will require instruction and training. Not only will the disciple grow as he is trained, his purpose for existence and spiritual growth will be understood and fanned to burn brighter. One of the greatest motivators for spiritual growth is when the disciple senses the Holy Spirit working through him. As he makes these fundamentals a part of his life, his spiritual maturity will be enriched and he will be encouraged in furthering his life of dedication and obedience to Christ.

3.   *Understanding of basic doctrine* is necessary for the disciple's protection from "wolves in sheep's clothing" (Matt. 7:15; 10:16; Luke 10:3). In Ephesians 4:14, Paul says that when we apply our understanding to biblical principles, "we will no longer be infants, tossed back and forth by the waves, and blown here and there by every wind of teaching and by the cunning and craftiness of men in their deceitful scheming" (NIV). Doctrine forms the foundation for faith and right living, and should be taught with emphasis on the practical application of these truths. Once again, if a class is available on Bible doctrine it would do the discipler well to enroll the disciple in the study of these truths. Take special care that he chooses to enroll in a doctrine class that is not too advanced. If a class is not available, I suggest material in the curriculum list from Appendix I, "Bibliography." Bible doctrine is an important tool necessary for mature spiritual growth; however, for that growth to be solid, make sure the disciple understands personal applications of various doctrinal truths.

4. *Independence in the Christian walk* also represents a necessary milestone for the disciple, as they no longer rely on the disciple maker or anyone else for spiritual nourishment. In order to achieve independence, the disciple must learn to study the Word on their own and live a consistent life without the discipler's constant urging. When the disciple nears this level of independence he is signaling to the disciple maker that he is coming closer to the place where the disciple maker's job is finished. He is becoming self-sufficient, relying on the Holy Spirit.

5. *Becoming like Christ* is an aspiration all of us must pursue wholeheartedly, while at the same time realizing we will never fully achieve it while we are in this body. We should nonetheless strive toward this goal throughout life, and encourage a consistent level of Christlikeness in the disciple. For instance, as he grows he should learn to confess and repent of sin soon after each offence in order to continue abiding in Christ (John 15:4). Moreover, the Christ-follower reflects Christlikeness as he or she develops the fruit of the Spirit, which include love, joy, peace, patience, kindness, goodness, faithfulness, gentleness, and self-control (Gal 5:22–23). In fact, all along the way the disciple maker must consistently tackle areas of the Christian life that need attention in order to grow in Christlikeness.

In addition, we must teach our disciple to practice self-denial by putting Christ first, others second, and ourselves last (Luke 9:23; Luke 14:26–27, 33). As the disciple continues to grow toward Christlikeness, he will continue to develop into the example necessary to one day become an independent disciple maker who impacts others by his own ministry.

6. *Discipleship reproduction* is the final milestone a disciple maker hopes to see his disciple achieve. In fact, one of the greatest expressions of becoming Christlike is to minister like Christ did as we obey his greatest command of making disciples. One of the greatest blessings God has given me occurs when a former protégé strives to reproduce a Christ-centered life in another person. At this stage, the disciple maker should become the new discipler's mentor, guiding the disciple by being available as they experience problems and face questions. Ask God to help you create in those whom you disciple a lifelong vision and passion to disciple others.

Content of Disciple Making

Earlier I stressed that the discipleship process is like a triangle with the three sides representing a triad of relationship, content, and prayer. I also asserted that the discipleship process will collapse if any of these sides are missing. In the final section of this chapter, let us take a closer look at the content side of discipleship. Content may take the form of a curriculum, Bible study, or simply an informal discussion. For purposes of discussion let's categorize our content into three divisions: Biblical Focus, Devotional Focus, and Outreach Focus.

The Biblical Focus of disciple making includes studies on basic Bible knowledge, Bible doctrine, apologetics, and biblical counseling.

Bible knowledge is the study of both the Old and New Testament, with practical application emphasized. Basic Bible doctrines include the topical study of bibliology, the study of Scriptures; Christology, the doctrine of Christ; the Trinity, study of the triune God; anthropology, the doctrine of man; soteriology, the doctrine of salvation; angelology, the doctrine of good and evil angels; and eschatology, the doctrine of future events as prophesized in Scripture. Apologetics is the study of defending our beliefs against nonbiblical philosophies, religious cults, and world religions. And finally, biblical counseling includes topics relating to life issues, difficulties, and temptations. All of these subjects can be taught in a classroom or in a one-on-one setting.

The Devotional Focus has to do with Christian disciplines such as personal devotions or Bible study, prayer, Scripture memorization and meditation, and Bible study methods.

The Outreach Focus has to do with involvement in the discipleship process and would include evangelism, writing and sharing one's personal testimony, follow-up with new converts, and learning to disciple others. For a complete list see Appendix II, "Discipleship Topics."

As I list these topics, I acknowledge our tendency to look at discipleship as being overly structured. Actually, it shouldn't be looked at that way. The disciple maker should follow the leading of the Holy Spirit as he prays over the direction of this ministry. Any list simply serves as a guide of important areas to cover in the process. Often, the discipler may choose to allow important issues his protégé is facing serve as a guide for a particular day. Repeatedly, the disciple maker must ask himself: What needs to be talked about that can move my disciple to the next step?

Now that we have spent considerable time discussing "Going to the Next Level," let us turn our attention to the problems we face in the discipleship process.

Review Questions

1. What often happens when a spiritual baby is neglected and not given proper spiritually palatable food? Cite examples, if possible.

2. Review the seven disciple-making principles. Which of these resonate with you most? Which ought to resonate with you more? In each case, why?

3. Review the "Major Milestones of Growth." If you're in a discipling relationship right now, where's that disciple at? How can you get him or her to the next level?

4. How can you build a greater desire for spiritual reproduction in those you disciple?

5. Review the "Content of Disciple Making." Which of these types of resources are you most comfortable using? Which could you become more "versed" in? And which resources does the disciple you're working with need most right now?

Chapter 9

THE OBSTACLES TO GROWTH: PROBLEMS AND SOLUTIONS IN DISCIPLESHIP

FOR MORE THAN TWENTY YEARS Professor Edwin R. Keedy of the University of Pennsylvania Law School used to start his first class of a semester by putting two numbers on the blackboard: 4 and 2. Then he would ask, "What's the solution?"

Immediately, one student would call out, "Six." Another would say, "Two." Then several would shout out, "Eight!"

But Keedy would shake his head in the negative and point out his students' collective error. "All of you failed to ask the key question: What is the problem?"[1]

Unless you know what the problem is, you cannot possibly find the answer. Likewise, if problems arise in your discipling relationship, be careful that you don't make the common mistake of jumping to the conclusion that you selected the wrong person to disciple. We must first pray for the disciple, for wisdom in discovering the real problem and dealing with it. After seeking God first, we can begin to approach these problems with his wisdom.

An Unwillingness to Meet

As the disciple maker begins the discipleship process he will occasionally observe a reluctance to meet. In this situation, the discipler should ask the young believer to level with him about his hesitancy. Once the disciple maker understands the reluctance, he can, with God's empowerment, deal with the issues or stumbling blocks.

There are a number of possible reasons why the person being discipled might display an unwillingness or hesitancy to meet for discipleship. First of all, he or she may not even have true saving faith. In an age in which our presentation of the gospel has become so very shoddy, we have evolved to an "easy believism," a kind of ABC pray-with-me formula for salvation. Often the person does not really understand what he is doing when he repeats a phrase-by-phrase prayer suggested by a counselor. Even when one understands, he is often just desirous of being saved from hell and knows nothing of the true repentance God expects of a believer.

Likewise, few evangelists or counselors make little if any effort to emphasize our responsibilities as believers. Romans 10:9 states, "if you confess with your mouth *Jesus as Lord*, and believe in your heart that God raised Him from the dead, you will be saved" (emphasis added). When one receives Christ as Lord, he is agreeing to be the Master's follower. This is not a works salvation; I am simply saying that God expects us to be disciples of his when we become children of God. If we were clearer when explaining God's expectations, perhaps one would make a more serious and genuine commitment at the outset.

Second, disciple makers must explain the importance of building a spiritual foundation to the disciple, so that she understands the purpose and importance that discipleship has on her overall Christian walk. If parents properly feed their children, they experience rapid, healthy growth. The same is true for the spiritual babe. Without proper nourishment from God's Word through study and practice, she will become malnourished and spiritually stunted. Therefore, the disciple maker must help the disciple to understand the importance of the systematic and sequential growth process that discipleship provides.

Finally, new believers will always experience some type of satanic opposition. Before salvation, Satan had the nonbeliever under his control and as part of his domain. With the new commitment to Christ, his hold is broken as the young believer becomes a new person in Christ. This being the case, Satan will make every effort to discourage and hinder the new believer's growth by any available method or tool. Peter warned of the battle we wage with our archenemy, "Be of sober spirit, be on the alert. Your adversary, the devil, prowls around like a roaring lion, seeking someone to devour. But resist him, firm in your faith, knowing that the same experiences of suffering are being accomplished by your brethren who are in the world" (1 Pet. 5:8–9).

For sure, Satan is our adversary who will often use any or all of the three reasons above to create reluctance on the part of the new believer. For instance, he will cause the new Christian to doubt his salvation and suggest current sin as proof that his salvation was not genuine. Satan will sometimes also lie and deceive the new convert by bringing him into contact with members of various cults who view him as ripe fruit to harvest for their purposes. In such situations, the naive young believer can be easily swayed, being impressed by the sincerity, commitment, and perceived knowledge of his new supposed friends. Truly, satanic opposition is one of the greatest difficulties we face; thankfully, the Holy Spirit can guide us and give victory as we face this enemy.

Not Confident That He Is Truly Saved

The lack of assurance concerning the validity of salvation represents another great problem that many people face. In his book, *Anecdotes, Incidents and Illustrations,*

D. L. Moody writes of the struggles John Wesley faced:

> After John Wesley had been preaching for some time, someone said to him, "Are you sure, Mr. Wesley, of your salvation?" "Well," he answered, "Jesus Christ died for the whole world." "Yes, we all believe that; but are you sure that you are saved?" Wesley replied that he was sure that provision had been made for his salvation.
>
> "But are you sure, Wesley, that you are saved?" It went like an arrow to his heart, and he had no rest or power until that question was settled. Many men and many women go on month after month, and year after year, without power, because they do not know their standing in Christ; they are not sure of their own footing for eternity. Latimer wrote Ridley (both bishops in the church of England and martyrs in the sixteenth century), once that when he was settled and steadfast about his own salvation he was as bold as a lion, but if that hope became eclipsed he was fearful and afraid and was disqualified for service. Many are disqualified for service because they continually doubt their own salvation.[2]

Counseling on the assurance of salvation

Every growing believer needs to know his condition as it relates to eternal life. As a disciple maker, we must be able to counsel people, helping them grasp whether or not they know Christ as savior. We must be careful that we do not try to be the source of a new believer's assurance because we can never know for sure if another person is a child of God. For anyone to insist that another person is indeed saved can perpetuate a dangerous false sense of assurance within those who in fact are not truly saved at all. Thankfully, God provides three evidences in his Word that help us know whether we have eternal life.

First of all, God's Word is the primary source of assurance. We should simply review Scripture that explains how one is saved and simply ask if they did what God's Word explained (John 1:12; 3:16; Rom, 10:9–10, 13). Did the person mean it when he or she received or called upon the Lord? Ask what the verse says will happen if he receives, believes, or calls upon the name of the Lord. If they did what God commanded, what is God's promise to them?

Second, we know we are his children because God gives us assurance. We may not be able to explain it, but we just know within. Romans 8:16 says, "The Spirit Himself testifies with our spirit that we are children of God."

Third, the changes and new desires within us are indicators that we are his children. Jesus said, "So every good tree bears good fruit, but the bad tree bears bad fruit.... So then, you will know them by their fruits" (Matt. 7:17, 20). Also, the apostle Paul said, "Therefore if anyone is in Christ, he is a new creature; the old things passed away; behold, new things have come" (2 Cor. 5:17). For example, the new believer has a desire to learn about this new life in Christ. He has a desire to go to church and to grow spiritually. He also has assurance that God has forgiven him, has a sense of gratitude, and a newfound joy. These changes and others give him confidence of his salvation.

If the disciple has considered the above information and continues to struggle with doubts concerning his salvation, there are other possible issues to consider. Indeed, we must continue to address the disciple's assurance because many young believers will grow very little until they come to grips with their status in Christ.

Confirming the validity of his salvation

As I said before, sometimes the reason the person has no assurance of salvation stems from the fact that he has never become a true believer in Christ. Perhaps he had the wrong motivation or did not understand how to be saved in the first place. A clear explanation of related Scripture can be used to help him determine how to become a child of God. Be sure you don't play the role of the Holy Spirit in giving him assurance. Only God knows for sure if a person is indeed his child. Our role is to review the appropriate Scripture so that the Spirit of God can provide the assurance.

Feelings of guilt being confused with the lack of assurance

Young believers often struggle with assurance of salvation because sins they committed were never completely resolved or dealt with, causing feelings of conviction or guilt. Someone has said that guilt is like the red warning light on the dashboard of the car; the driver can either stop and deal with the reason for the trouble, or break the light. Obviously, in this case the trouble light is guilt and the disciple maker must help the disciple deal with the cause of his guilt.

There are a number of reasons one struggles with guilt. First, sometimes people feel guilt because of their repeated struggle with temptation. Of course, temptation only leads to sin when we respond to it by disobeying God's Word, whether in thought or action. Therefore we should not assign guilt to temptation, but instead to unrepentant, unconfessed sin.

Second, often the disciple may have a nonbiblical disbelief that God can't or won't fully forgive them of some grievous past offense. Sometimes the problem is that the guilty person has not forgiven himself. In order to help a person who carries guilt, we need to first help them learn how to gain forgiveness. According to Scripture, we gain forgiveness as we confess sin. First John 1:9 says, "If we confess our sins, He is faithful and righteous to forgive us our sins and to cleanse us from all unrighteousness." Confession means that we admit our sin to God. Linked with confession of sin, Proverbs 28:13 says, "He who conceals his transgressions will not prosper, but he who confesses and forsakes them will find compassion." We must thus confess and forsake our sins for God to grant absolute forgiveness and cleansing.

The disciple must understand that confession involves more than presenting a big box of sins to God and asking him to forgive all we've committed in the past month. Rather, think of biblical confession like a man standing before a court hearing. The judge first asks if he is guilty of a particular crime. If the accused man were to list four or five crimes of which he is guilty, the judge would look at him and state that he did not ask how many crimes the man has committed. The judge would then ask once again if the plaintiff is guilty of the alleged crime yes or no. Like the man in the courtroom, the disciple maker should instruct the young believer to confess or admit and forsake specific sins. It's unlikely that anyone will forsake a list of sins all at once; but when one confesses and repents of a specific offense, he is forgiven and can forsake the practice of that particular sin.

One of the steps in fully correcting our offenses is to make restitution. Restitution may come in a number of forms. One may pay back what was stolen, replace or fix what was broken, or even repair someone else's reputation that has been damaged by a false accusation. Restitution is important if we are to live a life with a clear conscience. When our conscience is damaged or seared, our ability to follow Christ and to live a successful Christian life is inhibited. This guilt caused by our failure to make restitution may generate feelings that this sin has not been forgiven.

Third, a new believer's unwillingness to forgive others is a sin and will therefore cause him to be out of fellowship with God. Hanging on to an unforgiving spirit causes guilt and cannot be confessed until we forgive. God is so insistent on our forgiving others that Jesus said, "For if you forgive others for their transgressions, your heavenly Father will also forgive you. But if you do not forgive others, then your Father will not forgive your transgressions" (Matt. 6:14–15).

Also, as Jesus explains in the Lord's Prayer, we are to ask God to "Forgive us our debts, as we also have forgiven our debtors" (Matt. 6:12). Forgive as we forgive our debtors? Surely we want complete forgiveness from God. When sinned against, one tends to hold a feeling of resentment against the other person; if not dealt with as Jesus instructed, resentment turns into bitterness. Many hold on to a grudge, somehow feeling that the person deserves it and seeking to punish him by withholding forgiveness. Often the nonbelieving offender is totally unconcerned about how the offended feels about his wrongdoing. It is futile to try to make him pay by holding on to a grudge. God says to forgive, and that if we do not forgive we are acting in disobedience. To forgive may not make the hurt go away nor enable one to forget. To forgive means we no longer hold the offending person accountable. We release him to God, who is just and will take vengeance in his time according to his will (Rom. 12:19). If we obediently and genuinely forgive and let the offense go, God, in his perfect timing, will heal the wound caused by the offense.

Finally, many times people report that they have specifically confessed a particular sin and have completely repented of it but continue to feel guilty. These feelings of guilt are not from God. It is either from Satan who is called "the accuser of our brethren" (Rev. 12:10), or they are self-imposed. Guilt that is not from God is false guilt and must be rejected. If we have sincerely confessed sin, God says we are forgiven and therefore no longer guilty.

Opposition from Family and Friends

It is extremely difficult when loved ones and close friends begin to criticize and even ostracize a new believer for his faith in Jesus Christ. Many friends have walked away from relationships with new believers, and parents have even disowned their children. The apostle Paul also warned, "Do not be deceived: Bad company corrupts good morals" (1 Cor. 15:33, see also Ps. 1:1–3 and Prov. 13:20). Because of this biblical admonition, I encourage young believers to begin breaking close ties to nonbelieving friends.

Likewise, it may go without saying that to have a nonbelieving girlfriend or boyfriend is like playing with fire. Once a man or woman begin to "fall in love," it is very difficult to break off the relationship. In fact, most Christians who find themselves in this kind of emotional bond will begin to rationalize why dating a nonbeliever is OK. Many will eventually end up in an unequally yoked marriage (1 Cor. 6:14; 7:39b) that often brings many years of grief and pain.

I am not saying that we should have no relationship with nonbelievers, because they too need to be reached for Christ. However, we should not seek out nonbelievers as a major source of fellowship because such relationships often harm, or hinder, our walks with Christ.

Of course, one shouldn't break relationship with family members. They need to see Christ in your life so that they will eventually know Christ as their own Savior. We should not underestimate the power that a new Christian's life can have on those who are close and see the change up front and personal. The young believer may provide one of the greatest tools the Holy Spirit can use to draw family members and close friends to salvation. Therefore, we must always encourage the young believer to never hide his convictions but to let his light shine brightly. Of course, it never works to become a nag. Instead, the young believer needs to pray and look for God's divine appointments to share his faith with them. Ridicule will surely come; he should not take it personally but chalk it up to the fact that the unsaved often view the message of Christ's cross as an offense. Whatever the situation, the discipler should pray for and provide moral, understanding support to the protégé when he receives pressure from unsaved family and friends, as well as when he seeks to establish godly friendships.

It is also important to teach the new believer about the worth of knowing Christ. Paul said, "But whatever things were gain to me, those things I have counted as loss for the sake of Christ. More than that, I count all things to be loss in view of the surpassing value of knowing Christ Jesus my Lord, for whom I have suffered the loss of all things, and count them but rubbish so that I may gain Christ" (Phil. 3:7–8).

Involvement in a Theologically Liberal or Nonbiblical Church

When I was a young man I decided to build a shed in my backyard. Before I started construction I mixed cement and poured the foundation where I would build and permanently attach the structure. It was my first attempt and so I purposefully bought the needed tools to spread a nice smooth layer of cement. I then waited for it to dry, spraying it with water in the heat of the day so that it would not dry too fast. After about three days I decided to remove the wood forms I had nailed together, which provided the frame for the cement. Soon the job was done and I was very proud of my handiwork, so I proceeded to walk on the finished product. However, when I stepped near the edge a large chunk broke off, then another, and another. My project was a total failure. What went wrong? Why did the cement break up and why was my foundation so weak?

As I read the instructions, I quickly learned that when one mixes concrete he must add sand and gravel to the cement. In fact, I discovered there exists a "ready mix" with these ingredients that simply required me to add water. Embarrassed, I removed the old cement and started over.

The cement I mixed and laid looked good. It was smooth and dried nicely, but it was the wrong kind of foundation. It was a foundation that would not hold up under pressure. A solid foundation is made up of the "ready mix" of God's elementary principles. Hebrews 5:12 says, "For though by this time you ought to be teachers, you have need again for someone to teach you the elementary principles of the oracles of God, and you have come to need milk and not solid food." We need the "elementary principles" or milk found in the Word of God. A weak foundation is no better than having no foundation in the first place. As disciplers, then, it is our responsibility to ensure that new believers receive a strong foundation.

Many have built their new lives in Christ on the wrong kind of foundation—a foundation based on heretical doctrines as found in modern-day cults. Others have been a part of a church or denomination with beliefs based on nonbiblical presuppositions. Such is true of churches that believe that the Bible cannot be interpreted literally and contains error in its original manuscripts. Therefore, those who believe these concepts have to decide what to believe and what to allegorize, often interpreting biblical events as fictitious stories. In so doing, sinful man becomes the authority instead of the Word of God. Another flawed system is endorsed by the Roman Catholic Church which not only finds its authority in the Word of God, but also from the Pope and tradition. Indeed, when we add anything to the authority of God's Word, we end up with teaching and doctrine not found in Scripture. When believers accept such nonbiblical ingredients, their foundation will not hold up because it does not contain beliefs rooted in the infallible authority of the Word of God.

When a person receives Christ as savior, he or she may be attending a church that will confuse or erroneously instruct the young believer. Satan works very hard to discourage or sidetrack each Christian, and one of his most effective methods involves using a church that confuses or misleads the young, spiritually impressionable child of God. Often our adversary preys on the fact that a young believer does not understand that a Bible-centered church is God's ordained institution for fulfilling the Great Commission in this age. Therefore, the discipler must stress that the church exists to help the new believer grow to be more Christlike, rather than being a place where all we do is sing songs and listen to sermons. A disciple maker must encourage the young disciple to attend a church that will not confuse or mislead him as he continues to pursue Christ. A good church provides:

1. A new environment not unlike a hothouse providing the right amount of heat, necessary water, sun, and nourishment for the tender plant. The

church provides encouragement, fellowship, positive peer influence, and accountability.

2. Instruction in Christian living from the preaching and teaching of the Word of God.

3. A quality time of worship and praise for God.

4. A training center to equip the members to do the work of the ministry. Ephesians 4:11–12 says, "And He gave some as apostles, and some as prophets, and some as evangelists, and some as pastors and teachers, for the equipping of the saints for the work of service, to the building up of the body of Christ." This work of service is indispensable for the strong growth of disciples, giving them a sense of purpose in accomplishing something much larger than one's self. When it works together, the church is impacting people for eternity.

5. Many opportunities to serve God, using spiritual gifts provided by the Holy Spirit designed to be used by the believer to build up the body. These opportunities to serve God provide a major tool that fans the flame of spiritual growth.

There are several reasons the young believer might be reluctant to attend your church. If the new believer is from a background where the church experience is vastly different, it may be important to ease the person in. Draw the young believer to church a step at a time. The disciple maker, for example, could invite his protégé to accompany him to the church or a Bible study, particularly for new believers. Sometimes, the disciple maker should be slow to encourage a new believer from a vastly different church background to immediately attend too many programs and studies that might overwhelm the young believer. Pray for the Holy Spirit to convict and to motivate the new believer to become involved in the church. Also pray that the new believer will be hungry to learn and grow.

If a minor is reluctant to attend church, be careful that you as a disciple maker do not encourage the minor to rebel against his or her parents' refusal to allow the youth to go to church. Help the new believer to grow and pray for understanding and acceptance by the family members of the young believer's new faith.

In this day and age there are many churches that are weak doctrinally and in the practice of discipleship. The church is vital in the growth process, but the new believer will become confused if he attends a church that teaches non-biblical views. A strong church can be the greatest asset in the discipleship process; likewise, a poor church could be a great discouragement and even cause the young believer to lose interest or become apathetic. Therefore, disciple makers must pray fervently and counsel carefully to guide the young believer to a good local church—which preferably would be the same one the discipler attends.

Irregular Devotions or Personal Bible Study

Many believers never overcome their lack of commitment to personal devotions, and so it remains vital for disciple makers to instill within disciples a desire to spend time with God on a regular basis. Rather than thinking of a short time with God by reading a few verses and a few paragraphs from a devotional book, I have encouraged the people I have discipled to plan a personal Bible study time daily. The Bible tells us in 2 Timothy 2:15 to "Be diligent to present yourself approved to God as a workman who does not need to be ashamed, accurately handling the word of truth."

Why do so many Christians never develop a regular time with God? First of all, many people lack motivation and discipline; they somehow do not understand how important the Word of God is to help them grow in their Christian walk. The Word of God says, "All Scripture is inspired by God and profitable for teaching, for reproof, for correction, for training in righteousness; so that the man of God may be adequate, equipped for every good work" (2 Tim. 3:16–17). Hence, the equipping of God's Word provides many life principles that are indispensable in decisionmaking. These principles guide us in dealing with the many problems of life including dealing with finances, child-rearing, marital principles, communication problems, and maintaining our relationship with God and our fellow man. The Bible also provides many wonderful promises, many of which are conditional. However, if the person does not study God's Word he will never understand the promises and the conditions God expects.

Often the disciple is not motivated to spend time in God's Word because he simply lacks discipline. One of the roots of this problem stems from that fact that many children grow up today without a father living at home; or, if he does live at home, he is distant and does not model or teach his child how to be responsible. This especially impacts male members of the family and causes them to grow up with little self-discipline and follow-through. Often this even impacts his consistency in being on time for meetings as an adult and creates inconsistency as he seeks to practice regular, personal Bible study.

Developing consistency with fundamentals like personal Bible study is one of the milestones talked about earlier in this book. If a disciple doesn't break bad habits and develop consistency in this area, it will hinder his effectiveness in life and service for the Lord.

The second reason for irregular time with God is the lack of training. Often the young believer just doesn't know how to study the Bible. Therefore, the discipler must teach his protégé how to study God's Word. Granted, there exist numerous methods of Bible study but the most important is the inductive approach, which teaches the believer how to make observations and interpret the Bible as well as learn to apply its truths to life. In other words, this approach helps us discover what God wants us to know, namely, how we should live. Suitable training would also include how to use many Bible-study tools found in books and the Internet. I cannot overemphasize the importance of helping the disciple learn how to study the Bible. Learning this skill will benefit him in growth and service for the rest of his life.

Intellectual Stumbling Blocks

We live in an age where the educational system and the multifaceted media outlets, especially television and movies, revere science. Because of this, some people are often quick to label faith in God and belief in the Bible as archaic and full of fairy tales and error. Our society, on the whole, treats unproven theories based on unscientific presuppositions as fact. With this cultural understanding we have the challenge of nurturing new believers often faced with anti-God, anti-Bible belief systems. No wonder an immature believer may become confused and, without proper instruction, even disenchanted. The young believer wants to accept what the Bible says but in order to understand may need to ask some questions. Therefore, the protégé may begin to debate teachings based on his nonbiblical education. The disciple maker should not question the disciple's salvation simply because he is inquisitive and may be confused in his understanding. Instead, the discipler just needs to patiently take time to re-educate the new believer on his understanding so that it lines up with Scripture.

The disciple maker should not feel threatened when responding to nonbiblical arguments and beliefs espoused by the disciple, since such inquiries indicate that the disciple wants to know the truth. The disciple is usually parroting what he heard or was taught, and by his questions he is seeking biblical understanding. As we work with a disciple we should impress upon him the ability of the Christian faith to hold up under scrutiny. Indeed, the discipler should not be afraid of logic or science. When clearly understood, God's Word and science are in total harmony. In fact, the reason that the Christian faith can hold up under scrutiny is because it is rooted in God's infallible authority. We thus believe we can have full assurance in what we believe and attest that God's Word has never been proven in error and never will be.

I believe the best way we can help correct the disciple's nonbiblical teaching is simply to let him ask questions. These questions can provide excellent teachable moments; therefore we should encourage those questions. A discipler should never feel threatened that he will not be able to answer all questions. When asked a question that he is unprepared to answer, he can simply acknowledge that a great question has been asked, that it will require a little more research, and that the discussion can continue the next time they meet.

Lack of Doctrinal Clarity

Our society is inundated with a plethora of churches that espouse various doctrinal beliefs; therefore, we can expect many whom we disciple to experience confusion as to what God's Word teaches. Scripture refers to the word "doctrine" thirty-six times and stresses the concept of sound doctrine many more times. The only solution to doctrinal confusion is to study the Word of God. We must involve the disciple in Bible study so that he will gain biblical understanding. Paul says that the Word of God is "profitable for teaching" (2 Tim. 3:16); it is evident, then, that God has provided his Word to teach the reader doctrinal truth.

Early in the discipleship process, we should caution the disciple from attending meetings of any group or church that will confuse him. Young believers, with their zeal for growth, will often agree to have a cultist come to their house for personal, though unexpectedly biased and nonbiblical, Bible study. The young believer, not having the underpinning of solid biblical truth, will not recognize a wolf in sheep's clothing. He will not catch error and quickly become confused and even convinced in the beliefs of the cultist teacher. Jesus warned, "Beware of the false prophets, who come to you in sheep's clothing, but inwardly are ravenous wolves" (Matt. 7:15). Hence, our responsibility as disciple guardians is to protect our young sheep from this threat, warning of those people and ideologies that Satan uses to confuse and mislead believers.

Difficulty will not come from cultists alone. Even when the disciple attends a week night Bible study from another denomination, he can become confused when taught differing beliefs regarding Scripture. The disciple maker may continually find himself trying to un-teach and correct erroneous Scriptural claims. And so, I would caution anyone to be leery of discipling someone who refuses to attend the discipler's church, due to this danger of confusion.

Consequently, the disciple maker needs to have a clear grasp on who else is instructing the disciple and what topics he is studying. Keeping tabs in this way will allow the discipler to more fully make use of discipleship studies available and remain aware of how faithfully the disciple attends church services and activities. When we help the disciple clear up any doctrinal confusion by his involvement in classroom study and discussions with other well-trained church members, we are helping him progress in spiritual development.

Fear of Sharing One's Faith

One of our goals in discipleship must be to help disciples become mature enough to multiply themselves by winning others to Jesus Christ. Yet in the process we sometimes discover that the disciple has a fear of sharing his faith, which stems from a variety of reasons.

First, disciples fear sharing their faith because they lack a proper understanding of how to lead someone to Christ. As disciple makers, we must adequately train him or her. It may not be necessary for us to provide the training in every area, but we must make sure that the training is received and that disciples have opportunities to effectively practice what they've learned. For instance, after our evangelism training at my church, we usually go to the park two-by-two where a trainee can observe another person share his faith and in turn hopefully have the opportunity to share his faith as well. Good training will help the disciple to be more at ease as he or she shares the gospel with others.

Secondly, once trained, most people fear sharing their faith because of their lack of confidence that they will be able to answer the questions or objections they may face. Proper training helps, but in most cases one just has to jump in with both feet if he or she wants to overcome fear. It's always difficult to witness "cold turkey" to someone unknown. The most effective form of sharing one's faith is friendship evangelism. Witnessing to friends, neighbors, co-workers, and relatives may be easier for the one who shies away from talking to strangers. This form of sharing one's faith is also more effective then cold-contact evangelism and is more productive when it comes to following up with new believers and growing disciples because of the existing relationship. One will find it much easier to bring the new believer to church and to introduce the person to a new-Christian class if he has an ongoing friendship.

Third, many people have a fear of persecution, ridicule, or rejection. Because of peer pressure, this is especially difficult for teenagers. With growth one must learn that we need to be willing to suffer persecution if we're to follow Christ.

Fourth, many immature believers feel unqualified because they live inconsistent lives. For example, they are afraid the sins of the past will make it impossible to witness to anybody who knows them. However, a Christian's salvation serves as a bona fide example of how God changes a person, and thus can become a powerful testimony. Of course, if the disciple still struggles with some vice, he will need to have victory before he can be an effective witness.

Sharing one's faith is an important part of the life of every disciple of Christ. Jesus said, "Therefore everyone who confesses Me before men, I will also confess him before My Father who is in heaven" (Matt. 10:32). Every disciple must become proficient in sharing his faith, doing so as God prompts him.

The Discipler's Lack of Credibility

Dr. Stuart Briscoe, former pastor of the Elmbrook Church in Brookfield, Wisconsin, shared his experience after he had been hired for a position at a bank. He was young and just began learning the business. One day his boss told him, "If Mr. _____ calls for me, tell him I'm out."

Briscoe replied, "Oh, are you planning to go somewhere?"

"No, I just don't want to speak to him, so tell him I'm out."

"Let me make sure I understand. Do you want me to lie for you?"

The boss blew up at him. He was outraged, angered. Stuart prayed and God gave him a flash of insight. "You should be happy, because if I won't lie for you, isn't it safe to assume that I won't lie *to* you?"[3]

Briscoe's example illustrates that credibility is basic to the confidence and trust others have toward us and should be based on biblically driven honesty. It affects every relationship we have and is central to a life of someone who desires to impact others. But honesty is not the only factor that impacts our credibility. Our credibility is also affected by:

1. *Not living a consistent Christian life.* Is your Christian walk with Jesus Christ dependable? Perfection is not required, but consistency is essential. Do you remain in fellowship with Christ (John 15:5–7)? Do you spend time with God in the study of his Word and the communion of prayer, and do you live a life of obedience to that Word? Disciple makers often disqualify themselves by their inconsistency in practicing God's word. If instability marks your relationship with Christ, few young believers will desire your services and those who do will soon recognize your poor example.

2. *Not knowing what you believe and why you believe it.* If one is lacking in this knowledge there are a number of books that can help the disciple to sharpen his

understanding. See the bibliography in Appendix I, to get started.

3. *Not knowing where to find answers to biblical questions.* This is an indication of immaturity. I am not implying that the disciple maker needs to have an answer to every question, but he certainly needs to know where to look to find the answer. He also needs to help the disciple learn where to find the answers for himself.

4. *Lack of enthusiasm for serving Christ.* One's life speaks louder than his words. The disciple maker's enthusiasm should be demonstrated by his commitment and involvement in sharing his faith, discipling others, and serving the Lord with his spiritual gifts. The disciple maker should furthermore share often what God is doing through his life and ministry. He should share the blessings of being used by God to impact others for eternity.

5. *When the disciple maker doesn't show up, or is late for a discipleship appointment.* When a personal need comes up it is perfectly acceptable to contact the disciple to cancel or re-schedule an appointment, but the disciple maker should never be guilty of simply not showing up or even being late without a phone call to alert the disciple of some issue. Indeed, if the disciple maker expects the disciple to be faithful, this standard must be upheld by the disciple maker also.

6. *When the home displays a poor example of spiritual leadership.* A familiar adage says, "The proof is in the pudding." There exists no greater failure of Christian example and leadership than when one's family ceases to reflect God's biblical design—for example, when the discipler's marriage does not stand as a God-honoring example of a Christ-centered marriage, or when children are rebellious and undisciplined. When children are raised prior to the salvation of their parents, failure is understandable, but once a person begins discipling another person, the example of the home must begin to demonstrate success. That's why Paul told Timothy that a church leader must manage his family well and that his children must obey him with respect (1 Tim. 3:4–5). The quality of a Christian home will either become the discipler's greatest asset as a reference to his spiritual leadership or will shout as an alarm proclaiming "buyers beware."

There are many problems we face in the discipleship process. Yet when the discipler faces problems head-on with wisdom and direction from God, he will find solutions. With God's help, the disciple maker will bring the disciple to a mature level of growth—to help him become one who will one day be able to disciple others also.

Review Questions

1. Review the four reasons that a disciple is reluctant to meet with the discipler. Which ones have you encountered? How can you respond to each of these?

2. What counsel does God's Word give about hanging out with ungodly people? How can you use that counsel to guide disciples struggling with their old friendships, or with their current family relationships?

3. What is the primary danger of being involved in a biblically weak church? When have you seen this manifest itself?

4. Read 2 Timothy 3:16 and Matthew 7:15. What's the connection between these two verses? How can their counsel help us guide those we're discipling?

5. What factors can impair the disciple maker's credibility? Which of these factors need addressing, or at least shoring up, in your own life? And what steps will you take? Explain.

Chapter 10

TRANSFORMATION IN DISCIPLESHIP:
Producing Heart Change in the Disciple

ONE OF THE AMAZING MIRACLES we find in nature is the transformation of a caterpillar into a butterfly. The differences between the two are as different as night and day, as the insect changes from an ugly, sometimes detestable creature crawling on the ground to a gentle and beautiful creature flittering in the air. Though metamorphosis produces incredible change, the actual process can be considered quite boring to observe with the naked eye. All we can see is an ugly shell of a cocoon, while the insect undergoes a miraculous transformation inside.

The discipleship process entails guiding a spiritually immature believer through the process of life transformation toward Christlikeness. The Scriptures refer to this transformation, "But we all, with unveiled face, beholding as in a mirror the glory of the Lord, are being transformed into the same image from glory to glory, just as from the Lord, the Spirit" (2 Cor. 3:18). The word *transform* comes from the Greek *metamorphoo* from which we get our word *metamorphosis*. It is much like what a caterpillar experiences when it is changed, or morphed, into a beautiful butterfly. It's a wonderful truth to understand that when a person has saving faith in Jesus Christ he is already changed. Second Corinthians 5:17 says, "if anyone is in Christ, he is a new creature; the old things passed away; behold, new things have come." As a "new creature," the young Christian continues the transformation process by learning God's Word and obeying his commands.

The apostle Peter explains to the young disciples the basis for growth when he encourages them, "like newborn babies, long for the pure milk of the word, so that by it you may grow in respect to salvation" (1 Pet. 2:2). For the disciple maker, the apostle John further admonishes us, "Sanctify them in the truth; Your word is truth" (John 17:17). Just reading the Bible is not enough. Most people, at least in the early stages of their Christian walk, need encouragement and assistance in order to understand and practice basic biblical truth, or principles to which they are exposed while reading. Indeed, the practical teaching of God's Word given during discipleship, when done with clear application, constitutes the basis of a new believer's transformation process.

The truth is that God transforms believers' lives, not us; we are only tools he uses in the process. The transforming work comes from the Holy Spirit as he teaches, convicts, and encourages change. Paul referred to this sanctifying work when he stated his desire "that my offering of the Gentiles may become acceptable, sanctified by the Holy Spirit" (Rom. 15:16b). As we participate with this sanctifying process, we will experience the Holy Spirit conducting a work of transformation through us. Transformation may include change in all areas of our lives. Of course it would include spiritual growth, but it could also include the stewardship of our body (including weight adjustment, nutrition improvement, and bodily exercise), social life, educational needs, emotional needs, and financial stewardship.

Discipleship is not rocket science, but it requires thought and prayer. Since we must still combat our old nature, transformation takes time, effort and of course God's transforming work. One does not simply read a series of verses and voilà! He is transformed. Discipleship is a lifelong process. It takes many months and sometimes years for many to reach a basic level of maturity. To help us improve our effectiveness as guides in the transformation process, let's consider a number of elements needful to facilitate transformation in a disciple.

Systematic Topical Study of God's Word

The writer of Hebrews tells us to begin with the elemental truths and then progress to more solid food. He says, "For though by this time you ought to be teachers, you have need again for someone to teach you the elementary principles of the oracles of God, and you have come to need milk and not solid food. For everyone who partakes only of milk is not accustomed to the word of righteousness, for he is an infant. But solid food is for the mature, who because of practice have their senses trained to discern good and evil" (Heb. 5:12–14). One reason so many churches have failed to assist and encourage solid transformation is because there is no effort to help a person grow systematically. There are many disciplines, basic truths, and practices which must be incorporated early in the growing process if one is to continue to blossom spiritually. For a new believer to jump right into solid food would be unproductive and often discouraging. Ideally a systematic approach—stemming from his level of understanding and maturity, and prayerfully guided—will produce dramatic growth.

A Good Example

A living demonstration of what Christianity means is far more effective than a mere explanation. The disciple may quickly forget what it was that you said, but they will never forget how you lived. Some have asked, "Isn't it a little arrogant to ask another person to pattern their life after yours?" This was not the concern of the writer of Hebrews when he said, "Remember your leaders, who spoke the word of God to you. Consider the outcome of their way of life and imitate their faith" (Heb. 13:7; see also 1 Tim. 4:12; 2 Thess. 3:9). These writings inspired by God tell us that we should live lives worth imitating. We should expect those we are discipling to model our lives as we imitate Christ. Needless to say, if you do not live a life worth emulating, you should not begin such an important task as discipling another person until you consistently exhibit a godly example.

Consistent Accountability

Accountability provides a powerful sharpening tool in the transformation process. Solomon said, "Iron sharpens iron, so one man sharpens another" (Prov. 27:17). This wise proverb illustrates the kind of relationship that can be experienced during life-on-life discipleship ministry. This relationship included not only instruction and encouragement but personal accountability. Through the discipleship ministry, the disciple maker accomplishes inspection as he holds the disciple accountable. Honesty provides the basis for good accountability. In fact, it is impossible to practice accountability without transparency and honesty from the disciple. Thus, early on in the discipleship relationship, the disciple maker must emphasize the importance of total honesty while committing to confidentiality, assuring the disciple that nothing he says in confidence will ever be repeated to anyone.

In order to use accountability effectively, the disciple maker must get to know the disciple well enough to know where and how God's Word must be applied in his life. The disciple maker further needs to give his or her protégé specific examples of offenses made that demonstrate where changes need to take place. Some of the top areas with which we struggle and for which we need to be held accountable include materialism, pride, self-centeredness, laziness, anger, bitterness, sexual lust, envy, gluttony, and lying. As you practice tactful but thoughtful accountability, the disciple will be spurred on to a greater Christlikeness. (See "Accountability Questions" in Appendix V.)

As a good discipleship relationship develops, the disciple will soon hold a deep appreciation and respect for the disciple maker. Because of this relationship, the discipler will have the ability to confront the disciple on sin issues and hold him accountable, perhaps better than anyone else. Truly, God uses this relationship and this influence in a dynamic way to change the disciple's life.

A Biblically Based Counseling Ministry

A good disciple maker will always find counseling as a very powerful tool to guide the disciple in the transformation process. As the disciple raises questions or reveals problems he's facing, the disciple maker can counsel him informally through general dialogue and conversation. Sometimes counseling is initiated in response to something the discipler has noticed in the person's life, perhaps as a result of an accountability discussion. This counseling has powerful impact and must be integrated with the Word of God as the Holy Spirit uses it to transform the disciple's life. When a need comes up, the discipler may not be prepared with Scripture references at that very moment, but he can do the research and bring it up at the next meeting. (See "Topical Scripture Passages for Counseling" in Appendix IV.) Because the Word of God is sufficient, it makes an effective and powerful tool in the hands of the Holy Spirit to transform a life.

Renewing the Mind

In the early days of computer science, people typified the woes associated with imputing information into a computer with the expression GIGO, which stands for "garbage in, garbage out." When we input bad information into a computer and give the print command, the bad information will be printed just as it was inputted.

The same is true of our biological computer, the brain. We are conformed as we appropriate the input we receive. As Proverbs 23:7 says, "For as he thinks within himself, so he is." What we think becomes part and parcel of who we are.

Therefore Paul advises us, "do not be conformed to this world, but be transformed by the renewing of your mind, so that you may prove what the will of God is, that which is good and acceptable and perfect" (Rom. 12:2). This passage gives us the foundation for success as we struggle to have victory over sin, especially from sins that extend from our thought life. Exactly how does a person go about the process of renewing his or her mind?

The first step is to quit putting in the garbage. The disciple maker should have a discussion with every disciple to find out the sources of garbage they've been inputting into their minds. Each person struggles with "sin which so easily entangles us" (Heb. 12:1). These are areas of weakness which are very hard to resist. For example, most men have tremendous difficulty with lustful temptations. Discussing the disciple's source of lustful images and thoughts, for example, makes it possible to determine what can be done to eliminate this negative input.

Once we've begun prayerfully and practically eliminating the garbage in our lives, the second step is to begin inputting godly content into our minds. Examples include:

- Thoughtfully reading the Bible, studying the Word of God privately and in groups, meditating on a verse or passage, and memorizing Scripture. This attention to the Word of God requires that we claim the promises we read and respond to sin by confession, repenting, and obeying commands or principles.
- Listening to good sermons in person or in prerecorded form (CDs, mp3s, podcasts, etc.).
- Worshipping God privately and corporately.
- Good Christian fellowship and friendships.
- Meeting with a disciple maker to discuss growth topics.

The third step to renewing the mind and bringing transformation is obedience to God's Word. Information without obedience and practice is useless. The disciple maker should continually emphasize obedience to principles and precepts enumerated throughout the Word of God. As the disciple obeys, the Holy Spirit, using the positive input as listed above, will transform the disciple as he renews his or her mind.

The fourth step in renewing the mind involves submission to accountability by a trusted mature believer, ideally one's disciple maker. Loving accountability will motivate the disciple and help him experience victory as he strives to overcome weaknesses and sinful practices.

Finally, one must not undervalue the importance of prayer in the transformation process. Since it is God who transforms, prayer offered by the disciple maker as well as the disciple beseeching God to transform his life will have enormous impact, as God answers his prayers to renew his mind.

Actively Serving God

After the information provided above, I don't know of anything that will more deeply motivate the believer in the life-transformation process than Christian service. There is something about experiencing the Holy Spirit's work through us that thrills us within and motivates us to continue to pursue transformation toward Christlikeness.

Serving God also helps the disciple develop purpose and worth as an ambassador of Christ. When we come to realize that we have a purpose that is bigger than life itself, our whole motivation changes. Paul told us that "we are His workmanship, created in Christ Jesus for good works, which God prepared beforehand so that we would walk in them" (Eph. 2:10). God has planned our very creation, armed with abilities and spiritual gifts, in order to accomplish his work through our lives. We have value in God's master plan and have an important purpose for living.

Training for Service

Our service to God stimulates our desire for training so we can function better in our ministry. Jesus recognized the importance of training when He sent out the Twelve and also the Seventy to teach, preach, and heal the sick (Luke 10:4–11). He told them not to take any food or even a bag, thereby forcing them to trust his provision. Likewise today when we serve, God places us in situations that require we trust in nothing else but his enablement and provision. These experiences in turn provide opportunities for us to grow our faith and experience great joy, as we see from the results of the Seventy's mission experience (Luke 10:17).

We should look for opportunities and make suggestions where the disciple can begin serving the Lord. He may serve with you or on his own, but regardless of the arrangement serving will spur growth and transformation.

Discerning and Using Spiritual Gifts

One of the important areas of training in discipleship is to help the disciple to discover his or her spiritual gifts. According to Scripture, every believer has one or more spiritual gifts. Since we all have at least one gift it may be concluded that we received that gift or gifts at the moment of salvation. These gifts are part of God's gift to the church and serve as valuable tools for our effectiveness as we serve God.

God does not keep our spiritual gift, or gifts, a secret. In fact, the Holy Spirit wants each believer to know their gifts and to use them in service to edify the body of Christ. We discover our gifts as we experience the Holy Spirit using us and blessing our activity of service, so the disciple need not necessarily identify their gift or gifts before he or she begins to serve.

I often use the acronym DOG to explain how to discern our spiritual gifts. D stands for "DO it." One will never know if he has the gift of teaching if he's never tried to teach. Secondly, the O stands for OTHERS. Since gifts are designed to edify the body of Christ, our fellow church members will recognize the service and often point out how much of a blessing it was when, for instance, he took the time to help get their car started or when she spared some money for their bus fare. They don't call it a spiritual gift, but when people repeatedly recognize the same act of service as being a blessing to them, it is an indication that this may be a spiritual gift. Finally, the letter G stands for the truth that "GOD will bless it." When God blesses our service to him, it brings great joy to our hearts, often revealing a spiritual gift or gifts he has given us.

> **D** – Do it
>
> **O** – Others will recognize it
>
> **G** – God will bless it

Teach the disciple the gifts listed in Scripture (Rom. 12:6–8; 1 Cor. 12:8–10, 28; Eph. 4:11; 1 Pet. 4:9–10) and their descriptions. Encourage him to first pray daily that God will help him discover his gifts, then encourage him to begin trying different activities that would give him opportunity to exercise his gifts. Spiritual-gift inventories have become popular as a tool to help a person to discover his gifts. These questionnaires basically help the person to analyze what brings him joy and what others have recognized as abilities God has used to bless them. I believe a gift inventory can be helpful—as long as the disciple recognizes that it only indicates what he has so far experienced in his service to God. For example, if a person has never shared his faith, the questionnaire will not score very high in evangelism even though he may have that gift. Therefore, one should not treat a spiritual-gift inventory as a conclusive, completely accurate summary of our gifts. It is only a starting point and may become more accurate after one has served the Lord in a variety of capacities.

Having discovered his or her spiritual gifts, the disciple will likely require training in order to effectively use each gift. For example, a person with the gift of teaching needs instruction and practice in pedagogy. If a person has the gift of evangelism, he needs to be trained on how to share his faith. Whatever the case, the discipler must be prepared to guide his protégé in how to biblically practice his spiritual gift or gifts.

Training needed by every believer, regardless of one's gift:

- Inductive Bible study instruction
- General Bible study—Learning to use computer tools and various study books

- Personal testimony—Developing one's evangelistic testimony and becoming comfortable with sharing it
- Sharing one's faith—Learning how to lead a person to Christ including responding to objections made when one has the opportunity to believe in Christ for salvation, developing expertise through practice, and consenting to evaluation by an experienced evangelist
- Training in financial management—Learning about budgeting, debt reduction, and other biblical principles regarding finances

Leadership Development

Moreover, as we know, Jesus was actively involved in training his disciples to effectively serve him. From his training methods, we can identify six helpful steps our Savior used in training his disciples:

1. Tell them *what*. He told Peter and Andrew for example to "Follow Me, and I will make you fishers of men" (Matt. 4:19). Here, he tells them what he was going to train them to become. That is, he promises that if they follow him, he will train and develop them to evangelize and disciple men.

2. Tell them *why*. They learned that salvation was provided to all but that it was their job to proclaim the gospel and then to train disciples, so that the process would continue.

3. Show them *how*. "And He appointed twelve, so that they would be with Him and that He could send them out to preach" (Mark 3:14). The significance for the disciples of being with Jesus is that he would be their master in a discipleship relationship. They would learn from his instructions but they would also learn much by being with him and observing how the master lived and ministered. In fact, the first year or more was devoted to the disciples just watching Jesus live and minister.

4. Do it *with them*. The value here is the support and confidence that is built as the disciple serves with the experienced master. Doing so provided the disciples with various opportunities to put into practice what they had learned and at the same time receive feedback from Christ's on their performance.

5. Let *them* do it. Jesus didn't just suggest they serve him. When he sent them out, he issued several commands they were to follow (Mark 6:7–13; Luke 9:1–6). Once the disciples got back there was a sharing time, a type of debriefing in which they were able to share their thrill as they told him what the Spirit did through their ministry in the lives of many people (Luke 9:10).

6. *Deploy them*. Putting into practice what they had learned was the culmi-

nation of the two-and-a-half years spent with Jesus. Once fully trained, the master discipler deployed these twelve men with the filling of the Holy Spirit to reach others (Matt. 28:19–20; Acts 1:8). Christ intended that they not only grow to maturity, but ultimately that they would spiritually reproduce themselves in the lives of other men. As disciple makers today, we must likewise carry out Christ's intent with those we disciple.

1. Tell them WHAT

2. Tell them WHY

3. Show them HOW

4. Do it WITH THEM

5. Let THEM do it

6. DEPLOY them

Leading the Disciple to Move to the Next Step

Throughout the growth process, the discipler must encourage the disciple to strive to reach the next milestone, as well as be thoughtful in discerning how he can encourage the disciple's development. I would like to suggest ten steps of progress a discipler might consider. They are not listed in any particular order and they are not exhaustive:

1. Faithful attendance in the worship and praise services of a biblically sound church
2. Consistent Sunday Bible study attendance
3. Involvement in a week night Bible study and prayer meeting, or weeknight small group Bible study
4. Overcoming obstacles to growth—quitting a bad habit, sinful activity, or breaking off close friendship with nonbelievers
5. Church tithing and giving
6. Baptism
7. Church membership
8. Serving Christ
9. Advanced training perhaps offered by a church, Bible college, or correspondence school

10. Follow-up and discipleship of a new believer conducted by the disciple

Every discipler's constant goal should be to spur the disciple through biblical transformation. We need to give regular consideration to a given disciple's progress and growth needs. Yet more importantly, we need to pray every day for the disciple God has put under our charge. Remember, it is the Holy Spirit who brings transformation, with the disciple maker as his agent.

Review Questions

1. How does relationship provide the basis of good accountability? How have you seen this to be true?
2. What is the importance of the disciple maker's example in the discipling process? Explain.
3. Review the section "Renewing the Mind." Which of the three steps here does your disciple need the most help with right now? What could you use help with right now? In both cases, how can you help facilitate this?
4. How can the disciple discover his or her spiritual gifts? Which does your disciple need more in this part of the process right now, knowledge or opportunity? Explain.
5. Why is it important for the discipler to continually guide the disciple to the next step? What's the next step for your disciple right now, and how will you help him or her get there?

Chapter 11

THE PROCEDURE OF DISCIPLE MAKING: A STEP-BY-STEP APPROACH

MANY PEOPLE DESIRE TO HAVE the eternal impact I talk about. Most truly believe that God can guide and bless this discipleship ministry as they forge ahead. But when it comes down to actually beginning the process fear overcomes them, and feelings of inadequacy flood their souls. They just don't know where to start. If you're one of those people, this chapter is for you.

Regardless of what some may think, disciple making isn't difficult or complicated. It is simply a ministry in which one guides a motivated believer, with the help and wisdom of the Holy Spirit, to attain solid spiritual growth. As two people work together to achieve this common goal the Holy Spirit does something truly miraculous. He uses the disciple-maker—his words, his life example, discipleship materials, and the Word of God—to transform the immature believer into a God-honoring, motivated servant of God. Of course, we can't take credit for the transformation. Instead, we rejoice as we watch our great God use us to grow another person into a spiritually mature Christian—who further impacts eternity as he becomes a disciple maker himself.

To quote Allen Hadidian, "Discipling others is the process by which a Christian, with a life worth emulating, commits himself for an extended period of time to a few individuals who have been won to Christ, the purpose being to aid and guide their growth to maturity and equip them to reproduce themselves in a third spiritual generation."[1]

Remember, part of Christ's goal for discipleship involves the disciple ultimately reproducing him or herself, which requires that we prepare and motivate him or her to win others to Christ and then disciple them. This is the crown jewel, the ultimate end product—that the disciple not only obtains a solid level of spiritual maturity but that he multiplies himself. When the disciple maker reaches this pinnacle, he can rest assured that he has completed a task in which God is pleased.

Disciple Making Is Incarnational

When our Lord came to earth he became one of us, moving into the neighborhood, inserting himself into the culture, and becoming one of us through the incarnation—in which God, Creator of the universe, became a human child, eventually living as a man in order for mankind to have a personal relationship with him. To make this redemptive plan available our Lord began the most effective movement known to mankind. He devised a system that uses those who are changed by his salvation plan to share his gospel with others. God in his wisdom knew that if the process ended at salvation, the impact on the world would be minimal, and so he created a multiplication network of believers. Instead of simply organizing an evangelistic crusade, Jesus spent the vast majority of his life and ministry training a few people and ultimately commanding all his followers to do the same.

Incarnational ministry is relational. The only way to effectively train mature disciples is through that close relationship Jesus practiced. There must be intentional, relational contact guided by a specific strategy. That strategy should have a curriculum component, coupled with continual assessment by the disciple maker of weak areas that need to be dealt with in the discipleship process. Discipleship doesn't just happen because two people get together on a weekly basis. As Herb Hodges stated, "The simple rule is that *contact determines impact. Impact requires contact.*"[2] One may teach a person from a distance, but real lasting impact comes from close and ongoing contact with the disciple.

Additionally, there must be intentional, revelational, and logical communication. God's Word talks about nourishing young believers with "milk" first, then the "meat" of the Word. I find that most people seeking discipleship have missed much of the milk phase. Some whom I've discipled had been saved six or seven years, and yet still needed to be fed the basics. I worked with one person who had been saved twenty-five years and still didn't understand basic biblical truths and practices.

With this in mind, don't be too quick to skip over the "elementary principles of the oracles of God," as one biblical writer called it (Heb. 5:12). I usually start at the beginning and if I find the person has a good grasp with practical implementation of the material, I will not spend a lot of time with the basics except to provide a refresher, emphasizing the importance of practicing these truths.

As we study both basic and advanced truths, God will use biblically based content to transform the disciple into a mature follower of Christ. Paul tells us that "faith comes from hearing, and hearing by the word of Christ" (Rom. 10:17). All impact that leads to transformation during the disciple's growth process will come from the Word of God and will be applied through incarnational or relationship-based discipleship.

Developing a Relationship

Indeed, we must mirror Christ's incarnational discipleship approach. To do so, we must first become acquainted with the potential disciple. It is helpful to have him or her over to your home for a meal or out to lunch. This provides a low-pressure time of sharing and getting to know each other. The discipler may find that he and the disciple have little in common apart from their mutual relationship to Christ and common interest in spiritual growth, so it may take some intentionality to break the ice and get acquainted. Just remember, it is not necessary to develop a close relationship before the discipleship process begins; the relationship will grow as the meetings progress.

May I remind you that discipleship entails much more than a weekly meeting around a growth theme. Biblical discipleship insists that the disciple maker's life example impact the disciple. As disciplers, we must take advantage of opportunities to spend time with the disciple apart from the weekly meeting.

I will never forget one of the opportunities God gave me with a young man I was discipling. For years I served on the board of a Christian homeschooling organization. One of the responsibilities I had was to attend several conferences each year, where I would present several seminars and stand at a display table all day to answer questions and advise conference attendees. Prior to one such conference, I decided to take Bill with me. God really used this time to deepen our relationship. We traveled about 200 miles together, ate together, and stayed at the same hotel. While we were at the conference, Bill assisted me in everything I did. Even though he didn't have any money, he walked around the exhibit hall and kept looking at a particular creation-science book. Soon the vender noticed his interest and discovered he had no money, so he gave him a copy. Bill learned a lot, and told me that he would never forget this trip. However, the impact of our two days together did not come from the conference speakers or even the work we did. Our relationship grew as God used my life example to impact him.

I strongly encourage each discipler to incorporate as many opportunities as he can outside of the weekly discipleship meeting. Take the disciple to events. I take the men I disciple with me on visitations to the hospital and jail. It is the relationship in the midst of those opportunities that will allow the disciple maker to effectively reprove, correct, and instruct the disciple during regular meetings.

Providing an Effective Model

A godly role model's influence in the life of the disciple constitutes one of the most effective benefits of life-on-life discipleship. Thus, the discipler must ask if he has a life worth emulating because his influence will never be neutral. He either will have a positive influence—exhibiting love, humility, and patience—or he will have a negative, short-lived influence.

If a person doesn't have a life one can model, I would urge him to develop one before he embarks on such an important ministry as disciple-making. A life worth emulating is not a life of perfection; it is a life of spiritual maturity. It is the life of a person striving to be a godly man or woman. It is a life that quickly restores the breach with God as well as with his brothers and sisters in Christ when his sin has broken that relationship. A person whose life worth emulating doesn't wait until the offending party comes to him for reconciliation; he is the person who is humble enough, even when not guilty of wrongdoing, to seek reconciliation first.

When our dishonesty, selfishness, hypocrisy, prideful talk and actions, displays of ungodly anger, hurtful words, unholy language, and a host of other sinful actions weaken our credibility, there is only one thing to do: We must repent, restore our relationship with God and all who witnessed the sin. With God's help we must change that sinful weakness in our life, because it not only affects our life but the lives of those who are looking to us as an example. In brief, we must ask God for direction and strength to change the parts of our lives that cause us to be poor examples of Jesus Christ, so that we may have an effective discipleship ministry.

The Importance of Finding the Right Person

Since we will only have the opportunity to disciple a limited number of people in our lifetime, we need to select the right people to disciple—who will endure the process and ultimately become reproducing disciple makers.

The incredible power of prayer

Our effectiveness is not in any way based on our ability; it is the power of God that changes the life of the one we are discipling. In order to tap into this power, we must make prayer a part of the foundation of our discipleship ministry. Jesus demonstrated the importance of prayer by life example, retreating often to a private place. When it came to selecting the disciples, he prayed all night. Following

Jesus' example, one should not make a hasty decision when choosing a disciple, but instead fervently ask God to reveal the person God has given to him to disciple.

The disciple must agree to a commitment.

Remember, discipleship has eternal ramifications. The disciple maker will devote a significant amount of his or her life expending time, emotion, and even finances helping the disciple grow and eventually become a mature, reproducing disciple of Jesus Christ. Therefore, when meeting with a prospective disciple, it is important that we have them agree to a firm written commitment.

Once the discipler spends considerable time praying and chooses the person to disciple, the disciple maker meets with the prospect to discuss expectations. During this time, the prospect should be given a copy of the Discipler's Covenant (see Appendix III), which the disciple maker can go over point by point, making very clear what's expected. After they go over the covenant, the disciple can then take it home and pray about the decision. The next time they meet, the disciple maker should ask the disciple if he can agree to the covenant. If so, it's wise to have him sign it to signify its importance, and then file the covenant away.

All things considered, the time we spend with a potential disciple up front— emphasizing the seriousness of what will be undertaken and making the commitment clear— will save both the disciple and the discipler much headache and frustration later on.

The Regular Meeting

The foundation and anchor of the life-on-life discipleship process is the regular meeting. *The discipleship meeting must be frequent.* We live in a busy society and look for shortcuts in most everything we do. The foundational truth we need to grasp is that there is no shortcut to biblical growth. Meeting once a month, or even every other week, is not often enough for effective life-on-life discipleship. We need to understand that the disciple, spurred by the Holy Spirit, is hungry and that his growth desire needs to be satisfied or he will lose interest.

Also, meeting once a month or even every other week will stretch the discipleship process out far too long. Jesus lived with his disciples. He was with them twenty-four hours a day, seven days a week, from the time they began following him until his death. We cannot reproduce this intensity, and of course we cannot reproduce Jesus' expertise as a disciple maker. Nonetheless, in order to do the best job possible, we should meet at least once each week and include additional times when possible for social or ministry experiences.

The duration of the discipleship ministry depends largely on the disciple's knowledge, spiritual maturity, and motivation. The length of discipleship definitely should not last for only six weeks, nor even six months. In general, the average discipleship process lasts from a year to a year and a half; some, such as those who had a dysfunctional childhood, may need to be discipled for much longer. There are no short cuts. In discipleship, we cannot use a microwave approach; we need a crock-pot method.

Some disciple makers think that they've completed the discipleship process when they finish a series of materials with their protégé. This could not be farther from the truth. On the contrary, it is the discipler's responsibility to discern the person's spiritual needs. The disciple maker will need to determine whether the individual makes an effort to gain victory over major sin strongholds, spends time in God's word and prayer daily, regularly attends a biblically sound church, actively strives to lead others to Christ, and so on. Along with these areas, ultimately, the discipler has to determine whether the disciple demonstrates if he or she lives a life worth emulating and, therefore, is ready to disciple another person. Until the discipler has helped the person reach these objectives—particularly the final two—the discipleship process remains incomplete.

Consequently, each meeting must reflect a deliberate focus on reproducing the disciple. This strategy was modeled by Jesus where it says, "He appointed twelve, so that they would be with Him" (Mark 3:14). Why the necessity for them to "be with Him?" So they could emulate his life by multiplying disciples. Paul likewise used this model with Timothy and others, Peter with John Mark and others, Barnabas with Paul and others, and Timothy with faithful men. If, at the conclusion of the discipleship process, there is not a desire and plan for the disciple to become a disciple maker himself, the discipler will need to decide how his discipling should change for the next person he disciples. Regardless, keep encouraging the disciple in that direction. There may be circumstances preventing the person from discipling another believer right now. In the future you can circle back to challenge him to begin his disciple-making ministry.

The location of the meeting should be convenient and intentional. The location often depends on the disciple maker and the disciple agreeing on a locale convenient for both of them. For example, I usually meet in my office, but my wife meets with women either at our home or theirs, considering the needs of women with children. Sometimes one might meet over lunch or at the local coffee shop. Other times a topic can be discussed while en route to a special meeting or activity. It's great to be flexible and mix it up at times for variety, and in order to make the best use of time.

Use the discipleship curriculum effectively. As stated in chapter 7, content pertains to anything discussed during weekly appointments. Often the content is the next lesson in the curriculum used. However, while it is important to follow the curriculum, the discipler should never let the curriculum become a strait jacket.

Often the disciple will come to the disciple maker disturbed or confused about something he read or heard. He may be disappointed or discouraged in his ability in the past week to live victoriously over a particular sin. There may have been an event in his life, perhaps even a tragedy. Many issues like these or others trump the regular curriculum. In other words, the subject of concern, whatever it may be, becomes the important content for the day. In fact, any time the Holy Spirit leads the discipler to discuss another issue he should seize the opportunity to do so.

During most regular meetings the discipler will spend some of the time following the curriculum materials. This means that the disciple should have his own copy and prepare his assignment in advance, including verse memorization and any other material the discipler has asked him to read or research.

On most occasions, the meeting itself should go something like this: The appointment should begin with a few minutes in which the discipler and disciple catch up with events and experiences of the past week, followed by prayer asking God to bless the meeting and guide the disciple maker. The discipler may then ask appropriate accountability questions, including recitation of the particular week's memory verse. At some point, this conversation may turn to any lingering question from last week's discussion, or to anything of special concern to the disciple. If nothing else is pressing the disciple may then begin discussing the regular curriculum, or there may be an alternate discussion as the disciple maker feels led by the Holy Spirit. The discipleship meeting usually follows a discussion format, rarely a lecture, giving the disciple plenty of opportunity to ask questions. The final five to ten minutes should be dedicated to praying for any issues the disciple is facing, followed by a reminder of any assignments for the next meeting.

Content, such as answering questions and maintaining a prayer list, is indeed a necessary ingredient in the discipleship appointment. When we don't consistently regulate it, our meeting quickly loses its purpose.

Include each important ingredient in the discipleship appointment. Since a biblical

Suggested Meeting Schedule

1. Introduction, small talk and getting caught up
2. Prayer for the meeting
3. Asking accountability questions and verse memorization review
4. Answering lingering or new questions
5. Curriculum discussion, either the next lesson or a pressing discussion lead by the Holy Spirit
6. Prayer for application during the coming week

discipleship process requires the discipler to be intentional, there are certain ingredients that need to be kept in mind as one conducts the regular discipleship appointment:

1. Look for ways to encourage the disciple. By nature most of us are far too negative and critical in our approach to others. If the disciple will instead remain positive and affirming, our ministry will be much more edifying and will serve to motivate the disciple far more than simply through constructive criticism. Be complimentary when the disciple comes prepared with his or her assignment. Praise him when he has memorized a prescribed verse or even when he pulls out a notepad. Look for natural opportunities to praise the disciple for faithful attendance on Sunday or at weeknight Bible study. When the discipler hears someone say positive things about the disciple he should always pass on the encouraging comment. The fact is, the disciple maker can find many honest and heartfelt encouraging things to say—if he only looks for them.

2. Hold the disciple accountable. This responsibility serves as one of the primary strengths of life-on-life discipleship. Accountability can only be as beneficial as the disciple is honest. If he or she is not transparent and honest with the disciple maker, any efforts to hold the disciple accountable will be hindered.

Such instances support the importance of having disciples agree to and sign a covenant. One of the points in the Disciple's Covenant (Appendix III) states, "I will place myself under the spiritual authority of my discipler, participating in a spirit of honesty, trust and personal vulnerability." With this commitment in mind, continue to encourage honesty and transparency in the discipleship relationship, or accountability will be inefficient.

Whatever the circumstance or issue, accountability dialogue often leads to insightful instruction from the discipler and a special time of prayer. Indeed, accountability is a powerful and effective tool to help the disciple make changes that spark growth in his Christian life. If we use this tool prudently, it will yield huge dividends of growth.

3.   Practice the use of reproof, correction, and instruction in righteousness. Second Timothy 3:16 reminds us that the Word of God is "profitable for teaching, for reproof, for correction, for training in righteousness; so that the man of God may be adequate, equipped for every good work." The word "reproof" literally means to show someone their sin and to bring conviction. The idea here is for the person to clearly understand that he has offended a holy God. With "correction," the believer is directed to respond to the sin and make proper adjustments in his life practice. This means he will repent and confess his sin to God and to any offended people. This process may also include restitution and should always include an attempt to live in a different way as to not continually repeat the same sin. In brief, the disciple maker should use the Word of God as he or she holds the disciple accountable, whether through reproof or correction, in order to help the disciple become more Christlike.

"Instruction in righteousness" is the process of guiding the disciple to understand what is right and what is wrong, and to practice right living; and it is primarily accomplished through ongoing study of the Word of God. Some of the instruction will be from the disciple's personal study as well as life-on-life study with the disciple maker; other instruction will come from the curriculum used during the discipleship process; accountability also will provide discussion for additional instruction in righteousness.

Overall, when the disciple maker reproves, corrects, and instructs using the Word of God, he will ensure that the young disciple has ample opportunity to grow in righteousness.

4.   Address counseling issues or questions. As the process continues, the discipler will make note of issues that require counseling from God's Word. Often the disciple maker may choose to deal with an issue on the spot. Other times he may choose not to address it at that time but may reserve it for a future meeting. For example, the disciple will ask questions that the discipler may want to research for a more complete answer. Sometimes it may become clear that the disciple is incorrect in his understanding of some truth that relates to God's Word. In any case, taking extra time to prepare when faced with such inquiries allows the discipler more time for a complete presentation. It also allows one to print

out reading materials and record verses to give to the disciple or to even go through with him. Also, the disciple may often reveal the need to spend some time on some personal growth issue with which he needs help.

5.   Keep the next step in mind. In chapter 8, I talked about "Milestones in Discipleship." These are major steps each discipler should strive for in the discipleship process. These milestones include: assurance of salvation, which entails helping the person come to grips with his security in Christ; consistency in the fundamentals, such as developing a consistent personal Bible study, consistent involvement leading to membership in a good Bible-teaching church, becoming baptized, and beginning to actively serve the Lord; understanding basic bible doctrine; growth to consistent and relative Christlikeness; independence in one's Christian walk, meaning that the disciple no longer depends on any other human for his growth; and reproduction as the disciple leads others to Christ and in turn disciples them.

The Importance of Prayer in the Discipleship Ministry

Jesus' life forever remains the best illustration of the importance of prayer in discipleship ministry. His disciples quickly learned this as they observed him. Hearing people pray out loud is a common experience for us because from early childhood—or at least since we became believers—we have heard pastors, Christian family members, and friends pray out loud. However, Christ's twelve disciples were not privy to this kind of experience. The only prayers they likely heard out loud were the prayers of the Pharisees who prayed out of their hypocrisy to be seen and heard by those around them. But thankfully, the disciples were able to see and hear Jesus praying throughout the day and often spending large portions of time, sometimes all night, in prayer. Undoubtedly they could sense the importance of prayer in his life. In fact, one day they asked him to teach them how to pray, resulting in what we refer to as the Lord's Prayer in Matthew 6:9–13.

As the Lord instructed the disciples on prayer, he gave a parable that we find recorded in Luke 11:5–8, illustrating the importance of perseverance in prayer. Particularly, in verse 9, Christ says, "So I say to you, ask, and it will be given to you; seek, and you will find; knock, and it will be opened to you." The disciple must persevere in prayer for the one he is discipling, often without ceasing. That does not mean continual prayer, but it means that we should have an open communication with the Father all day, praying often, sometimes just a few words but overall maintaining an open communication with God.

Jesus prayed against Satan's determination to destroy Peter and for Peter's protection and perfection (Luke 22:31–32). He also prayed for the twelve disciples and for us, his future disciples (John 17:6–24). In this prayer Jesus is praying that you and I will have victory against the attacks of Satan, and that we will be sanctified in God's truth. Likewise, the discipler should follow Jesus' example and pray earnestly that God would protect the person he is discipling from Satan's attacks, while also praying for their growth toward perfection and sanctification.

Satan will try to minimize the impact of God's Word. In 1 Thessalonians 2:17–18, Satan tried to hinder Paul's impact in the lives of the Thessalonians. The word translated "hindered" here means to *cut in*. Paul charged Satan with cutting in on his path, preventing him from coming to see them. Just as Satan desired to hinder Paul's ministry, he also wants to keep us from traveling the path of God's leading and, if possible, to drive us off-road toward another direction, far from God's will for us.

Paul, by the inspiration of the Holy Spirit, left many examples of prayer for those he discipled. In Ephesians 1:15–19, he prayed for their enlightenment; in Ephesians 3:14–20, he moreover prayed for their enablement; and in Philippians 1:9–11, Paul prayed for the enlargement of their spiritual growth. Likewise, the disciple maker needs to pray on a regular basis that the ones he is discipling will have enlightenment, so they can truly understand God's Word in a way that will bring transformation into their lives. He should also pray for enablement in their battle against Satan and their service for Christ. And finally, he should pray for enlargement, an ever-increasing growth in Christlikeness.

I believe a lack of prayer constitutes one of the greatest weaknesses in any discipleship ministry. With the busy schedule of the average disciple maker, it is easy to go days without ever praying for the disciple. Yet he need to always remember that transformation comes from God as the Holy Spirit intervenes to grow us. This same Spirit responds to our intercession. James tells us that "The effective prayer of a righteous man can accomplish much" (James 5:16b). Each discipler must practice daily prayer for the disciple.

Always Seek to Produce a Multiplier

The New Testament approach to discipleship entails equipping disciples to reach others for Christ, and the desire to disciple additional people who in turn become multiplying disciples of Jesus Christ. I usually clearly state that ultimate goal early on and work toward achieving it throughout his ministry with each disciple.

The importance of producing a multiplying disciple. First, far greater eternal impact will be achieved as disciple makers grow others who are winning and discipling people to become reproducers than if they were the only ones who win people to Christ.

Secondly, it is important to produce multiplying disciplers because life is short. James tells us that our life is "just a vapor that appears for a little while and then vanishes away" (James 4:14). Life will be over before we know it and we can never turn back the clock. Since we have one life of service to give to Jesus Christ and one opportunity to make an eternal impact, how can we redeem the time? How can I make my life count for something? I am convinced the best way to do that is to obey the last command with which Jesus left us, to make mature multiplying disciples of him (Matt. 28:19–20).

Thirdly, producing multiplying disciples is important because God will hold us accountable. I am a steward of this short life that God has given me. Paul said, "For we are His workmanship, created in Christ Jesus for good works, which God prepared beforehand so that we would walk in them" (Eph. 2:10). God expects us to work in a way that will bring eternal impact, because one day we will stand before him and give an account. Since Christ gave the Great Commission to all his followers, I believe we will be held accountable for whether or not we obeyed it.

To continue multiplication, the disciple maker should become a mentor. Once the discipleship process is finished and the disciple is ready to become a disciple maker, the original disciple's new role is that of guide, encourager, and prayer partner. This does not require a weekly meeting but perhaps weekly phone discussion and prayer as the disciple goes through the selection process. After he begins discipleship the new disciple maker will face problems and difficulties in his new discipleship relationship. Thus, he needs a mentor to contact who will give a listening ear, provide advice, and walk him through the process. The objective here is to help the mature disciple, now the disciple maker protégé, successfully disciple others.

Continue the Process

What a blessing to see the fruit of one's labors, to rejoice in the expanded influence carried on by the protégé. But now the original discipler must look for a new, God-given disciple with whom to begin a new discipleship relationship. Continue the process and one day each disciple maker will stand before a pleased Savior, the one who commanded him to make disciples, with real joy followed by a host of discipled believers, branches from his spiritual family tree of disciplers. And he will say to the discipler, "Well done, good and faithful servant!" (Matthew 25:21, NIV).

Review Questions

1. What does it mean that disciple-making is incarnational? What does that look like to you? What might it look like to those you're discipling?
2. Why is it important for the discipler to have a life worth emulating? What relationship or ministry opportunities might you be able to invite your disciple(s) into, where he (they) can observe and/or participate?
3. What is the duration of the average discipleship process? In your own words, why does it need to take this long?
4. What reasons would cause the discipler to deviate from the printed curriculum? Give examples—personal ones if possible.
5. Where does counseling fit into the discipling process? How can you bring God's Word deeper into that process?

Chapter 12

SMALL GROUP DISCIPLE MAKING: A COMPANION TO THE LIFE-ON-LIFE APPROACH

FOUR OUT OF EVERY TEN AMERICANS attend a small group meeting regularly, according to Harley Atkinson's book *The Power of Small Groups*. That means that 80 million of the 200 million adults in this country participate in small groups and that sixty percent of these people participate in groups affiliated with a church or synagogue.[1]

Many groups are conducted by churches for the purpose of spiritual growth, and some are promoted as discipleship groups. Unfortunately, most of these groups are not systematic disciple-making tools, especially for people who are relatively immature in their level of growth. It is common for small groups to study the Bible or other topical interests, but its members usually grow at a slow rate. Most small groups simply are not organized to produce disciples of Jesus Christ. It would be better if church leaders would view most of these small groups as continuing discipleship, designed for those at mid-level or greater in maturity.

Without a doubt the best approach in making a person a disciple of Jesus is the life-on-life approach, usually an intentional one-on-one relationship. Small groups can never be as effective in disciple making because relationships are weaker, and, therefore, will never be a good substitute. However, small-group disciple making can be used effectively by churches along with the life-on-life approach, if the group design is altered.

Among the advantages of small-group discipleship is the close fellowship and camaraderie that comes from a small group, enabling people to have intimate fellowship. The dynamic environment of friends who are motivated to grow spiritually can be a catalyst of encouragement using positive peer influence. These types of groups provide an emotional home where the believer can feel accepted, while providing an atmosphere for spiritual development through instruction and interaction.

The Composition of the Disciple Making Group

For churches desiring to use small groups to make disciples I would like to outline ten important principles and procedures that should be followed in order for the small group to have greater effectiveness as a disciple-making tool:

Recruit groups that are of optimum size

As we have discussed at some length, one of the important elements in making disciples is relationship. The larger the group, the less impact the relationship of the leader has on group members. Many will respond that Christ had twelve in his small group; however, as I stated before, Christ lived day and night and traveled with his men seven days a week for at least two and a half years. They didn't even rise in the morning and travel to their various places of employment; instead, they followed him throughout the day and into the evening as he ministered. Also, we must admit that we can never expect to have the disciple-making expertise our Lord had. Therefore, I suggest keeping the group to a small band of committed and hungry followers of Christ. The number of people in the group could range from six to no more than ten members. A smaller number of members in the group allows for some leader accountability and private counsel. Therefore, pertaining to the optimum size of the small group let me affirm the axiom "smaller is better."

Recruit members of similar spiritual growth level

In order for each person to grow in a disciple-making group it is important for the members—excluding the leader, or leading couple if it's a mixed group—to be near the same spiritual level, usually initiating the group with members at the beginning stage of spiritual growth. If the group is composed of people at varying levels of maturity, the content need will vary from person to person.

Some have promoted a mixture of spiritual maturity so that the more mature members can be an example to the spiritual infants. Unfortunately, I have found a maturity mixture can be more of a hindrance than an asset. One of the problems is that the members of a mixed spiritual level group will experience dissatisfaction. Mature individuals will know much of the content and will tend to introduce more advanced questions and sometimes controversial subjects that go over the head of the spiritual infant, causing the group to be sidetracked. Their desire for deeper study will force the leader to choose material that will be inappropriate for the immature believer. The type of discussion often introduced by more mature members may have value in more mature groups but not for the young believer. There is a content progression that needs to be followed, and which can only advance effectively when the members are close to the same spiritual level.

Another concern is that those who seem to be more mature, having been around many Christians and church activities, seem to be knowledgeable but are often very carnal. Many young believers will seek them out for advice and friendship, but their failure to practice the Christian life can be the stumbling block Satan uses to derail the growth process of the immature. For these reasons I recommend that groups designed for discipleship with young believers be composed of members with the same approximate growth level.

Determine the sexual composition

Disciple-making groups can have men and women mixed or separate. There are real advantages of keeping the group gender-separate. A men's or a women's disciple-making group can allow sensitive discussion that relate to subject matter such as sex, lust, and other sensitive topics otherwise inappropriate for mixed groups. Mixed groups of married or engaged couples can work well if the leader has a partner, usually his or her spouse, who interacts with members of the same gender in private for counsel and accountability. When a mixed group discusses sensitive topics they can easily divide sexually, to discuss gender-specific or sexually intimate content.

Members should only include adults

The intentional disciple making process is very important, affecting the rest of the life and ministry of each disciple. Planning an uninterrupted group meeting is necessary for the focus and total involvement of each member; therefore, children should not be present. Some parents have pooled their resources to hire babysitters to watch children at the home where the meeting is being held. Inevitably, children will still interrupt the meeting, making it necessary for care to be provided at a location other than the meeting home.

Closed to visitors and new participant enrollment

Effective small groups designed to make disciples should be closed to new members and visitors, for several reasons. Members of a disciple-making group are near each other in spiritual maturity as they progress in their growth. If new members are allowed to join, they would likely be at a different level. Second, the new member would not have the benefit of the content and discussion that had already transpired. Finally, if group members paired off among themselves for accountability (as we will discuss shortly), the new member would not have a partner, or at least a partner at the same level. For these reasons, it is important that the group be closed to new members and visitors.

Determine the duration of the group's existence

Obviously, the group goal is not to lead its members to ultimate maturity; its goal is to lead members to a consistent walk with Christ with a life worth emulating. Each disciple should be able to take responsibility for his own spiritual growth, know how to search Scripture for answers, know what his or her spiritual gifts are, to know how to lead another person to faith in Christ, and be able to disciple another person through a life-on-life procedure. Therefore, a disciple-making group should have a specified end, usually between to two years. This is not the type of group a person would be a member of for the next five or ten years. It is a group requiring a high commitment from its members, who are dedicated to a continual growth process for a specified period of time, during which the members are held accountable to live the principles studied.

Select curriculum that is systematic and progressive

The purpose of small-group disciple making is not fellowship, nor is a Bible book or topical study sufficient to accomplish the goal needs. I believe in the study of the Word of God, but just having a Bible study does not ensure that the material needed at the members' growth level is being covered at the needed stage of the young believer's life. In making disciples, the leader must follow well thought-out content that leads those who are growing disciples in a topical Bible study which proceeds through material that will systematically aid their growth. The new believer needs basic instruction in what the Bible calls the "elementary principles" or "milk," before he or she is introduced to "solid food" (Heb. 5:12–14).

I believe the violation of this principle is the reason many new believers never grow or grow very slowly. They're invited to church and, if they come at all, get a few morsels of solid food that are usually above their understanding level. They receive food that cannot be digested by spiritual infants. When they get a few swallows of milk, the teaching is inconsistent and non-progressive. It is not the type of food needed for their level of development and therefore does not bring effective growth. A good disciple making group begins with very basic but practical content taught with illustrations in a discussion approach; the growing believer is then held accountable to practice the new principles. As the disciples are ready they progress to more "solid food," all taught with clear application of how each member should be practicing the truths being discussed.

If the members have not gone through a good new-believer series the group should start with this material first. I have used the series, *Growing in Christ,* published by NavPress, for many years and have not found material that better covers the "milk" or "elementary principles." After finishing with *Growing in Christ,* I recommend the group go through *The 2:7 Discipleship Series* (taken from Colossians 2:7). This three-book series, also published by NavPress, is very good following *Growing in Christ.* For a women's group I recommend the *Woman's Journey of Discipleship,* also published by NavPress. This is a three-book series on the level of the 2:7 series, but covers topics that women new in their faith would appreciate.

Young believers also need to know what the Bible teaches on the major Bible doctrines. Often doctrinal classes are too deep for young believers. I suggest taking them through *Meat* and *Bread,* both published by Positive Action Bible Curriculum. *Meat* covers eight major doctrines, and *Bread* goes deeper into the doctrine of Christ, which is necessary to understand as one is challenged by members of cults. These materials and many more are listed in the bibliography (Appendix I).

Simply going through systematic and progressive content does not ensure that a person will grow to a relatively mature level. The example of the leader, accountability, and sometimes private counsel must all be covered by prayer so that the Holy Spirit will do his transforming work. These elements are all necessary if members are to grow in their desire to become more like Christ.

Include a training component

An effective disciple-making group should include training. One type of training each person must go through is how to share one's faith. I recommend three stages as part of the evangelism training. The first stage is a workshop on developing one's personal testimony of salvation to be used as a witnessing tool.

I suggest these testimonies follow a three-part outline. The first is "what my life was like before salvation," which includes a short opening fifteen to thirty seconds in length. The second part of the outline is how they came to faith in Christ. This is not a sermon or a Bible study, so it should include no more than one or two quoted verses relating to how a person is saved. The final portion of the testimony should include what their life has been like since salvation. This is a short conclusion of no more than fifteen to thirty seconds in length. The entire testimony should not exceed more than two minutes in duration.

Once developed, each person should share their testimony in the group with the members making a few helpful suggestions for the quality development of each testimony. The second stage of evangelism training would include a seminar on how to share one's faith and how to handle common objections faced when witnessing. The third stage should include an evangelistic outreach where group members have the opportunity to practice what they've learned. I have often taken disciples to a city park on a warm Saturday or Sunday afternoon. Once there, we would pair off two-by-two and look for opportunities to share our faith. A park experience can make a great laboratory where the disciple learns by practice. After the experience it is profitable to have a debriefing time where each person shares what was learned. The second year of the group's existence could include an outreach every quarter in which each person participates in planning, promoting, and conducting an evangelistic event. One example is a simple backyard barbeque, where each group member invites a nonbelieving friend. At the outreach one person could share their testimony of how they received Christ as personal savior. The following week after each outreach have a debriefing to share the blessing, results, and how to follow up with the friend each person brought.

Along with evangelism, other types of training conducted by the group should include understanding and discovering one's spiritual gifts and how to conduct a personal Bible study, including how to use various Bible study tools available in books and/or on the Internet.

Include built-in accountability

The best accountability, normally, comes from the group leader(s). The difficulty in this is the workload created for the leader, especially when the group consists of six to ten members. An alternative is to organize accountability partners early in the group's life. Members are asked to choose another person in the group of the same gender, and each week fifteen minutes could be devoted to a time of accountability and prayer. Accountability can also be conducted during the week at a coffee shop or over the phone. Accountability can be effective in helping members practice what is being taught and to also have victory over sin issues the person is struggling with.

Recruit using a disciple making group covenant

A disciple-making process carries a very high level of importance. Therefore, it is very helpful to include in the recruiting process a Disciple-Making Group Covenant that is presented to each prospective member. After praying about it for a few days, each would sign the covenant as a confirmation of their commitment to growth. Each agrees to meet the requirements in order to get the very most out of the process of intense growth in Christ, as they practice the wonderful truths they learn over the life of the group.

Agreeing to a covenant seals the commitment of members to the group. It establishes what's expected from each member and it assists the group leader in explaining its purpose, goals, and intentions. The covenant clarifies when and where the group meets, how long each meeting will last, the length of time the group will exist, and what the group will do during meetings. A suggested covenant is included in Appendix III, and can be used as written or as a starting point in drafting your own covenant.

The Qualifications of Disciple-Making Group Members

Being selective will assure that the group will be committed to the process of spiritual growth. First, since this group will be starting at the beginning level it is important to look for spiritually young prospects. It is common for a person to be a believer for many years and still be at the spiritual-infant stage. Therefore, the potential members we are referring to here are not necessarily just new believers but other believers who are young in their maturity level. Secondly, I suggest that you look for prospective group members who have the FATHER qualities discussed in chapter 6; one would do well in reviewing this chapter before starting the process of recruiting. These members should be: faithful, available, and teachable, have a heart for God, are eager to serve, and have a respect for authority. No one is perfect in any of these qualities, but even a new believer can have a measure of each of these traits. If they don't have these character qualities, they will not have the behavior necessary to become mature disciples of Jesus Christ. They can be urged on by members of the church and encouraged to grow in these qualities, but are not ready for intensive disciple making at this time.

Besides considering those who attend church services, I would recommend you consider members of the new-Christian class, if there is one available in your church, as a prime resource. I believe every church should have a class ministering to new believers at the beginning level, whether the class has one student or a dozen. It could be held at church or at another location, but new believers need this class very soon after their salvation. If it is a continuing class, a new believer can join at any point in the series, and by the end of the class the leader will have a good idea which members have the FATHER qualities listed above.

Suggested Schedule for a Disciple-Making Group

The schedule for most groups usually should not last more than two hours and would usually include opening prayer; topical Bible study discussion; group sharing time, which includes sharing God's blessings and victories the past week; and accountability time with an accountability partner. This is an opportunity to be transparent and honest, asking the hard questions about sin struggles and consistency in meeting the growth demands as the members hold each other accountable. (I have included accountability questions for men and women in Appendix V.) Following the accountability time I suggest you include a prayer time, either with accountability partners or with groups of three or four, and ending the evening with light refreshments and fellowship.

Suggested Small-Group Meeting Schedule	
Activity	Minutes
1. Opening prayer	5
2. Topical Bible study discussion	45-60
3. Group sharing time	15
4. Accountability time	5
5. Prayer time	15
6. Light refreshments and fellowship	15-25

How to Multiply Disciples through the Group

One of the weaknesses of small-group disciple making is multiplication. Part of the plan should be to prepare disciples to be multipliers. Instead of challenging each person to multiply the group with each one leading a new group, it would be a better objective to train and encourage each person to become a life-on-life disciple maker. Therefore, the last study of this course should include training on how to disciple another person. The material to discuss could come from the chapters in this book or other books listed in the bibliography (Appendix I). Small-group disciple making can be very effective, provided that the elements in this chapter are integrated into the organizational plan. Whether done by the use of a small group or through life-on-life disciple making, we must do a better job at our churches in making disciples of Jesus Christ.

Review Questions

1. What are some of the plusses and minuses of using small groups for disciple making?

2. Why is it important to have the members of a disciple-making group at roughly the same spiritual maturity level?

3. Why is it important that the disciple-making group be closed to new members and visitors?

4. What does the author mean by systematic and progressive content? Why is this type of content important?

5. What are some topics that should be taught in the training component of the disciple making group?

6. What questions do you have about small-group disciple making that you'd like to explore further? How does this model differ from other small-group models you have seen or worked with before?

Chapter 13

DISCIPLESHIP AT HOME: PARENTS—THE PREMIER DISCIPLERS OF CHILDREN

WE HAVE SPENT MOST OF THIS BOOK FOCUSING on our Christ-given responsibility to disciple adult Christians. However, I believe that there is no grander task, no more profound undertaking, than our mission to guide our children toward becoming mature disciples of Jesus Christ. In spite of its importance, past and present authors of discipleship books say little about this responsibility. Perhaps it has been assumed far too long that the normal Christian upbringing by committed Christian parents would automatically produce followers of Jesus. As we observe the common track record, one would have to conclude that disciples of Christ are not the automatic byproduct of Christian parenting.

Also, let me state that one does not disciple children as one would disciple adults. The process of discipling children does not come primarily from discipleship Bible studies and discussions. As children become mature followers of Christ they are developed primarily through the teachable moments that God gives us, correctly administered Biblical discipline, and the provision of a godly example from parents along with biblical instruction with practical application. Some information in this chapter could be classified as child-rearing instruction, but it is included only because I believe it to be important in the task of discipling our children.

While some discipleship surely takes place in children's ministries at church, God intends for spiritually mature Christian parents to be the primarily disciplers of their children. God has given parents the responsibility to guide the lives of their children toward Christ. It is the work of the church to develop the parents and support them in the discipleship of their children.

Several influences war against spiritual growth of children—and as in any war, we must know our enemy. First of all, most Christian parents have not come to realize their profound, God-given responsibility. They may realize the importance of good child-rearing, but most parents do not intentionally create disciples of Jesus. Indeed, the overall failure of Christian parents is extremely serious when one realizes the negative spiritual impact society has on our children and, more importantly, the negative impact their lack of spiritual development can have on their eternal existence.

Secondly, the vast majority of parents tend to farm out their children's upbringing to the public-school system, day-care organizations, nannies, sports, television viewing, and so forth. In general, this cultural practice stems from the passionate desire in the United States to experience the "American Dream." In other words, we deliberately or unintentionally relinquish our responsibility as parents to pursue our own aspirations. In our modern society both Mom and Dad work outside the home in order to experience a desired lifestyle. And yet, God mandates that believers "seek first His kingdom and His righteousness" (Matt. 6:33). Sadly, we often look to further our own kingdom and, in governing our lives this way, have sacrificed our children at the altar of materialism. Thus, many children are raised by nannies or sent to pre-school programs, followed by traditional government-run school. In these public schools they constantly face ungodly peer pressure, humanistic-based education, as well as exposure to sexual promiscuity, drugs, and homosexual lifestyles, to name a few. And when the children are home in the evenings, parents often spend little time or effort capitalizing on the remaining few hours of their children's day.

To further complicate this problem, the US has become overrun by a large number of broken homes, void of the benefit of a father's involvement on a daily basis. This much too common single-parenting environment has devastated our homes at an epidemic proportion. As Viv Grigg said, "Fatherless children are at a dramatically greater risk of drug and alcohol abuse, mental illness, suicide, poor educational performance, teen pregnancy, and criminality."[1] Likewise, "Four out of every ten children in the United States will go to sleep in homes where their fathers do not live. Before they reach the age of eighteen, more than half of America's children are likely to spend at least a significant portion of their childhood living apart from their fathers."[2] No wonder we have so many problems in our society. We tend to blame the school system when the greatest problem is the lack of both a father and mother, and often neither parent is raising their children. In short, children will never be raised with moral attributes and never be correctly discipled until parents once again function the way God intended.

The third influence that wars against the spiritual growth of children, as mentioned briefly above, is the influence of ungodly peer influence on children and teens. In 1 Corinthians 15:33 the apostle Paul said, "Do not be deceived: 'Bad company corrupts good morals'" (see also Ps. 1; Prov. 4:4; 13:20). We should never underestimate the impact of peer pressure on the lives of youth. I am not saying parents should shelter their children from the world. We need to teach them to be "in the world but not of the world" (John 17:14–16). We shouldn't shelter them from every aspect of the world's influence, but we do need to teach them to not live as the world lives. The challenge is finding the proper balance. For those who have their children in traditional public schools, the influence of peer pressure will be much greater in intensity and quantity than most children or teens can bear.

Though I appreciate the mission and effort of many Christian schools, they also often become a substitute for parents. Instead of discipling their own children, parents often pawn them off to a Christian school. This source of spiritual development on average is better than what can take place in a public school; however, no matter how good the school or the faculty, Christian-school teachers are always a poor substitute for godly parental discipleship. School teachers simply have too many students and must focus primarily on academics instead of life issues. Another element that hinders spiritual development in most schools, including Christian schools, is the fact that many peers are not believers or live an ungodly life often unknown by busy parents. Therefore, the negative peer pressure multiplied by the number of hours at school often has a negative impact on the student.

What about our responsibility to be light and salt in a needy world? Many well-meaning parents believe that their teenagers need to be missionaries to their unsaved friends in the public school. This desire may be a great aspiration. However, most Christian youth are not spiritually able to withstand the negative pressures from other students, as well as the humanistic philosophical teaching they face day in and day out. If your child is somehow ready for that challenge, he or she is much more mature than most Christian teens. A fourth and final influence that wars against the spiritual growth of children is the danger of public education vastly indoctrinating children from Christian homes with a secular and humanistic worldview. This has colored their philosophical foundation, impacting their presuppositions and conclusions used to direct their life decisions. This worldview promotes feminism, lessens the sanctity of life, and encourages the quest for a materialistic self-seeking lifestyle void of God and the moralistic life he purports.

As you can clearly see, there are many battlefronts Satan has created to prevent our children from becoming disciples of Christ. No wonder our society is declining year after year. The solution falls directly on parental responsibility.

Basic Truths We Must Understand

There are a number of important truths we must understand and embrace if we are to effectively disciple our children:

God owns all things. Psalm 24:1 says, "The earth is the LORD's, and all it contains, the world, and those who dwell in it" (see also Ps. 50:9–12). God owns our children and has graciously given them to us to steward their upbringing. Thankfully, he has not left us without direction, having given us principles and specific instruction from the Bible. We should seriously study and practice these principles, because we will be held accountable by God for effectively managing our children's development.

Humans are born with a sinful nature. Children are not born as a blank slate that simply needs to be programmed. Addressing mankind's sinfulness, Jeremiah 17:9 says, "The heart is more deceitful than all else and is desperately sick; who can understand it?" According to this passage and many others, our children, as cute and loving as they can be, are sinners—just like their parents. The child is not a sinner because he sins; he sins because he is a sinner (Jer. 17:9; Prov. 22:15; Rom. 3:10–12). A child doesn't have to be taught how to sin, but we have to begin training them to abstain from their sinful impulses.

I remember each of my infant children, watching as they had their little temper tantrums. There were times when they clearly expressed outright anger because they were not fed quickly enough or simply because they wanted to be held. Not surprisingly, no one ever taught our young children to lie or to be self-centered. Instead we had to teach them to tell the truth and to share with other children. When we understand their sinful condition, we are less likely to make excuses for them. Instead we will instruct and, when needed, discipline them in order to encourage godly convictions.

The importance of example. Children learn much from observation; therefore, the example of parents significantly influences their lives. They not only adopt mannerisms and characteristics from Mom and Dad but also learn how to be godly fathers or mothers. It is during childhood that one learns about the husband and wife roles in the family. It is during these years that a child learns how a man relates to a woman and how a woman relates to a man. More than anything else, what he or she learns from their parents' example prepares the child for the relationship with his or her future spouse. Children also learn leadership and discipline, which is critical as they function as adults.

The greatest way a father and mother can teach wholesome character qualities is to live a godly example. Have you ever noticed that when a sexually provocative image comes on the television screen, an adolescent son or daughter looks to see how Dad responds? They are looking to his example. It doesn't matter whether the father's life reflects godliness or carnality; a child will look to him as a model. Children learn by watching their parents and they will naturally assimilate these examples into their understanding of how they should respond and act as they grow up. Their moral framework also comes primarily from their parents' example, so we cannot underestimate the importance of the parents' example in the discipleship process of children.

Behavior needs to radiate from correct heart attitudes. It is extremely important that parents do not raise their children to just develop good behavioral habits. Often these habits are not based on the proper motivation, and so once children leave their parents' home they no longer have to obey them because they are now their own supervisor. Instead, their behavior needs to be based on heart attitudes motivated by a personal desire to obey God. Developing these heart attitudes, based on the Word of God, should be one of the priorities as the parent goes through the discipleship process.

Time with children is foundational to the discipleship process. Very critical to everything we cover in this chapter is the amount of time parents spend with their children. Deuteronomy 6:6–9 challenges parents as they raise their children: "These words, which I am commanding you today, shall be on your heart. You shall teach them diligently to your sons and shall talk of them when you sit in your house and when you walk by the way and when you lie down and when you rise up. You shall bind them as a sign on your hand and they shall be as frontals on your forehead. You shall write them on the doorposts of your house and on your gates." Here Scripture stresses the necessity of teaching our children all day long. The "words," or content, to which the verse refers, is the Law or the Word of God, which parents must teach not so much through family devotions as through lifestyle. Practicing the principle in this passage takes a major commitment of time—far more time than the lifestyles of most parents allow.

In the Old and New Testament period as in most of the history of the world, until the beginning of the Industrial Revolution around the middle of the eighteenth century, parents spent time with their children throughout the day, every day. Fathers would take their sons to work with them, whether it was to work in the family trade or out in the field. Daughters, likewise, worked with their mothers cooking, mending cloths, cleaning, and gardening.

At great spiritual cost to their children, both parents in the twenty-first century usually go off to work and farm their children out to others such as a nanny, preschool nursery, and public or private schools. The primary reason both parents spend their life outside of the home in vocational pursuits is the debt trap. Early in their relationship many young couples go into debt in order to get all the things they desire such as furniture, cars, a home, etc. Because they bury themselves in debt, both parents have to work—requiring that their children be raised and educated by other people.

When children are home from school their time is taken up in activities away from parents such as homework, soccer, baseball, gymnastics, music lessons, and recreation with friends. Dad plays golf or joins the baseball or bowling league, while Mom takes care of shopping, cleans house, and updates her Facebook page. What little time the parents have is not used in a way that guides children to become disciples of Christ.

When I got married, my wife and I decided that in order to faithfully nurture and disciple our children, my wife needed to be a stay-at-home mom. However, we could never afford for her to do that unless we stayed out of debt. That meant that we had to sacrifice the things we desired, or at least wait until we saved money to purchase them. We didn't buy anything on credit and therefore paid no interest, except for a house. This lifestyle allowed us to live on less so my wife could stay at home. My ministry was near enough so I could have most meals at home. I also prioritized my life so I had time with my family in the evenings and on weekends. I did not allow my occupation (ministry) to always be the priority, and thus rob my family of time with me.

Discipleship requires that both the father and mother spend time with their children, in order that the impact of the parent-child relationship is at its strongest. Through interaction and observation children will begin to understand what a Christian adult looks like in various social roles. Through these experiences children learn how a man and woman relate to one another. It is also when parents spend time with their children that they receive adequate affirmation to bolster their sense of self-worth; they share family affection and provide an anchor the child can cling to throughout life. When a child observes his parents' Christian moral lifestyle, it forms a Christian worldview and provides a godly example the child can follow and build his life around.

Without question, the rich involvement of parents in the life of the child will provide a primary lifestyle teaching tool: the teachable moment. These moments in which a child asks questions provide an opportunity in which his interest is peaked. These are golden opportunities for discipleship. Answering the "why" questions from a biblical framework will help the child develop his own convictions based on God's Word. They are not just "sit-down moments" of instructional discussion, but often occur "along the way," as described in our passage from Deuteronomy above. They may occur while riding in the car together, while mother and daughter prepare a meal, while father and son work on the car. Therefore, we should not, unless absolutely necessary, tell our child, "not now, I'm busy." Even when we are truly busy, we must exercise a measure of discipline.

Remember, teachable moments are gemstone opportunities for child discipleship—but they usually don't occur at a time that's convenient for *us*. But by taking advantage of these divine appointments, we reflect Christ's approach to discipling his twelve disciples. Indeed, he always took time to use life circumstances, such as answering his disciples' questions. Discipleship that impacts a child's character development does not come primarily from a class or a devotional, though these materials have a level of worth when taught correctly, but by way of conversations and events that take place during everyday life.

Preparing Your Children for Salvation

Every Christian parent has a deep desire to see each of their children become believers in Jesus Christ, but it is incorrect to think that it happens only by means of a timely gospel presentation. We must remain wary of such dangerous thinking because children, without understanding or even truly desiring salvation, can easily be led to say a prayer if encouraged to by an adult. Instead, parents should seek to know when the child understands and is ready for a true, repentant heart decision. In guiding children toward belief in Christ, parents need to consistently and lovingly cultivate their children's desire through the spiritual nurturing process.

The first place to start is with prayer. Pray daily that God would prepare the heart of your child for salvation and that he will guide you, as a believing parent, to spiritually nurture your child. Secondly, remember that the child learns much from their parents' example of devotion to God. This truth is foundational and very critical in creating a desire in the child's own heart. Thirdly, teach your children the nature of man's fallen state and separation from God. They need to learn of God's character and how Jesus paid the debt of sin, making it possible for each person to be restored to fellowship with God. Fourthly, expose them to God's truth by taking them to church and Bible study. Respond to the teachable moments generated from exposure to God's Word.

Children who are spiritually nurtured will often make a solid decision to receive Christ as Savior by the time they are five or six years old. Don't push them, however; let their understanding lead you, trusting that God will show you when they're ready. For example, at the age of five, one of my sons was riding with us in the car after we had visited his grandfather, who had just undergone bypass heart surgery. On the way home he began to sing a made-up song, "I want to be with Jesus whenever I die." I looked over at my wife and asked, "Are you listening to what our son is singing?" He continued, "I want to become a Christian but I don't know how. I know I'm a sinner and Jesus died for me." As he went on, it seemed clear that he understood all the ingredients the Bible requires for one to be saved. When we got home we sat down in the living room, asked a series of questions to make sure, and then we guided him to become a child of God. Each of our children had their own story, and each one received the Lord as their savior around age five or six. They began showing fruit of salvation and we began the process of discipling them.

Discipline: A Powerful Tool of Discipleship

God has much to say about discipline, whether applied by God to his children or about parents applying discipline to their children. Discipline is never pleasant for either parent *or* child, but yields wonderful life-changing results if applied consistently and correctly. Though discipline is commanded by God, there is both faulty and correct implementation.

Non-Biblical Methods of Discipline

Unknowingly, parents tend to develop much of their own child-raising methods from their personal upbringing. They also incorporate some of their culture's popular and trendy methods into their parenting philosophy, which are sold to them by psychologists and educators. However, God's Word is all-sufficient and gives clear direction to parents in their child-rearing responsibilities. Christian parents must be cautious in discerning whether popular cultural parenting methods, or even methods their parents used, coincide with God's design. Some current non-biblical parenting methods include:

Bribery—a form of behavior modification. Behavior modification is a form of child-rearing that seeks to modify actions by simply rewarding good behavior and punishing bad behavior. With this method, the parent often makes deals with the child in order to manipulate his or her behavior toward a desired outcome. By simply choosing an incentive desired by the child and offering a particular reward for the right action, one can coax the child to act or exercise certain behavior. This method is seen every year at Christmastime. The "Santa Claus incentive" dictates that the amount and quality of toys children get at Christmas is directly related to how good they are. Most of us were coaxed by the following lyrics, "He's making a list and checking it twice; gonna find out who's naughty and nice. Santa Claus is coming to town." Older children are often encouraged to agree to an unwritten, informal contract which is another form of bribery. If he disobeys, his cell phone or computer may be removed. With the right behavior, the child may be allowed to go to a friend's house for a sleepover.

I'm not saying that this method is always wrong, but it certainly does not develop godly character. The child learns that behavior is based on self-interest. He learns nothing about being under parental authority, nor does he learn responsibility or integrity. This method does not deal with the child's heart but only seeks to manipulate behavior and teaches the child that they only have to obey when Mom or Dad is watching. The heart is not changed, and behavior is only temporarily influenced.

Punishment—a punitive form of discipline. With this method, the parent adopts a punitive response to undesired behavior for the purpose of manipulating it. The threat of punishment becomes a natural way to simply control behavior, as opposed to correcting it. I am not only talking about corporal punishment; for example, parents often use grounding and time-outs as a form of punishment. The problem with these forms of discipline is that they do not adequately address the reason for the poor behavior. The next time you use these forms of discipline, ask yourself what this punishment has done for the child. You'll usually have to concede that nothing was done *for* the child; it was only done *to* the child. The punishment didn't help to biblically correct the child's heart attitude or desire. It was just another attempt at behavioral modification.

Emotionalism as a manipulative form of child control. Perhaps because the parent doesn't desire to use negatively viewed forms of discipline, many resort to another method in which they appeal to the emotions of the child, coercing him or her to alter their behavior. During my childhood, the primary method of control my mother used was emotional manipulation. She would make me feel sorry or guilty for my behavior, whether indeed sinful or otherwise. As I got older and more independent, she would tell me she would have to stay home alone if I went out. Other times she would tell me that I should be ashamed for a particular behavior she didn't like. Another parent who practiced emotional manipulation sang this old song to her children, which poetically demonstrates this type of discipline, "Nobody likes me, everybody hates me, guess I'll go eat some worms."

Actually, what this method attempts to do is to appeal to childhood fears—fear of being shamed, fear of disappointing my mother and making her sad, or even fear of losing her love. Some parents have used fear to control their child by telling them that they will be left home alone if they don't obey. Other emotions parents have tried to manipulate to change the child's behavior include happiness, anger, worry, and even humiliation. Sometimes, because of the emotional and often degrading hurtful feelings, this technique backfires, causing rebellion or a belligerent attitude. When we analyze this emotionally manipulative form of discipline we can see that the benefit is more for the parent than the child. Again, these methods do not provide the results needed in discipling children, but simply manipulate his emotions instead of changing his heart and creating God-honoring character.

Principles of Biblical Discipline

One of the most important discipling tools that Christian parents have is biblical discipline. In understanding biblical discipline there are three principles each Christian parent must learn to follow. Foundational to the subject of correct discipline is understanding the nature of the child's heart. Where does negative behavior come from? Some say, "Boys will be boys!" or "They're just kids!" But what is the source of their actions? Our actions reflect our hearts. In Mark 7:21–23 Jesus said, "For from within, out of the heart of men, proceed the evil thoughts, fornications, thefts, murders, adulteries, deeds of coveting and wickedness, as well as deceit, sensuality, envy, slander, pride and foolishness. All these evil things proceed from within and defile the man" (see also Luke 6:45; Prov. 4:23). Once we understand the source of our child's actions, we can begin to seek transformation of his or her sinful attitudes.

Correcting the source of the problem—the sinful heart—requires that parents be intentional in their focus on the heart throughout the child's early developmental years. Yet parents often get sidetracked with how their children act and feel an urgency to change the negative behavior, and so we seek to change behavior rather than helping to spark a change of heart. Even though there may be some behavioral changes, the child's negative behavior will simply surface in a different way if he or she does not experience biblical heart transformation. If parents can really get hold of this concept, it will change their parenting goals as well as their methods.

The first principle, as we have just stated, is that Christian parents must deal with the heart issues, not just the behavior. We need to understand that God has called parents to be his stewards, with the responsibility of molding the lives of our children. We are their authority, their teacher, their guide, and their moral compass, as the Holy Spirit enables. We are not called to be the child's best friend.

If we really love our children, we must not raise them in a way that pleases us or them. Instead, the Christian parent must raise them in a way that pleases God.

> PRINCIPLE #1:
> The Christian parent must deal with the heart issues, not just the behavior.

To be sure, discipling children require that parents, both father and mother, practice consistent discipline. It doesn't work to leave the discipline to one parent, because that person is not always present. Dealing with heart issues will be undermined by parental inconsistency, and as a result the discipline will be less effective and the child may draw the wrong conclusions.

Secondly, discipline must always be corrective, not punitive. We must never discipline children out of unholy anger. When we enact punishment out of this kind of anger, we simultaneously risk injuring our children and train them to fear man instead of God. We must therefore discipline children according to God's direction, not based on our own agenda which sometimes results in venting our frustration or irritation because our own personal rights or desires were violated (James 1:19–20). Punitive discipline can be interpreted as unloving since the parent seems intent on just meting out judgment. On the contrary, corrective discipline has a loving purpose with minor pain, when implemented, never being the end but the means of bringing change and growth.

> PRINCIPLE # 2:
> Discipline must always be corrective, not punitive.

The fact is that discipline is an expression of love. Two dads were talking during a break at a conference. One dad said, "I'm too hard on them. I really have to; my wife loves them too much to discipline them." The other dad replied, "I guess you and your wife need to strike some sort of balance." The first dad responded, "Yes, we need some balance between discipline and love." We might chuckle at this absurd statement that there needs to be a balance between discipline and love because discipline is an expression of love. Proverbs 3:12 says, "For whom the LORD loves He reproves, Even as a father corrects the son in whom he delights." Concerning a permissive parent, the Word of God further says, "He who withholds his rod hates his son, but he who loves him disciplines him diligently" (Prov. 13:24). Proper corrective discipline is an expression of love, and the lack thereof is described as an expression of hate. Using discipline to help the child to become a follower of Jesus is thus one of the greatest expressions of love that parents have to offer their children.

Finally, we must help the child understand that parental authority originates from God, as recorded in the Bible (Eph. 6:1–3). Parents have surrogate authority and as such, must teach their children to obey them primarily out of their desire to obey, honor, and love God. If our children see us as their sole authority, we have not correctly taught who the child ultimately obeys—and when he is no longer under our roof, he will follow the dictates of his sinful nature. "Dad isn't there to discipline me, so I can do as I please." In order for children to develop godly character, Christian parents must raise and disciple their children in such a way that encourages them to obey and fear the Lord first and foremost. One of the important elements that will help the child to obey their parents out of obedience to God is the way we handle teachable moments created from physical discipline, as we will discuss shortly.

> PRINCIPLE #3:
> Character is developed as the child learns to obey God
> and His Word, not merely his parents.

Methods of Biblical Discipline

The Bible promotes several methods of discipline that are effective to help the child grow to become a man or woman with biblical character. Each method is necessary as we seek to grow the child to become a disciple of Jesus Christ. It all begins with communication.

Discipleship requires communication from both the parent and the child. Communication between parent and child must involve a mutual effort to listen to and understand each other, not merely to have your child understand you. With good communication, there is no cold, oppressive, punitive action. The Bible emphasizes the importance of good communication, understanding each other so one can act accordingly (Prov. 18:13; Eph. 4:25–32; et al.). Developing an open communication in which the child will be listened to develops a relationship of respect. This aspect of discipline is critical as the child becomes a teenager. My wife spent hours at a time talking to each of our children, especially when they became teenagers. She was available whenever the need or desire called for it.

If this open communication is established in the grade school years it will greatly smooth out the teen years. On the contrary, it will be difficult to develop open communication if it hasn't been established prior to the teen years. Sometimes our approach hinders effective change. Our objective is to understand the cause for the bad behavior so we can deal with heart issues.

Tedd Tripp, in his book, *Shepherding a Child's Heart*, states that the "'Why did you…' line of questioning never works with children." He states that questions applying to the specific situation are more productive:

1. "What were your feelings when you hit your sister?"
2. "What did your sister do to make you mad?"
3. "Help me understand how hitting her seemed to make things better."
4. "What was the problem with what she was doing to you?"
5. "In what other ways could you have responded?"
6. "How do you think your response reflected trust or lack of trust in God's ability to provide for you?"[3]

As you can see, questions like these above help the parent get at the root of the sinfulness of the heart. They help us understand if the problem is pride, jealously, selfishness, and so forth. Parents need to help the child understand the choices he had prior to his actions and how he responded sinfully. To be sure, communication remains an important aspect of discipline. Sometimes it is all that is needed. Tripp lists eight forms of communicative discipline that are helpful in various circumstances: encouragement, correction, rebuke, entreaty, instruction, warning, teaching, and prayer.[4] Each of these forms are useful during the discipleship ministry that godly parents must have with their children. Communication is foundational to the entire discipleship process and is even basic to the next form of discipline referred to in the Bible…..

Physical discipline. The use of a rod—or in modern terminology, spanking—should not be avoided as a method of discipline, as it is rooted in biblical principles (Prov. 13:24; 22:14–15; Heb. 12:11; et al.). Following God's methods always pays high dividends. When wise parents correctly apply spanking, it has extraordinary potential to provide teachable moments to create godly character traits in their children.

Some object to such discipline, saying they love their child too much to spank them. Yet God's Word says that spanking expresses love (Prov. 3:12; 13:24). To withhold spanking can in fact be harmful to the child, as will be explained later in this chapter.

Some parents have objected to spanking because they fear causing rebellion and anger in their child. Proverbs promises just the opposite: "Correct your son, and he will give you comfort; he will also delight your soul" (Prov. 29:17). The child will not become an angry person because he will know the right way to live and, if practiced properly, the child will have confidence that he is loved and respected. His lifestyle and convictions will, more often than not, give the parents comfort and cause them to have joy because the correction that accompanies spanking will help the child to develop respect for parents as well as help him develop moral character qualities.

Parents have also been afraid that they run the risk of hurting their child by spanking them. After many years of using the rod—or in my case, a paddle—I believe no child will ever be hurt if one uses the proper technique, as I will explain later.

Finally, some have claimed that spanking just does not work for them. We must remember that this is not man's method; it comes as a command from God. The question, then, is not whether or not we spank but rather the methodology of carrying it out. Based on years of pastoral experience, Tripp states that if the rod does not work it is due to one of four reasons:

1. Inconsistent use of the rod. The child never knows what could provoke its use.
2. Failure to persist. The parent quits after a few attempts.
3. Failure to be effective. Some parents are too gentle in their use, or try to spank through thick diapers or layers of clothing.
4. Doing it in anger. Children often do not yield to parents who spank in a rage of anger. It comes out of a sense of justice.[5]

When it seems as though spanking is not working, parents should seriously consider these possible errors in methodology, even if they are raising strong-willed children. Spanking is a method designed and instructed by God; therefore, Christian parents should exercise it as one of the methods used.

Incorrect techniques/reasons for spanking. First of all, we must not spank our children while angry, because then the discipline becomes punitive instead of corrective. Punitive discipline, especially expressed in anger, runs the risk of harming the child and causing him or her to obey out of fear of the parent instead of obedience to God. Also, outbursts of anger cause the parent to jump to incorrect conclusions concerning the child's misbehavior and of course provide a very poor example for the child.

In instances when a child's sinful behavior necessitates spanking and has provoked a parent's anger, he or she should send the child to his room and take some time to pray and cool down. Once the parent is under total control, he or she can go to the child's room to carry out the discipline.

Second, never spank your children in front of others. Take them to another room. The objective here is not to humiliate or embarrass the child. When you are in public, inform the child that as soon as you are home he will be disciplined. Then be sure to follow through with it.

Third, never make threats that you will not carry out. The child will quickly recognize false coercion and will ignore it. In general, these false threats are merely a technique of manipulation and will never create heart change.

Fourth, don't warn multiple times, raising the pitch of your voice until you can no longer tolerate further misbehavior. Tell the child once in a stern but calm voice. The second time should be followed by discipline. Some object that this is a little strict. It is much healthier to be strict than to yell and nag at the child. When you consistently discipline the child after one warning, the child knows exactly when he must obey.

Correct technique of spanking. The Bible refers to the use of a rod, which could be compared to a dowel rod available at the home-improvement store. But I don't think that the Scriptures teach that the rod is the only type of implement that may be used. I preferred to use a sturdy paddle. The one my wife and I used was a five-inch-wide paddle we bought in a thrift store. Soon after purchase, she cleverly painted on it, "The board of education will be applied to the seat of knowledge." For my part, I've never liked using a wooden spoon because it is too light; also, there is danger of the spoon turning on its edge, which could injure a child. In any case, the paddle or whatever you use needs to be thick enough so it won't break when used and yet heavy enough that it will penetrate clothing. I think it is significant that Scripture never suggests using the hand to spank a child. The hand is a part of the body used for expressing affection and should not be used for spanking. I would say the same with daddy's belt. It is better to use a neutral object that is not associated in any way with the parent.

The spanking should only be applied to the muscle and fatty portion of the buttocks. A parent should never spank, even with your hand, on the face or head, on the legs, or any other part of the body. The only exception may be a slap on the back of the hand when a young child takes something he has been told not to take, accompanied by a brief but strong verbal "no, no!" to remind the child of the prior instruction.

Spanking, if done properly, is designed to have a strong impact on the child's heart. To illustrate how this is accomplished, let me share the procedure that has consistently proven to work.

I usually first sent my child to his or her room, giving the child an opportunity to reflect on the offence and the consequence. A minute or so later I would then go to the room and have the child lay over my lap with his or her arms straight down. I could then put my left arm down behind the child's arm. This would prevent the child from protecting his backside by putting his hand behind him or herself, which most children will do instinctively. This eliminates the danger of injuring their hand by accident. Some people like to have the child lean against the wall with outstretched hands. Others have the child bend over, holding on to their ankles. Both techniques are designed to keep the child's hands out of the way. I like my method because it allowed me to have complete control in order to prevent injury.

Once they were over my lap, the swat intensity and number of swats was based on the severity of the offense. I always felt that moral offenses such as lying, defiance, disrespect, or harming another person were more serious then mischievous or careless acts, but in most cases I generally used two or three swats. Following the spanking, I then left the room and let my child cry for a little while. In response to those who are afraid of an injury caused by spanking, I can say with certainly that in my years of raising four children there was never a bruise or any kind of injury, only a little red bottom.

After he or she was through crying, it was time for the real impact that spanking makes possible. I would have my "Daddy talk." I would sit down on the bed next to my child, and have him explain to me why I spanked him. Once it was clear that he understood, I would then explain why this action was wrong. I made it clear that I spanked him because what he did was a violation of one or more of God's commands. Whenever possible, I quoted a verse. More than anything, I wanted them to know that they were spanked not because Daddy was upset with them but because they disobeyed God. Once the discussion was complete, I lifted my child onto my lap and affirmed that there was nothing he or she could do that would ever stop me from loving them. And after giving them a big hug, I let them go play. With that, the discipline was over and the child felt loved and in good graces with Daddy—and, of course, with God. This quick recovery time is not possible with discipline such as withholding meals or grounding a child, which puts the child in disfavor with parents for a long period of time.

Developing Christian character is one of the primary needs in the discipleship process. Character is always based on obedience to God's Word. Along with what God's Word says on the matter, my experience as a parent has convinced me that it takes the spanking method to bring the child's disobedient heart to a teachable moment. In contrast, during a time-out for example, all the child can think about is how soon he can get down and play. It is very difficult to get the child to focus on the offence, and thus create a teachable moment. I don't think other methods apart from spanking can provide the kind of teachability that brings about real heart change.

One mother told me she would not spank her child until he was at least five year old, that preschoolers were too young for physical punishment. Parents that skip the preschool years to initiate spanking are making a great mistake because these years lay the foundation for affecting behavior. Controlled and measured spanking for bad behavior between ages one and four will eliminate eighty percent of the behavior problems most children display in the grade-school years. In fact, most behavior problems will be eliminated before the child is two years old if the parents are unified and consistent. I even began minor physical discipline before my children turned one year old. When my crawling child reached for something that he couldn't have I would simply say "no" and if my child grabbed the item in spite of my warning, I would simply slap the back of his hand while I said the words "no no." He quickly learned what "no" meant and obeyed.

When parents do a good job during the childhood years, very little discipline is necessary during the teen years when physical punishment may occasionally be replaced by grounding and taking away privileges. Spanking, especially during the childhood years, is one of the best tools God has given parents to teach godly behavior. I have also found that well-behaved and spiritually motivated teenagers have a profound influence on their younger siblings, as they look up to them and follow their example.

Indeed, when a child begins to alter their behavior based on the Word of God, they will develop the biblical character for which we strive to help instill within them. As difficult as spanking can be on both parent and child, we can rejoice knowing that we have impacted the heart, not just behavior.

Appealing to the conscience. God has given us the wonderful gift of conscience to help us live in a way that pleases him, and it is a tool that Christian parents should use in the discipline process.

When a child sins it is good if he feels a guilty conscience, and if he is a believer the Holy Spirit uses the conscience to bring conviction. When a child doesn't feel guilty, the parent should appeal to the conscience by helping the child understand that what he has done is sin according to God. Remembering the power of the Word of God, it is helpful to read or quote from his Word, which "is living and active and sharper than any two-edged sword, and piercing as far as the division of soul and spirit, of both joints and marrow, and able to judge the thoughts and intentions of the heart" (Heb. 4:12). God uses his Word to convict children and adults alike of sin.

As I elaborated on in a previous chapter, not only should each offending believer confess sin, but he or she also needs to forsake or repent of the sin, asking God for help to stop committing that particular offense (1 John 1:9; Prov. 28:13). Therefore, part of the process of discipling children involves teaching them how one is cleansed by confession of sin and what it means to repent of those sinful actions.

Natural consequences. Another helpful tool God has given us is the law of natural consequences. We should not shelter our children from this instructive tool—unless, of course, it will cause serious harm. For example, let's say you told your child to stay off the wet kitchen floor. A few minutes later he or she impulsively forgets and runs across, slips and falls, banging his elbow. This is a good opportunity to remind the child of the consequences of disobeying mother by running across the wet floor. When possible, allow the natural consequences to do the disciplining. Natural consequences are beneficial because they teach that our actions in life often result in undesired penalties.

Warned consequences. By warned consequences I am referring to the consequences the parent warns the child of if he commits certain actions. For example, a parent tells his child that he can go to a birthday party if his room is clean. When it is time to go, however, he comes to the parent asking for an exception because he forgot or procrastinated. Out of sympathy, many parents give in and let the child go. If the parent expects the warned consequences to be an effective discipline tool, he should not give in. By giving in and allowing the child to go to the party, the child has learned that the warning was not serious and that many parental consequences are not enforced. Consistently enforcing warned consequences is necessary, as we seek to teach obedience and responsibility.

Other Discipleship Tools

As we continue to disciple our children, there are a number of tools we can use to develop needed qualities:

Good work ethic. Children should learn to work as though they are working for God, putting in a good day's work without complaining. In our home we never gave our children an allowance. We believed that each child should participate in daily chores in our home just by virtue of the fact that they were part of our family. Even though we didn't give our children an allowance, we encouraged and helped them earn their own money.

For example, as part of our homeschooling, my wife organized short-term family businesses in which she determined each of our child's responsibilities based on their skills. Usually our business included an incentive of something we were going to earn money to purchase, thus motivating our children. One winter we made and sold Christmas tree ornaments. Several times we funded projects by a banana bread-baking business. As a family we contributed to our daughter and her fiancée's dream honeymoon by operating a concession stand at Northwestern University, in the northern suburbs of Chicago. During such experiences, my wife and I tried to empower our children to not only earn their own money but also become good stewards of it, as they learned to save, invest, and be generous in their giving to God through the church and giving directly to people in need. I am convinced that my children continue to have an entrepreneurial spirit as adults today because my wife and I used such moments to instill a good work ethic in each of them while they lived at home with us.

Along with stressing that parents take advantage of everyday opportunities to disciple their children, Deuteronomy 6:6–9 also teaches that parents should display Scripture passages in practical places within the home. Specifically, the passage says to place Scripture on the "forehead," "doorposts," and "gates." My wife never wore verses on her forehead, but she did print out strategic verses, put them on wood plaques, and placed them all around the house at strategic locations. They were found on the child's bedroom door, on the bathroom mirror, on our bedroom door, and other places in the house. Employing Scripture in this way, and encouraging children to memorize the verses, not only teaches the importance of God's Word but also serves to remind children of key biblical truths, and in so doing advancing the discipleship process.

Words of affirmation. Words of affirmation are very important in the discipleship of children. Comments like "I am so proud of you," "You sure are growing up to be a fine young man/woman," "I love you," and "You're a good boy/girl" go a long way to encourage and motivate the child in the growth process. As parents, we tend to be negative and overly critical, which is often counterproductive. Positive and honest words of praise go a long way in reinforcing proper behavior. They motivate children to act and live in a way pleasing to his parent—and, hopefully, to God. Words of affirmation also increase the bond between parent and child and widen the door of communication, allowing parents to further the discipleship process.

The role of the church. As I have said all along, consistent spiritually mature Christian parents are the God-ordained primary disciple makers of children and should not transfer the discipling responsibility to another person or to the church. However, the church does play an important role in the process. For instance, parents should teach their children of the importance of faithful church attendance. Hebrews 10:24–25 says, "And let us consider how we may spur one another on toward love and good deeds. Let us not give up meeting together, as some are in the habit of doing, but let us encourage one another—and all the more as you see the Day approaching" (NIV 1984). Here, the author, under the inspiration of the Holy Spirit, emphasizes meeting with fellow believers. For children, their future church attendance habits hinge, in part, on whether their parents faithfully take them to church. Part of the disciple-making responsibility is to instill in the child the importance of the local church in their life. To truly be a disciple of Jesus means that we are faithfully involved in the church, in which Jesus is the head.

Realizing Scripture's command to faithfully attend church, I would like to highlight four benefits of regularly attendance for child discipleship:

First, God designed the church to satisfy important needs in our Christian walk. Specifically, meeting at a local, biblically sound church provides a place for worship, ongoing Bible study, fellowship, and accountability. If a child is not raised by parents who place great value on regular support and faithful attendance in a Bible-believing church, they are apt to grow up with a low commitment level to the local church— and likely pass that on to their children (your grandchildren) as well.

Second, the church provides a place for older children to begin to discover, develop, and use their spiritual gifts by providing opportunity to serve in various capacities and types of ministries.

Third, the church provides an environment for your children to find friends their age who are being raised in Christian homes, and also mature adult teachers who serve as additional role models.

Fourth, the church provides training that becomes a supplement to the parents' discipleship. For this reason, parents should stay abreast with what the children are studying and use it as a springboard for discussion and further application.

God has provided the church as a dynamic gift for the entire family to meet numerous needs. Without the family's involvement in the church, the child would likely grow up with little commitment to this God-ordained institution, missing all the things I mentioned above and much more.

Family devotions. Depending on the number of family members and the diversity of ages, family devotions can be a challenge. When families have younger members, the focus of devotions needs to be placed on their understanding level and limited to their attention span. For five years of age and younger, it might be best to keep the time to just a few minutes, extending it as they get older. Also for young children, it's best to use lots of Bible stories and conclude sessions with simple application discussions. When a family has children in both the preschool years as well as in grade school, it's good to let the little ones down to play after about five minutes. For grade school and older I recommend the devotional time be kept to about ten to twenty minutes. Also parents should consider recruiting those who are eight years old or older to assist and, in some cases, lead the devotions. Devotions not only afford parents the opportunity to add to their children's discipleship through instruction and discussion but it also provides an opportunity to enhance the development of older children as they prepare and share devotionals.

One of the first questions parents have concerning devotions is what they should teach. Along with the use of some of the curriculum resources I have included in the bibliography, other elements can be included: reading through and even singing some of the great hymns, reciting memorized Scripture, prayer time (including adoration, thanksgiving, and supplication, with confession encouraged privately), with Mom and Dad praying for the growth of each child and for God's guidance for the future.

Many families struggle to find a good time to have family devotionals. Some have picked a time in the evening, while others have chosen to start the day with devotions. I think the most workable time is before the dinner meal. If you wait until after the meal the children will be antsy to get down. This is the period of the day when everybody is most likely to be available in one place with potentially the least amount of interfering, or conflicting, events planned. Obviously, there are some nights that may not work, but this time presents the best options for most families.

Some have been hesitant because of unsaved family members, but many have found that these kinds of short studies and discussions will prepare them for salvation. There is a wealth of material available for family devotions, and I have included some suggestions in the bibliography.

In any case, family devotions further the discipleship process by providing children with experiences they can use as we encourage them to begin having their own devotions. In fact, once the child is reading, he or she can spend a little time each night reading small sections from the Bible by themselves, talking with God about what they read and often discussing with him what was read with parents.

Family devotions provide a good way for parents to instruct their children on various life issues, and at the same time open the lines of communication.

The Biggest Obstacle and Solutions to Discipling Children at Home

How can a parent follow the teachings of Scripture when they hardly see their children? In our modern society full of child activities and events including homework, Boy and Girl Scouts, 4-H, video games, Little League, and so on, I am convinced that the biggest obstacle to parents discipling their children is the lack of time available.

My children were enrolled in a Christian school. They would come home, take a play break, eat supper, and then start on homework until bed time. On the weekend they had collateral reading and other homework assignments. Frustrated, my wife and I lamented over the fact that we are commanded to nurture and disciple our children but that we had so little time to spend with them. As we prayed and explored our options, God led us to homeschool our children.

Homeschooling is not the answer for everyone, for various reasons I will state later; however, for those who can, it provides the ample time and opportunity for parents who are committed to discipling their children.

In the last twenty-five years, homeschooling has skyrocketed in popularity in the United States. According to a USA Today article, in 2007 there were 1.5 million children being homeschooled nationwide;[6] as a result, many companies have begun producing quality Christian as well as secular curriculum. Though the restrictions and requirements vary from state to state, the practice of homeschooling is legal in all fifty states and in many countries. One of the great advantages of homeschooling is that it enables parents to protect their children from many immoral influences. As stated earlier, the Bible warns us about the impact ungodly influences have on our children. Based on the principles in these passages, it is clear that it is dangerous for parents to allow their children to grow up spending massive amounts of time with nonbelievers or even carnal Christians, especially away from the supervision and knowledge of their caring parents. With teen pregnancy, drug and alcohol use, and high-school dropout rates on the rise, homeschooling not only allows parents to exercise guidance toward the selection of spiritually positive friendships but also allows parents to take control of their child's education.

The greatest advantage of homeschooling is it allows parents the time necessary to disciple their children. My wife was able to spend all day with our kids, and they were able to complete all school assignments before I got home so that I also had much more time with them in the evenings and also on weekends. They did well academically, but the real advantage was in the area of discipleship. They are all grown up now, and, as I look back, I strongly believe that without teaching our children at home we could have never done an adequate job of discipling them. Because of this discipleship, all of our children are believers and serving the Lord. Our two boys are planting and growing a church together, our oldest daughter and her husband are beginning to plant their second church, and my youngest daughter and her husband are raising support and currently serving the Lord in youth and young adult ministries at the young church my two sons are serving in.

Even though I am an advocate of homeschooling, I do not believe home schooling is for everyone. First of all, because of debt or financial commitment it is not possible for some families to have one spouse stay home to educate their children. Secondly, it is necessary that you have good control of your children. Parents with unruly and disobedient children will have a very difficult time trying to supervise their education each day, and would find homeschooling to be exasperating. Third, both the husband and wife must be committed to home education. Homeschooling one's children is not easy and takes a major commitment of time and energy. Homeschooling requires perseverance, and a person who attempts to tackle such a great task without the support and blessing—if not the help—of his or her spouse will find it very difficult and discouraging.

For parents who cannot homeschool their children, I believe that the best discipleship-driven option is to avoid preschool child care or hiring a nanny, if at all possible. The preschool years are very important for laying a biblical foundation for salvation and discipleship. And the most effective people—in fact, those primarily responsible before God for this task—are parents. Furthermore, when children are of school age, I recommend attempting to place them in a strong, bible-centered Christian school. Look for a school that will not put excessive pressure for homework so as to allow you to have as much time with your children as possible.

Parents who have limited time with their children must protect what time they do have. That means not spending their days off on the golf course or away from the children in other activities. That means that neither parent takes extra employment or work overtime, if possible. And that means that all vacations need to be with the family, not separated from them. For parents serious about discipling their children, they need to "redeem the time" (Eph. 5:16; Col. 4:5), to make most of the little time available with their children. Even though it can be difficult, with God's help and the assistance of a good church, children can grow and become real, devoted followers of Christ.

A Promise of Success

One of the verses that most Christian parents cling to especially when they have wayward children is Proverbs 22:6. The wise counsel in this well-known verse gives parents instruction on how to raise their children. It exhorts parents, "Train up a child in the way he should go, even when he is old he will not depart from it." This verse can be interpreted in two ways; both interpretations, I believe, are instructive.

The first interpretation of the phrase "Train up a child in the way he should go," according to commentator Albert Barnes, can be correctly interpreted, "The way he should go—Or, according to the tenor of his way, i.e., the path especially belonging to, especially fitted for, the individual's character. The proverb enjoins the closest possible study of each child's temperament and the adaptation of 'his way of life' to that."[7] This interpretation instructs the parent to understand their child's abilities, talents, and leanings, so as to nurture these qualities with the goal that the child will take them into his future as life practices.

In his book *Raising a Modern-Day Knight*, Robert Lewis shares the experience one man recalled of his childhood, which he recorded in a letter. He says: "My dad tried to teach me how to play baseball when I was a kid, but I was never interested in sports. This made him real mad. I could feel his constant displeasure over this. I later got real interested in electronics, but he wasn't any more interested in that than I was in baseball. At my request, he would take me to an electronics store on Saturday and drop me off for a few hours, but that's about as far as our interaction went."[8] As this example illustrates, one of the things the child needs is for the parent to help him understand his life skills, so that as a teen or young adult he can plan his life with a career in mind that utilizes these abilities. When a parent takes interest in a child's talents, or the wholesome things the child is interested in, it becomes very affirming to him and he will be more motivated to develop these interests or talents.

According to commentators John Walvoord and Roy Zuck, the second interpretation hinges on the meaning of the word "way." They assert, "Since 'way' in Proverbs does not mean personality or stage in life, it is preferable to say that 'way' means *proper* way…behavior pattern or godly lifestyle,"[9] ensuring that he will not depart from that lifestyle if trained properly. Moreover, Walvoord and Zuck state that "the Hebrew word for 'train' means to dedicate. It was used of dedicating a house (Deut. 20:5) and the temple (1 Kgs. 8:63; 2 Chr. 7:5)."[10] Applying this interpretation of Proverbs 22:6, then, one would expect a parent to dedicate a child to wise godly living rather than to dedicate the child to innate personality practices or abilities, as in the first interpretation.

The problem is that many parents who claim Proverbs 22:6 with the second interpretation are baffled by the way their adult children are living. But as we look at the parenting styles used to raise their children we will usually find they were parents who, though sometimes faithful in taking their children to church, have neglected to provide the nurturing and modeling that God requires. In general, the average Christian parents send their children off to day care or public school while they both work away from the home, leaving little time for serious discipleship. They have relegated their responsibility of education, nurturing, and spiritual growth to others, yet claim Proverbs 22:6. God requires more of parents than that.

The child needs godly character qualities so he will be equipped to face a life filled with many temptations and influences. One of the alarming characteristics of our modern society is that many adults do not possess the positive moral qualities that were once common. A few years ago, a Christian contractor shared with me the difficulty of finding honest and trustworthy employees. He said that if necessary he could teach a man to read but he could never give him integrity. He could not survive as a contractor if his employees stole from his clients or performed substandard work. We need to train our children to have godly qualities of integrity, reliability, respect for others, humility, sexual purity, and control of their tongues. No school instruction on character development will ever replace what can only be effectively taught in the home.

Discipling our children is a demanding responsibility, but one that will yield huge dividends if we commit to the task and stick with it to its completion. There is no greater privilege and no greater responsibility than discipling them life-on-life as they progress toward adulthood. Yes, by the grace of God, our children will develop the solid moral values and Christian commitment that they require, and we will never, for one minute, regret the sacrifice and time that discipling them required. This time and commitment will enable us to experience a profound closeness and respect not found to this degree by most parents. We will enjoy our adult children as they remain our friends and co-laborers, and one day, they will be given rewards because of their labor for Christ that they will enjoy throughout eternity.

Review Questions

1. Would you agree with the statement, "Time with children is foundational to the discipleship process"? Why or why not?
2. Where are you most liable to delegate the discipleship of your children to others? How can you take back responsibility in those areas?
3. What are the four greatest influences that wars against the spiritual growth of children? Where do you see these issues crop up with your children?
4. Why is it necessary to impact a child's heart, rather than just his behavior?
5. Which of the discipleship tools offered in this chapter do you most use, currently? Which tools could use some "sharpening"—or at least to be taken out of the box once in a while? Explain.

Chapter 14

DISCIPLING CHILDREN THROUGH THE CHURCH: WHEN PARENTAL DISCIPLESHIP IS UNAVAILABLE

AT NO TIME IN HISTORY HAVE CHILDREN been more unparented than today. As stated in the last chapter, it is godly parents whom God charges with the responsibility of leading their children to Christ and growing them spiritually to become mature disciples of his. Unfortunately, many parents do not disciple their children for a number of reasons. Some parents, for instance, are themselves nonbelievers or spiritual infants. Others find themselves experiencing financial difficulties that require both Mom and Dad to work outside the home, thereby affording them little to no motivation or time to disciple their children. Yet children need Christ and, once they are believers, need to be discipled. Thankfully, God has commissioned church leaders to train Christian adults to not only disciple their own children but, when necessary, to disciple children who do not have parents to meet this need.

Many Young Adults with a Christian Background Leave the Church

In 2011 the Barna Group conducted extensive research of American Protestants between the ages of eighteen and twenty-nine. They reported that sixty-one percent of participating young people with a Christian background dropped out of church after going regularly. Additional research indicates that forty-one percent have gone through a period when they significantly doubted their faith; another thirty-five percent describe a period when they felt like rejecting their parents' faith.[1] Surely the fact that the vast majority of parents do not disciple their children fuels this great dropout rate, but churches across the United States have also done a poor job discipling children. Yes, they have worked hard to provide Sunday School classes, children's churches, and other programs; nevertheless many children continue to enter adulthood with a negative attitude toward the church and Christianity because collectively we fail to biblically guide them to become disciples of Jesus Christ.

Intensive discipleship should not be postponed to adulthood. A newborn baby must be fed appropriate food when he is hungry; if he is not fed he will become malnourished. When a child receives Christ as savior, he is spiritually hungry. If he is not appropriately fed spiritual food, the child will enter adulthood apathetic and self-satisfied in his immature state and likely will remain a spiritual infant, not realizing that God has so much more for him. However, children who are discipled by godly Christian adults will be much stronger in their walk and, with ongoing spiritual guidance, stand a greater chance of being spared the terrible mistakes so many of our teens and young adults make.

Biblical Support for Childhood Discipleship

Jesus demonstrated his concern for the spiritual nurturing of children. The gospel of Matthew tells us of Jesus' response when the disciples attempted to keep some children from him. "Then some children were brought to Him so that He might lay His hands on them and pray; and the disciples rebuked them. But Jesus said, 'Let the children alone, and do not hinder them from coming to Me; for the king-dom of heaven belongs to such as these'" (Matt. 19:13–14). Jesus demonstrated that the time we spend in effective ministry to children is necessary in our efforts to build the kingdom of God.

We must not neglect these pliable years to disciple children because these are the impressionable years when positive attitudes toward God and church, as well as Christian character traits, become part of a child's life. These are the years when children are learning the things that will become the foundation for their faith. Second Timothy 1:5 tells us that Timothy's grandmother Lois and his mother Eunice were women who had sincere faith; Paul says he is confident that this faith resides in Timothy as well. Even though Timothy had a Greek father who was not a believer, his mother and grandmother made sure that Timothy was spiritually nurtured in his early years. His example demonstrates that, if children are faithfully discipled when they are young, they are much more likely to follow Jesus as adults and less likely to bring into their adult lives the personal baggage many carry.

As I explained in the last chapter, I believe that childhood discipleship is the responsibility of godly parents. When they are raised in a solid Christian home where Christ is truly in the center, most children will receive Christ while they are young. In these homes, the work of the parents in discipling their children becomes primary and the ministry of the church becomes supportive in their work of discipleship. Unfortunately, many children are not raised in Christian homes, and many Christian parents lack the required spiritual maturity to disciple their children. It is in homes like these that the church must encourage and train its members to stand in the gap and nurture these children to become disciples of Jesus. This need offers a goldmine of opportunity for believers as they fulfill the Great Commission in the lives of children. But can children become true disciples of Jesus?

The Amazing Receptive Qualities of Children

Let's first consider a child's receptive qualities to believe in Christ for salvation. Children are extremely pliable and receptive to adult guidance and instruction and are quick to become believers in Christ, once they understand the truths about their need and God's provision for salvation.

Clear back to the first century, Polycarp, a disciple of the apostle John and pastor at the church of Smyrna, received Christ at nine years old. He grew to be a great leader of the early church and died a martyr for Jesus Christ. Isaac Watts, born in the seventeenth century and also converted at the age of nine, has lifted thousands to Christ in worship through his many hymns. In the eighteenth century, Jonathan Edwards, saved at the age of seven, became a renowned minister who God used to ignite the First Great Awakening, which brought millions of people to salvation and millions of others back into fellowship with God. What a tragedy it would have been if the people who led these three men to Christ had neglected the opportunity because of an erroneous belief that these children were too young.

Indeed, Jesus confirms that young children can be saved. During his earthly ministry, he said, "Truly I say to you, unless you are converted and become like children, you will not enter the kingdom of heaven" (Matt. 18:3). In this verse, Jesus affirms that children can be saved. In fact, he uses a child as an illustration of the simple faith required for the salvation of adults as well. In fact, children are far more responsive to the gospel and faith in Christ than people of any other age group. Another recent Barna study indicates that nearly half of all United States citizens who accept Jesus Christ as their savior do so before reaching the age of thirteen (forty-three percent), and that two out of three born-again Christians (sixty-four percent) made that commitment to Christ before their eighteenth birthdays.[2] These figures indicate that children are ripe for the gospel; therefore, we should be aggressive and at the same time very sensitive and non-manipulative as we strive to lead them to Christ. Not only are children receptive to the gospel but, once saved, a child is extremely curious and hungry to grow in his faith.

John L. Thompson

Growing Children in Their Christian Walk

When the children of Israel crossed the Jordan River, God told Joshua to make a memorial from twelve stones taken from the middle of the Jordan. The purpose was to erect a small monument they could bring their children to, providing an object lesson that would give parents the opportunity to tell how God mightily dammed up the Jordan so the Israelites could cross safely on dry ground (Joshua 4). As in ancient times, God desires twenty-first-century children know of his great deeds and come to know him and become his followers. God has always desired for parents to teach their children about his character, demonstrated through his great deeds, because this lays the foundation for their salvation and discipleship.

My wife and I practiced this principle all through our child-rearing years. Our children watched as we served as missionaries, living by faith in the inner city of Chicago. They lived through lean years of financial hardship, which became some of the greatest object lessons in our life, with God demonstrating his faithfulness as we trusted in him for our daily bread. We tried to always share with them our need and asked them to pray so they could see our great God answer prayer and provide. Observing our faith and love for God, and seeing our faithful God provide for our family prepared them for salvation. Also through these experiences, having received Christ as savior, they learned to become men and women of faith as they watched and experienced many foundational lessons while growing up in our home. I believe that part of the reason God allows life trials is so that he can use them to teach spiritual truths to children as well as adults. Children are indeed capable and desirous of growing in their Christian faith, but is the average church developing children to become disciples of Jesus Christ?

Church Workers and the Discipleship of Children

Overall, many church workers endeavor to reach children with the gospel. However, these same volunteers continue, inadvertently in most cases, to do a poor job of discipling children who have professed saving faith in Jesus Christ. At the same time curriculum companies, with their goal of teaching the entire Word of God to every age group, do a great job telling the amazing biblical stories and are used by God to bring many children to faith in Christ. However, while being strong in evangelism, the same companies do not help to facilitate strong growth in children. Instead, they often take children through a repetitive review of the great heroes of the faith but are weak in helping children learn the basic truths needed for their growth in their Christian lives. In the discipleship process children should be taught basic truths as spiritual babes, and more solid spiritual truths as they are ready. Children are able to grasp so much more with the aid of the Holy Spirit. Most churches have adopted a classroom, peer-influenced approach in which all children learn at the same level and speed. We simply have not imagined that there are other ways that children could be discipled more effectively.

My wife became a believer at the age of five and went through this traditional approach of childhood teaching. Many years ago God gave her a deep conviction that we need to change our mindset in order to create more effective disciple making of children. After forty-five years of experience working with all ages, she can testify to the fact that young Christian children live in a spiritually dormant state because of the lack of effective discipleship in their lives.

The graded-educational approach most churches use in their educational program prevents children from progressing at their potential rate. A graded program, by its very nature, takes all the children in that grade or class through the same materials. However, children learn at various levels of understanding. Some are unsaved, some are academically and spiritually at the beginning level, others have moderate academic and spiritual understanding, and some are more advanced in their understanding and walk with Christ. Contrary to the graded approach, the Bible instructs us to teach people at their spiritual understanding level, not their grade level. When we lump kids at different spiritual levels into one "age-appropriate" group, we cause them to grow at a repressed pace that generally does not mirror their potential spiritual growth rate. Specifically, we must follow an evangelistic strategy with appropriate content for nonbelievers, and then with maturity-appropriate material for Christian children using basic "milk" topics for new believers and more advanced, "solid food" materials for more mature believers (1 Cor. 3:2; Heb. 5:12–14; 1 Pet. 2:2.) To be most effective, this ministry, whether held as part of churchtime programs or outside the church, should emphasize a portion of time for one-on-one ministry in the life of the child.

God has tremendous blessings in store for those who faithfully make disciples of children. What a great blessing this will prove to be in this life and the next for that young person, as well as for the disciple maker. Let's examine this maturity-specific approach more closely.

"Milk" Lessons for Spiritually Young Children

In this beginning level, the young believing child should learn the very basics. Of course any teaching must also be presented on his educational level, taught with vocabulary he can understand. Topics include:

1. *Understanding salvation.* Such lessons should include information about the need for his salvation, how God made it possible, and how he or she became a believer. It is appropriate here to offer one major caution: Children's workers should be careful not to tell a child he is saved simply because he repeated a prayer. Many children have followed our evangelistic instruction but either did not understand or did not make a sincere request for salvation and, therefore, may not be true believers. Another concern is that a child will often pray a prayer for salvation to win peer acceptance or leader approval; the leader needs to counsel the child privately and make sure the child's motivation is correct. In the final analysis, only God knows for sure if a child has become his child. But we can look for spiritual fruit and allow God, through his Word and the Holy Spirit, to provide assurance.

2. *Assurance of salvation.* This topic is important because many children, especially children between four and seven, are quick to believe that they need to receive Christ again every time an invitation is given. He needs to know that once he has sincerely received Christ as savior he does not need to reiterate the action repeatedly.

3. *Reading the Bible.* The child needs to understand that as a new believer he should begin to read the Bible. As soon as he can read, he should build a habit of having his own personal time with God. It is best if he has a Bible with a vocabulary consistent with his reading level. Below is a chart that may help in Bible selection:

Bible Translations by Grade Level			
Translation	Grade Level	Translation	Grade Level
KJV	12th	NKJV	7th
RSV	12th	NLT	6th
NASB	11th	GW	5th
NRSV	11th	CEV	4–7th
ESV	10th	Message	4–5th
CEB	7–12th	NCV	3rd
NIV	7–8th	NIRV	3rd
HCSB	7–8th	ICB	3rd

*King James Version (KJV), Revised Standard Version (RSV), New American Standard Version (NASB), New Revised Standard Version (NRSV), English Standard Version (ESV), Common English Bible (CEB), New International Version (NIV), Holman Christian Standard Bible (HCSB), New King James Version (NKJV), New Living Translation (NLT), God's Word Translation (GW), Contemporary English Version (CEV), The Message Bible (Message), New Century Version (NCV), New International Reader's Version (NIRV), International Children's Bible (ICB)

4. *Praying to God*. Learning to pray is an important exercise for all Christians, regardless of age. Teach that God listens to prayer and will answer every request with a "yes," "no," or "wait" according to his perfect will. Even as adults, we tend to think that God did not answer our prayers unless he granted our wishes. Since each answer is God's will, each of these three responses from God is a good answer to prayer. Moreover, we must teach children how to pray alone and practice the various elements of prayer, described by the acronym ACTS: *adoration* (express appreciation, esteem, and worship), *confession* of personal sin, *thanksgiving* for what God has given and how he has helped us, and *supplication* (our requests to God).

5. *Victory over sin*. All believers must learn and practice to have victory over sin. The child needs to know that God will help him or her do as he requires, but the believer must choose to obey. When we do not obey, we have sinned against God and must seek....

6. *Forgiveness from God*. The child will find forgiveness as he is cleansed from sin through confession to God. He should begin confessing specific sins soon after the offense. He should know that confession should include the repentance of sin and, when applicable, asking forgiveness of others we have offended and making restitution whenever possible.

"Solid Food" for Spiritually Growing Children

Due to their youth, most children are not ready for adult-level spiritual "solid food." Nonetheless, we can still teach more advanced topics to them based on their respective academic and spiritual levels. Some of these include:

1. *Basic Bible doctrine*. Doctrinal truths that teach about God's character qualities and attributes are especially important, because each truth has personal application to the child's life and should be taught on his level of understanding. Whether the learners are adults or children, the teacher must always help the student understand how doctrinal truths apply to his Christian life.

2. *Lordship of Christ*. Most children are too young to understand this concept completely, but it is good to begin helping them learn this principle to the degree they're able. Help them understand that to put Christ first means seeking to obey what God says in the Bible. God presents commands and principles believers need to follow. God also makes conditional promises. For example, Ephesians 6:1–3 says, "Children, obey your parents in the Lord, for this is right. Honor your father and mother (which is the first commandment with a promise), so that it may be well with you, and that you may live long on the earth." Here Scripture

teaches that God will reward children as they honor their parents by giving the child a long good life. When we place Christ as Lord of our lives, we obey what he says. Therefore, the discipler should begin exploring commands and principles he can encourage the child to practice.

3. *Following God's direction.* Learning to follow God's direction for one's life is a valuable lesson on Christian living. In other words, we should base our decisions on principles from God's Word. Begin teaching these principles as soon as a child is able to understand. He or she also needs to understand the importance of praying for God to give direction as they make decisions. Over time, the child will become more sensitive to the Holy Spirit's guidance as he or she follows and obeys God.

4. *Love in action.* Another important lesson for a child to learn and practice is the *agape* love principle of putting others ahead of ourselves. Our world is very self-seeking and self-centered. Children grow up learning to do what feels good to them, or to strive to satisfy their desires. Disciplers of children must teach that satisfying self should not be the focus of the child's life. Instead, he must be taught to put God first, others second, and himself third. When a child learns to be a servant and practice humility, he will experience much contentment, and his service will spur him on in spiritual growth.

5. *The importance of the local church.* A child should also learn the importance of being faithful to his church. This not only involves regular attendance but includes praying for his pastors and leaders and the importance of financial giving. Encourage children to give their own money, not money their parents give them to put in the offering.

6. *Learning to worship.* Help the young believer to understand what worship is and how to participate in it. She should know that worship is the act of giving worth and praise to our great God, and that it can be done at church or in the privacy of her home. We worship by singing songs of worship and praise to the Lord, in giving to the Lord financially, by listening to our teachers and pastor as they teach us, and by serving our great God.

7. *Christian service.* As stated above, serving the Lord is a very important part of our spiritual growth. The child should be given opportunities to serve in his class; and as he is ready, he can become a junior leader helping out with the younger children during Sunday and weeknight children's ministries.

8. *Memorization of Scriptures.* It has been long understood that children from four years to ten years old have the greatest capacity for rote memorization of Scripture than during any other time in their lives. But memorizing Scripture is

not enough. The child should understand the application and meaning of the verses he memorizes because they become tools in his victory over sin. Memorizing Scripture also becomes material a child can meditate on, repeat or think about in worship, and ultimately use all through life as he or she ministers to others.

As indicated earlier, there are Bibles available based on the child's reading ability. Rather than memorizing from several different translations at various age levels, I suggest that you use a translation the child would likely use as an adult. It would be better to use the New American Standard Version (NASV), English Standard Version (ESV), or even the New King James Version (NKJV) for verse memorization, so as to provide more consistency throughout life.

As he proceeds in the discipleship process, the disciple maker will find that simple discussion with a child on both milk and solid food topics will have a profound impact on the child's Christian walk as well as his commitment to Christ.

As We Move Forward

Effective discipleship training will begin to correct the nonbiblical instruction children have gained from their public school, nonbelieving or confused parents, and friends. Solid growth can be experienced as they go through the process of hearing, believing, and implementing what they are taught. Each child should be instructed in a vocabulary he can understand, with a curriculum that is doctrinally sound.

There are not a lot of topical materials available that effectively aid the discipling of children. (Suggestions are included in the bibliography.) Many curriculum materials finish the process in six to thirteen weeks, but I recommend that church disciplers extend the development time to three to four years. During this discipleship process it is important that ministry volunteers commit to a minimum of at least one year. If the method used is small groups, the number per group should not exceed six children; the smaller the group of children close to the same *spiritual* age, the better. However, the one-on-one approach continues to be most effective method one can use to disciple children.

For the second and third year, the topics for discipleship could be the same as the first year but in an expanded form. In the fourth year the child could begin actively serving the Lord as an assistant or trainee, working with younger children. Some of the materials I suggest in the bibliography include materials for children ranging from three years old through age seventeen, and written to emphasize the life-on-life approach of discipleship.

Churches could adopt this type of format on Sunday morning, Sunday evening, or during the week. Some churches, for instance, have an after-school program for young believers where children spend time in recreation, homework, and approximately twenty to thirty minutes meeting with a disciple maker for life-on-life discipleship, depending on a given child's attention level.

It would be prudent at this point for me to caution each church leader on the importance of having a screening program for children's workers. It is unfortunate that the church has to go to this extreme, but sexual predators find their way into the church as well as public and private schools. This is especially important as you expand your life-on-life discipleship ministry to children. You might not have any problems in church, where there are other child workers around, but the real problems may come as a worker seeks to be involved in the child's life outside church. It is the church leader's obligation to make sure that no children in your ministry are ever harmed. Therefore, I recommend that all churches have a screening program. This program would include the requirement that all children's workers be members in good standing of your church; that they fill out applications for service in the children's department that include at least three references; that each person pass a background check (organizations that can help with this are in the bibliography under "Sexual-Abuse Prevention"); and that all children's workers go through sexual-abuse awareness training. Our children are precious and we need to take special precautions that they are safe in our ministries.

As the child gets into the older grade-school ages and into middle school he should be guided in developing skills of personal Bible study, understanding the basics of Bible doctrine, the importance of following Jesus as the Lord of his life, and should learn how to deal with the specific sin issues with which he struggles. During these years he can even learn how to lead another person to Christ, follow the Lord in believer's baptism, and discover the importance of becoming a member of his local church (as church procedures allow). Moreover, during the middle-school years the disciple maker can help the child begin to discern some of his or her spiritual gifts and begin to use them for the Lord. The workers will also provide encouragement and counsel as he goes through teen peer pressure and youthful temptations.

Is the Traditional Structure Working?

In most churches, we segregate children from adult services and other ministries by means of a nursery, Sunday school, children's church, club programs, etc. Many churches pride themselves in the variety of entertaining activities they offer on a weekly basis for children and youth, but they rarely integrate children into adult services and ministries. On those Sundays when they have to sit in an adult service, they become bored quickly because they are used to being entertained and haven't learned to listen. Moreover, teens do not feel accepted and valued by the adult congregation because we rarely train them in ministry responsibilities. All of this, coupled with the lack of effective discipleship, causes far too many young children and teens to feel detached from the church's adult ministries, and so they drop out as soon as they graduate from high school. To them, the church has become irrelevant to their new adult lives.

What if we made more effort to have children and youth become a part of adult services? What if preaching was applied to their lives as well? What if youth were taught to share the responsibility in various areas of service such as ushering, Scripture reading, prayer, and even serving on the worship team? Wouldn't they be more likely to feel valued members of the church as they graduate from high school? Perhaps the church would seem more relevant, and young adults would be less likely to drop out. After all, an integrated church service was the type of service that was conducted by the early church as they met in homes. Perhaps it is time for a change. Instead of a flashy, entertainment-steeped, musical youth ministry with all its fluff, what if we changed to a more integrated church service in which the youth are intentionally involved? If we would couple this approach with a youth ministry where the emphasis is placed on intensive life-on-life disciple making, we would see revolutionary spiritual growth in our young people.

Children need a strong spiritual foundation. They need to progressively understand how to live the Christian life. Unfortunately, most children don't gain this foundation, so they stumble and even backslide spiritually as they go through their teen years and into young adulthood. The church, therefore, should emphasize discipling children—while they still exhibit spiritual hunger for the things of God. They need more from us than to simply read and teach Bible stories to them. Instead, we as the church must first of all train spiritually able parents to disciple their own children. And for those children who will never be discipled at home, the church needs to come alongside parents to actively and lovingly nurture children in order that they might learn practical Christian principles and pursue a lifelong relationship with the Lord and dedicated involvement in their local church. Every Bible-believing church can and should have success as they cultivate children as tender plants, so that one day we will see much fruit harvested and can bask in the joy of knowing what God did through us and will do through these children as they serve him.

Review Questions

1. If discipleship can be accomplished best in the home, why should the church tackle this task as well? Give specific examples.

2. Why is it important to begin discipling children as soon as they understand, rather than postponing it until they're at a higher grade level, or adults?

3. What are some of the flaws of discipling children through traditional church programs? Where have you wished the church would better come alongside you, as you disciple your children?

4. Review the examples of "milk" and "meat" lessons above. Which ones are lacking in your current children's programs? How can these shortcomings be addressed?

5. What's your reaction to the idea that the discipleship process with children should last three to four years? Explain.

Chapter 15

WHY HAVE WE FAILED?
A COURSE CORRECTION FOR
REVOLUTIONARY IMPACT

THE GREAT COMMISSION RANKS as Christ's most important command to the church. And yet, we cannot help but marvel at the fact that the twentieth and twenty-first-century church has done an ineffective job growing and maintaining a spiritually mature church. Chuck Colson said, "The church is 3,000 miles wide and an inch deep."[1] Most Christians have so little spiritual depth we have to ask: Where is the discipleship?

It is even more disconcerting to see that many Christian leaders make little real movement toward adequate changes to correct our stifled progress. Therefore, in this final chapter I would like to talk about the reasons we are not accomplishing his most important command and what we can do to make an effective course correction.

We have misapplied the Great Commission.

In many evangelical churches it appears that the application of the Great Commission is to make converts. Many other churches seek to fulfill the Great Commission by adding baptisms and church members to its roster. Neither application is in keeping with what Jesus said in Matthew 28:19–20. Because of this incorrect application of the Great Commission, church members think their job is to add souls to God's kingdom. When he has led a person to Christ, his job is over.

Often I hear a brother or sister share joyfully an experience in leading a person to Christ. After rejoicing with them, I usually ask if they've invited the new convert to our new believer's class. When they say no, I ask if they got the person's address or phone number. They usually say, "I didn't think about that," or "I forgot." Most believers do not grasp the fact that evangelism is only the beginning of our mission in that person's life.

In the parable of the sower (Luke 8:1–15), Jesus illustrated the perils preventing spiritual seed to germinate when the birds of the air snatched up the seed before it began to take root. Unfortunately, I think this is what often happens. The seed falls by the side of the road and the birds—or shall I say, Satan's demons—snatch up the seed before it has the opportunity to take root (verses 11–12). I think that is why many who receive Christ, whether with an individual counselor or at evangelistic meetings, are not true believers. The seed is snatched away before it can take root.

Our method of evangelism has become so watered down and so simplified that many who "say the prayer" do not really have saving faith. They may have followed the instructions but believe only intellectually. Perhaps they even desire to be saved but do not grasp the concept. If we would faithfully follow up on the salvation decision and begin to explain how a person becomes a child of God, the intellectual belief may become a heart belief.

We need to help people see that the Great Commission is not completed when a person receives Christ as savior. Our responsibility is to make mature disciples. If the one who leads another to Christ cannot continue the disciple-making process, he should make sure that the process is continued in another way. That is, disciple making could be transferred to another disciple maker; he could use remote discipleship (email, or phone conversations), as discussed in the first chapter; or at the very least he should find a Bible-centered church near the new convert's home who can follow up with him. Our greatest need is to change the way people think about their responsibility in obeying the Great Commission. It is every believer's job to make disciples.

Christian workers do not understand the time required to make disciples.

We must practice the best methods to help immature believers experience transformation in their lives, and this takes time. We live in a fast-food society that wants everything right now. This is not the way the physical body grows, and it is surely not the way the soul grows. Most churches don't even offer a class for new believers. Many churches that have a new-believer class promote their six-week discipleship program or something similar. Though there may be some value, a six-week class is not sufficient. A crash course on discipleship will not accomplish our objective. How long does it take to become a relatively mature disciple? Technically, it takes a lifetime, but our primary objective is to help a person grow to a solid level of maturity in which the person is able to live a consistent Christian life, take responsibility for his own growth, knows what he believes (practical basic Bible doctrine), can lead another person to Christ, and disciple that person as he was discipled. This length of time varies from person to person because we learn and grow at different speeds. Some may take a year, but others much longer. The person who was raised with poor training in areas of personal discipline and who had poor role models growing up will often take much longer. We must train the people we work with so that they understand our job is to help the young believer be transformed to a mature believer—and this takes time and effort.

Disciple making is a process, not a program.

First, we think of discipleship as a series of classes or a course of study. We have defined "discipleship" as an intellectual pursuit, teaching that a disciple is simply a "learner" rather than a process of transformation. Knowledge, though needed, is insufficient. The Pharisees illustrate what should never be the product of our ministry (Matt. 23:27–33). They had great knowledge but were lacking in proper attitude, godly character qualities, and life application that demonstrated spiritual transformation. In other words, they had a lot of knowledge but little practice.

Secondly, we have mistakenly assumed that if we have enough programs for all ages, and run them with a level of quality, that somehow people will successfully grow to maturity. As Greg Ogden, has stated in his book *Transforming Discipleship*, "Programs tend to be information-or knowledge-based. Programs operate on the assumption that information will automatically lead to transformation. In other words, right knowledge will produce right living."[2] The lack of disciples in our churches has proven that this kind of thinking cannot be farther from the truth. Producing disciples requires a customized approach encouraging individual growth. This is not possible in classroom teaching where each person has varying degrees of knowledge, different levels of maturity, and where individuals have various degrees of motivation.

A necessary element missing from program-based discipleship is the necessity of a profound relationship between the leader and the disciple. The influence of a mentor or role model is essential for the immature believer. This is not only true in the church but in the Christian home as well, and it is especially needed for a person who was not raised in a stable Christian home. Life-on-life disciple making makes possible several necessary elements of discipleship such as a godly example, affirmation, accountability, rebuke, correction, and instruction. The disciple maker becomes the spiritual guide, remaining available for prayer and problem-solving as the protégé braves new responsibilities and difficult times. The disciple maker also directs the disciple in areas of training including spiritual disciplines, life skills, and the discovery and development of spiritual gifts.

Third, when it comes to discipleship, we promote programs rather than people. We usually conclude that of life-on-life discipleship takes too long and requires an approach that is too leader-intensive, and so we resort instead to programs to get the job done. On the contrary, spiritual growth comes through relationships, as demonstrated in the Word of God.

John Koessler, in his book *True Discipleship*, says, "One of the greatest obstacles we face in making disciples is the church's tendency to allocate its resources based on the amount of return it will receive for the time, effort, and money it has expended."[3] In other words, most churches claim they are devoted to growing people, but the most effective developmental procedure known to man—the life-to-life mentoring or disciple-making process—is almost completely ignored in favor of programs such as Sunday school and small groups. Surely all available programs can contribute to growth, but they are missing the most important element for life transformation: the powerful and indispensable dynamic of a relationship. As Greg Ogden has stated, "Programs can make it look like we are growing disciples, but that is more illusion than reality, and we know it."[4] When we see numbers of people involved in our programs, it looks good because we have something to validate the effectiveness of these ministries. We hope for growth and may see slow growth, but the fact is that the growth is not only slow but it is spotty. In reality, these programs are actually better suited for those who are already relatively mature. Effective discipleship does not come from programs, but through strategic relationships.

We teach people in random order, rather than with a systematic progressive approach.

One might think of church Bible studies, sermons, and other programs like a giant "connect the dots" game—only our page doesn't have any numbers and usually is without any systematic order. The "player"—in this case, the disciple—is unable to connect the dots as intended.

The systematic order prescribed in the Word of God is milk first, then solid food. With a systematic approach we can teach young believers in a very practical way so that they know and begin to live biblical truths. As a result of our failure to properly practice disciple making, young believers know the characters and stories of the Bible, and are familiar with many verses, but somehow don't grasp their importance or internalize their application. In other words, they have not made the connection between what they were taught and how to implement it into their own faith and lives.

There is little or no accountability.

People who want to grow spiritually and experience life transformation will benefit greatly from personal accountability. Regrettably, while some evangelical churches encourage members to have accountability partners, most accountability is not continued successfully over a long period of time. When accountability is practiced, it is only as good as the participant is honest, and the one who needs accountability is often not forthcoming with the most serious and sometimes embarrassing struggles.

I have found that the most effective personal accountability is between the disciple and his disciple maker, for three reasons. First, the confidentiality practiced between disciple maker and disciple grants the latter the trust needed to be honest with his discipler. Second, there is a respect level for the mentor that encourages serious accountability; and third, by submitting himself to the disciple maker, the disciple has shown that he seriously desires growth and wants help in breaking sinful strongholds. With a mentor-protégé relationship, accountability through life-on-life discipleship is effective in helping the disciple grow to a significant level of maturity.

*The church has not treated relational disciple making as a
fundamental priority ministry.*

Most churches tend to be so committed to growing programs and events that they overload people to the point that they have little time for the commitment that disciple making requires. Often, the leaders of the church do not teach or encourage life-on-life discipleship. Other leaders unintentionally treat life-on-life discipleship as simply one's personal ministry, or an "extra-curricular activity," rather than a key ministry of the church. The results suggest otherwise.

After analyzing research, George Barna stated that "Only half of the believers we interviewed felt that discipleship is one of the two or three highest ministry priorities of the church."[5] Emphasizing his belief that the church has not treated life-on-life discipleship as the important irreplaceable tool, Robert Coleman asserted, "My conviction is that if making disciples of all nations is not the heartbeat of our life, something is wrong, either with our understanding of Christ's church or our willingness to walk in His way."[6] It's no wonder we are not experiencing spiritual growth and multiplication as the early church did.

*Small groups—the primary method many churches depend on
for spiritual development—typically fail to provide adequate growth.*

The reason small groups fail to bring life transformation is because leaders are poorly selected and trained; they are given poor materials that are often superficial and contain insufficient life application; and because they are often designed as fellowship groups and/or Bible study groups, and therefore do not have the objective of making disciples. Along with this: I believe the greatest reason small groups rarely make disciples is because they are almost never designed for that purpose.

I devoted chapter 12 of this book to explaining the needed principles and structure that we must put in place in order to make small-group ministry an effective disciple-making tool. I have put together and led small groups that have had extraordinary impact on their participants, and therefore I believe it can be a good tool for disciple making. However, it should never be considered a substitute for life-on-life discipleship.

We do not effectively disciple children in most churches.

Given that most people place their faith in Christ as children, the church truly can have a profound impact on their lives through its children's ministries. However, we must remember that God intends for the discipleship of children to come primarily through godly parents. In order to equip future parents, we as the church need to provide quality discipleship to all believers—from the moment of salvation until they are mature disciples of Christ. After this, they in turn will be capable of making wonderful committed disciples of Christ of their children. The church, for its part, needs to supplement such disciple-making parents and, at the same time, provide strong topic-driven and relational discipleship ministries for children who do not come from homes with spiritually mature parents.

Church leaders do not emphasize the importance of spiritual development.

Most pastors would say that spiritual development is important, but their actions often demonstrate something entirely different. After his research of senior pastors across this nation, Barna concluded, "While they give verbal support to the idea of spiritual growth, they often are not personally devoted to strenuously advocating spiritual transformation." He also found that the vast majority of pastors do not make disciple making a top priority of their ministry. In fact, pastors in his survey described success in terms of attendance, revenue, programs, and square footage of their building.

Overall, Barna concluded that when senior pastors downplay discipleship, whether by their public statement or by their lack of involvement and support, the message is very obvious: Discipleship is helpful, but optional.[7] If spiritual growth is considered important by the pastor—and most would agree that it is required in the Great Commission—then it's time for pastors to demonstrate it in their personal lives, giving public support in sermons, and testimonies from the pulpit as well as in other venues.

We divert our best leaders to ministries other than relational discipleship.

Department leaders and ministry staff members quickly approach discipled people to ask them to fill positions in the hefty list of church ministries. As a result, the potential disciple maker cannot devote his time to discipling another person, and his busyness often gets in the way of discipling his own children. When a disciple continues the discipling process of multiplication and begins to disciple another person, there is pressure to serve in the authorized church programs.

For sure we have fumbled the ball in this past century. It is time that we church leaders institute new methods in order to become more effective in accomplishing Christ's command to make disciples.

The church has failed to select qualified believers to become disciple makers.

The church has often failed to produce mature disciples because churches that do attempt to make disciples have allowed unqualified people to disciple others. One does not qualify just because he is a member of the church. Just as there are qualifications in other positions of the church, there are also qualifications to be a disciple maker. It is necessary that potential disciplers possess the following qualities:

1. The disciple maker must have a deep conviction and commitment to the truth of God's Word so he can use it in teaching, reproof, correction, and instruction.
2. He must be a person with a life worth emulating, so that his life can be modeled. I am not implying perfection, because we are always in the growing process, but the discipler must have grown to a consistent level of spiritual maturity. This quality is absolutely essential for effective results.
3. The discipler must be transparent with his own weaknesses so that he does not present a level of spiritual perfection that seems to be impossible to imitate.

4. He must be able to keep confidences. The disciple needs to feel totally safe, believing that things spoken in confidence will not be shared with others.

5. The disciple maker needs to be committed to the process, which will take a significant amount of time. He must not drop out halfway and should not allow himself to take on too many responsibilities, thereby dwarfing his effectiveness.

6. The FATHER (or MOTHER) qualities described in chapter 6 are recommended in determining if a person is a good candidate for extensive life-on-life discipleship, and are qualities every disciple maker should also have.

Qualities for Creating an Effective Disciple-Making Church

There are a number of principles we must implement if we will effectively change the DNA of our church into a strong disciple-making body.

First, we need to reject the Western church growth notion that more is better. It is not the number of programs and ministries that determine success; it is the growth of its participants. An Italian proverb says, "Often he who does too much does too little." Most churches in the United States today endeavor to develop as many programs as they can staff, and thereafter struggle to maintain quality leaders. In the process, we burn out staff and lay people with programs that are simply not growing mature disciples. Our aspiration of running quality programs actually gets in the way of the responsibility of parents to disciple their own children because, in many cases, parents are left with little time to accomplish their God-given responsibilities.

So what are really the most effective methods? We must learn to major on the majors—the ministries that have the greatest impact for the kingdom—and to focus on what will really produce the results desired. There are a small number of ministry components that we must maintain. Craig Groeschel, in his book *It*, discusses what the truly successful churches across the country have in common. The "It" factor is a way of describing the churches that really have the qualities exhibited by a body of believers filled with the Holy Spirit and working together to accomplish the Great Commission. According to Groeschel, one of the factors is that these churches keep their ministry focused on a few areas they consider most important in accomplishing their vision. Currently his large church has only five components in its ministry focus.[8]

By keeping programs to a minimum, we then can focus on quality and major on what is really important in order to accomplish the Great Commission. Doing so allows us to begin a ministry that will more completely fulfill Christ's final command. We will have a ministry of effective small-group discipleship, along with an emphasis on life-on-life disciple making.

Second, we must recognize that disciple making is a process, not a program. It is a process of growing people from the new-believer stage to mature, multiplying disciples of Jesus Christ. In the last hundred years, evangelical churches in the United States have reduced discipleship to a series of activities. In order to achieve greater impact, we have continued to expand our programs only to find the church in a frail and impotent condition, no longer producing the results commanded by the Lord. Thus, the world has written off Christianity as irrelevant to their lives—and we are to blame.

Programs, by their very nature, do not create disciples. On the other hand, a study of Jesus' discipling method illustrates the relational impact that true discipleship has in a person's walk with Christ. In today's church, we have substituted person-centered growth with program growth as the means for making disciples. These types of programs often have value but miss the central and necessary ingredient: Every person has a different growth potential and rate. They also possess a different knowledge and spiritual growth level. Each immature believer needs individual attention through a life-on-life relationship in order to grow and to flourish into spiritual maturity.

In addition to a lack of relationship emphases in church discipleship, programs are generally based on merely filling believers' heads with knowledge. Most will agree that information by itself does not produce transformation. Simply completing the program does not produce a godly, mature disciple. And yet, some programs produce a sense of self-satisfaction on the part of the participant, nurturing a false sense of having reached the desired outcome.

Another problem with programs is that they tend to lack accountability, which is needed for real growth and transformation. As stated earlier, effective accountability can only occur when the disciple humbly subjects himself to the oversight of his discipler. If consistently practiced, the disciple-making process will have extraordinary impact upon the disciple—an impact he can then eventually extend to those God gives him to disciple.

Third, the typical church pastor and other ministry staff leaders have become so immersed in the process of pastoral care that they continue to ignore the primary purpose of church leaders, specifically, "the equipping of the saints for the work of service" (Eph. 4:12). Believers need to know and use their spiritual gifts, to be trained to use them effectively, and to understand and support the work of disciple making. The membership has grown to expect the pastor(s) to be responder(s) to all of a particular flock's needs. Specifically, they are expected to make regular hospital visits, provide counseling, organize assistance to people in need, perform funerals and weddings, and deal with wayward members—to name a few. By the time they prepare several sermons and lessons, they have little time for the primary responsibility of equipping the saints. Therefore, pastors must raise up others to assist them in the area of pastoral care, as the early church did, calling them deacons, so that they can develop the church into a disciple-making body.

Fourth, while all pastors should personally disciple people, the senior pastor must spearhead the process of effective life-on-life disciple making by his example if he expects to see others become disciple makers. He must become the prime cheerleader, encouraging these men and women. He needs to also lift this ministry up often by way of testimony and sermon illustration, to keep the importance of making disciples primary in the minds of the people. By doing this, he nurtures the process as those who need to be discipled seek a disciple maker and those who develop the ability to disciple others come out of the woodwork. The senior pastor does not need to direct this ministry himself, but support and commitment to this process must come from him first and foremost.

Fifth, the discipleship process is not likely to succeed unless a church develops a simple but intelligent plan for growth. To accomplish this, the plan must reflect an understanding of the process of disciple making. The church, for example, may conduct Sunday Bible studies and small-group Bible studies, but the emphasis must be on application of biblical truth. Likewise, for the most effective disciple making, emphasis must be placed on life-on-life discipleship.

Sixth, the process of discipleship will not continue on and generate mature disciples in a relatively short period of time unless it has a designated supervisor who facilitates the process. This person's responsibility should be to lead by example as a disciple maker; to train others to effectively disciple people; to assist and encourage in the selection process, assisting those who are looking for someone to disciple; to provide recommended discipleship curriculum; to help solve problems when the disciple maker needs advice; to organize ongoing training; and to encourage enthusiasm, training, and expansion through monthly or quarterly rallies. The plan of growth could include small-group discipleship but must include life-on-life discipleship as well. In short, the intent of every church should be to emphasize what it takes for solid spiritual growth and service, which will always include developing disciple makers who will reproduce themselves.

What Will the Future Hold?

Many have made it clear that we are falling short of what should happen in and through the modern church as we act in obedience to Jesus' Great Commission. We have the complete Word of God with not only precepts but models of what God wants us to do. We have the omnipotent, indwelling Holy Spirit who instills us with the enablement, wisdom, and guidance necessary to get the job done. And we have a plethora of modern technological tools to which the early church never had access. Yet, even with all these advantages, we simply do not produce the kind of Christians who produced the book of Acts!

I am convinced that we can and must do better. We can impact our world as the early church did, so that once again nonbelievers will acknowledge that "we have turned the world upside down" (Acts 17:6, ESV). But we must follow the example of Jesus and the apostles. George Martin takes the strategy of Jesus and challenges pastors to apply it in their ministry:

> Perhaps today's pastor should imagine that they are going to have three more years in their parish (church) as pastor and that there will be no replacement for them when they leave. If they acted as if this were going to happen, they would put the highest priority on selecting, motivating, and training lay leaders that could carry on as much as possible the mission of the parish after they left. The result of three sustained years of such an approach would be significant. Even revolutionary.[9]

Since we don't know what's ahead, we should initiate a plan that will continue our impact into the future. Jesus followed a three-year plan, knowing the profound need of it being successful. He knew he had a short time to provide salvation for all present and future believers. This plan had to include the continual expansion of the evangelization of the world as well as the constant growth of men and women to become mature disciples of Christ who would go on to make disciples, continuing the process. With this goal always in view, he selected twelve men with whom he lived with over the next two and a half years. Everything he did centered on training the Twelve, which he did by example as well as through teaching, exhortation, rebuke, correction, and accountability as they followed him. Every day drew him closer to his last day on earth when he would turn the task over to them—even telling them (and us) at one point that they (and we), assuming we followed his directions, would accomplish greater things then he had (John 14:12).

Jesus could have used another method. Instead he spent his precious three years pouring his life into twelve protégés. As Robert Coleman stated, "Jesus' concern was not with programs to reach the multitudes, but with men the multitudes would follow."[10] His strategy was to initiate a world-changing movement. He not only provided salvation for all who would receive it during the next two thousand-plus years, but a relationship-driven method to carry on this message. With the eternal destiny of billions of people at stake, he chose to reach the world through a system focused on multiplying disciples.

Clearly, Jesus wants us to continue following his master plan. And for those who obey his commission, he promises to be with them, even to the end of the age (Matt. 28:20). What a glorious plan! But will you use his strategy?

What a day we live in. We are in the right place at the right time. God intentionally planned our existence at the end of this age to accomplish something very special. We were created for "such a time as this." We have an opportunity to *change the landscape of eternity*—to change the destiny and rewards of thousands of people for all eternity. I am ready for that opportunity. How about you?

Review Questions

1. In your own words, why has the church been ineffective in producing disciples?
2. Explain the author's statement that "disciple making is a process, not a program." What does that process look like?
3. Why is it so important that the senior pastor (or top leader of the church) be committed and practice life-on-life discipleship? What would it mean to you personally to see this kind of commitment and support?
4. If you had only three years of ministry, what would be your priorities? How can you make them your priorities now?

APPENDIXES

Appendix I
Bibliography

Books on Making Disciples

As Iron Sharpens Iron, by Howard and William Hendricks. Chicago, IL: Moody Press, 1995. This book focus on the ministry of mentoring.

Big Truths for Young Hearts, by Bruce Ware. Wheaton, IL: Crossway Books, 2009. This is a good book with the focus on explaining doctrinal truths in a simple way so the information and application can be transferred to children.

Design for Discipleship, by J. Dwight Pentecost. Grand Rapids, MI: Kregel Publications, 1996 (originally published Grand Rapids, MI: Zondervan Publishing House, 1971).

Disciples Are Made Not Born, by Walter A. Henrichsen. Colorado Springs, CO: David C. Cook, 1998 (originally published Wheaton, IL: Victor Books, 1996).

Following the Master, A Biblical Theology of Discipleship, by Michael Wilkins. Grand Rapids, MI: Zondervan Publishing House, 1992.

Fox Fever: Exploring Both the Will and the Skill to Obey Christ's Great Commission to "Turn People into Disciples," by Herb Hodges. Chelsea, MI: Sheridan Books, 2006. *Growing True Disciples*, by George Barna. Colorado Springs, CO: Waterbrook Press, 2001.

Intentional Disciplemaking, by Ron Bennett. Colorado Springs, CO: NavPress, 2001.

Organic Disciplemaking, by Dennis McCallum and Jessica Lowery. Houston, TX: Touch Publications, 2006.

Parenting Is Heart Work, by Dr. Scott Turansky and Joanne Miller. Colorado Springs, CO: David C. Cook, 2006. This book is a good resource for parents on child discipleship.

Personal Disciple Making, by Christopher B. Adsit. Orlando, FL: Campus Crusade for Christ, 1996.

Shepherding a Child's Heart, by Tedd Tripp. Wapwallopen, PA: Shepherd Press, 1995.

Spiritual Discipleship, by J. Oswald Sanders. Chicago, IL: Moody Press, 2007.

Tally Ho the Fox: A Foundation for Building World Visionary, World Impacting, Reproducing Disciples, by Herb Hodges. Manhattan Source, Inc., 2001; order from Spiritual Life Ministries at 1-901-758-2777 or email at: herbslm@mindspring.com.

The Complete Book of Discipleship, by Bill W. Hull. Colorado Springs, CO: NavPress, 2006.

The Cost of Discipleship, by Dietrich Bonhoeffer. New York, NY: Touchstone Books, 1995 (originally published New York, NY: MacMillan Publishing, 1959).

The Disciple Making Pastor, by Bill Hull. Grand Rapids, MI: Baker Books, 2007.

The Lost Art of Disciple Making, by LeRoy Eims. Grand Rapids, MI: Zondervan, 1978.

The Making of a Disciple, by Keith W. Phillips, World Impact Press, 1981.

The Master Plan of Evangelism, by Robert E. Coleman. Grand Rapids, MI: Revell, 2010.

The Master Plan of Discipleship, by Robert E. Coleman, Grand Rapids, MI: Revell 1998.

The Training of the Twelve, by A.B. Bruce. Grand Rapids, MI: Kregel Publications, 2000.

Transforming Discipleship, by Greg Ogden. Downers Grove, IL: InterVarsity Press, 2003.

True Discipleship, by John Koessler. Chicago, IL: Moody, 2003. This book is designed to help a person to grow to be an effective disciple of Christ.

True Discipleship, by William MacDonald. Port Colborne, ON, Canada: Gospel Folio Press, 2003.

OUT-OF-PRINT BOOKS ON MAKING DISCIPLES (MAY BE AVAILABLE FROM USED-BOOK DISTRIBUTORS):

Discipleship, edited by Billy Hanks. Grand Rapids, MI: Zondervan, 1981, 1993.

How to Disciple Your Children, by Walter A. Henrichsen. Wheaton, IL: Victor Books, 1981.

Multiplying Disciples, by Waylon B. Moore. Colorado Springs, CO: NavPress, 1981.

New Testament Follow-up, by Waylon B. Moore. Grand Rapids, MI: Eerdmans, 9th printing, 1978.

Successful Discipling, by Allen Hadidian. Chicago, IL: Moody, 1979.

The Dynamics of Discipleship Training, by Gary W. Kuhne. Grand Rapids, MI: Zondervan, 1978.

The Dynamics of Personal Follow-up, by Gary W. Kuhne. Grand Rapids, MI: Zondervan, 1996.

RESOURCES FOR BIBLICAL COUNSELING

The *Christian Counseling and Educational Foundation* provides a large assortment of books on most counseling topics, courses on biblical counseling, many free blog articles and videos, as well as a national conference. Review their materials online at http://www.ccef.org.

The *Association of Biblical Counselors* offers many books and resources, along with free articles on various counseling topics. Review their materials online at http://christiancounseling.com.

The *American Association of Christian Counselors* also offers many books, along with a biblical-counseling course. Review their material at http://www.aacc.net/courses.

SEXUAL-ABUSE PREVENTION

Protect My Ministries, a sexual-abuse screening ministry. Contact online at http://protectmyministry.com, or call (800) 319-5581.

LifeWay Background Checks, a sexual-abuse screening ministry. Contact online at http://www.lifeway.com/Article/composite-home-background-checks, or call (800) 464-2799.

RECOMMENDED DISCIPLESHIP CURRICULA

A Book You Will Actually Read, a small book series by Mark Driscoll. Wheaton, IL: Crossway Books, 2008. This is a simple and brief series that would be good for homework assignments. Order online at http://www.crossway.org /books/list/?sort=featured:
On Who Is God
On the Old Testament
On the New Testament
On Church Leadership

Design for Discipleship, a six-book Bible Study series by NavPress, Colorado Springs, CO, 1973, 1980, 2006. Order toll free at 1-800-366-7788 or online at http://www.navpress.com/store/search.aspx?q=2:7series&page=all:
Book 1: *Your Life in Christ*
Book 2: *The Spirit-Filled Christian*
Book 3: *Walking with Christ*
Book 4: *The Character of the Christian*
Book 5: *Foundations for Faith*
Book 6: *Growing in Discipleship*

Discipleship Essentials, A Guide for Building Your Life in Christ, by Greg Ogden. Downers Grove, IL: InterVarsity Press, 1998. Order toll free at 1-800-843-9487 or online at http://www.ivpress.com/books.

Growing in Christ, published by NavPress, Colorado Springs, CO, 1980. In my opinion, this is the best material available for new believers. This thirteen-week series can be used as a small-group class or one-on-one. It is a self-guided topical Bible study with fill-in-the-blank questions. Also included are tear-out-verse cards for memorization.

Journey to Your Spiritual Gifts, by Tommy C. Higle. Marietta, OK: Tommy C. Higle Publishers, 1991. This is designed as material to teach in a classroom but would be an excellent resource. Order toll free at 1-800-635-5346 or online at www.journeyseries.com.

MasterLife, A Biblical Process for Growing Disciples, by Avery Willis, Jr. Nashville, TN: LifeWay Press, 1996. Each book contains six weeks of lessons with five lessons per week. It is designed for young believers and works well for someone who has been faithful going through the basics. It can be used one-on-one or in a small group and is designed to take the person to a deeper level of knowledge, commitment, and Christian service. Order toll free at 1-800-233-1123, or online at: http://www.lifewaystores.com/lwstore:

Book 1: *The Disciple's Cross*
Book 2: *The Disciple's Personality*
Book 3: *The Disciple's Victory*
Book 4: *The Disciple's Mission*

Positive Action Bible Curriculum Discipleship Series. Whitakers, NC: Positive Action Bible Curriculum. These are self-guided topical Bible study materials, excellent for young believers with fill-in-the-blank questions and can be used one-on-one or in a small group. Order toll free 1-800-688-3008, or online at http://www.positiveaction.org:

Milk for New Christians
Meat for Growing Christians
Bread for Hungry Christians, a basic Bible doctrine, providing a more thorough study of the doctrine of Christ.
Fish for Witnessing Christians, a basic evangelism course.

Share Jesus without Fear, by William Fay. Nashville, TN: Broadman & Holman Publishers, 1999. This book is especially good for relationship evangelism and could be assigned reading for a motivated disciple.

Spiritual Gift Survey, Nashville, TN: LifeWay Christian Resources, 2003, download free at http://www.lifeway.com/lwc/files/lwcF_wmn_SpiritualGifts_Survey.pdf.

Survival Kit, by Ralph Neighbor, Jr. Nashville, TN: LifeWay Press, 1979. This study for new believers is laid out in a reading style with few questions. It is best used in a small group or for self-study. This material has five weeks with five lessons per week and includes memory cards for verse memorization. I would especially recommend this material as a good resource to mail to new believers who live too far away for personal follow-up. Order toll free at 1-800-233-1123, or online at http://www.lifewaystores.com/lwstore.

The 2:7 Discipleship Series, Colorado Springs, CO: NavPress, 1974, 1978. This three-book series is a course in personal discipleship, designed to strengthen your walk with God. Order toll free at 1-800-366-7788 or online at http://www.navpress.com.

Book 1: *Growing Strong in God's Family*

Book 2: *Deeping Your Roots in God's Family*

Book 3: *Bearing Fruit in God's Family*

Woman's Journey of Discipleship, Colorado Springs, CO: NavPress, 2010. This three-book series is a course in personal discipleship designed especially for women. Order toll free at 1-800-366-7788 or online at: http://www.navpress.com:

Book 1: *Bridges on the Journey*

Book 2: *Crossroads on the Journey*

Book 3: *Friends on the Journey*

DISCIPLESHIP MATERIALS FOR CHILDREN

Bibleman DVD Series. Nashville, TN: Thomas Nelson,. This is an excellent series to teach basic concepts to children (especially boys) from three to ten years old, depending on the DVD.

Character Sketches. Oak Brook, IL: Institute of Basic Life Principles. This is a full-color, three-book series with each book available individually. Each section begins with a captivating nature story that introduces the character quality being taught, and continues with interesting facts on the selected animal's qualities and physical features. This is followed by a story from Scripture that illustrates the character quality. Generously illustrated with stunning lifelike watercolor and pencil drawings, this oversized book (9 1/4" by 12 1/4") will be treasured and enjoyed for generations. Call toll free at 800-398-1290 or online at: http://store.iblp.org.

Children's Discipleship Series, by Bill Bright, Joette Whims, and Melody Hunskor. Orlando, FL:

New Life Publications (a ministry of Campus Crusade for Christ), 2002. This four-book series is designed for children nine to twelve years old. Each book has thirteen lessons and are recommended for one-on-one, small group, or classroom study. Among its strengths are the many activities designed to help the child understand and apply the truths personally. There are no student workbooks necessary, and each book has handouts designed for the leader to photocopy for the students.

Book 1, *Beginning the Christian Adventure*. Designed to introduce children to the thrill of walking with Jesus day by day.

Book 2, *Discovering Our Awesome God*. Introduces students to the wonders and awesome nature of God the Father, the Son, and the Holy Spirit and how to talk to our loving God.

Book 3, *Growing in God's Word*. Gives student a foundation in how the Bible is arranged and how the Old Testament is God's plan for humanity. This book also uses practical applications for using God's Word daily.

Book 4, *Building an Active Faith*. Shows students how to build their faith through obeying God, giving back part of what they have to him, and sharing their faith with others.

DiscipleLand, Fort Collins, CO. An excellent series that can be used one-on-one or in a classroom setting. *DiscipleLand* has a pre-school program for ages three through five; a kindergarten program for ages five and six; and a core topical Bible program for children in grades one through six, recommended for Sunday school. Also available for grades one through six is *The Adventure* curriculum, ideal for midweek programs, and *DiscipleTown* curriculum, ideal for kids' church. Leaders and parents would benefit by reading material in the blog at www.discipleblog.com and children and parents would benefit from the home resources support site at www.disciplezone.com. Order toll-free from 1-800-284-0158 or online at: http://www.discipleland.com.

Partners in Discipleship, by Jan VanDyke, published by Camp Beechpoint, Allegan, MI. This is a unique program in which its impact is attributed to its foundational emphasis on one-on-one discipleship. Even when used in the church setting, the program requires a period of time given over to the leader spending quality one-on-one time with the child, helping him grow spiritually. The one-on-one time is not only for instruction and encouragement but also emphasizes accountability. The child is held accountable for Scripture memory, lesson retention, church attendance, personal church offering, Christian service, prayer, and personal Bible study. The material includes five series that are progressive:

Series Number 1—*Who God Is,* for ages 8 and 9

Series Number 2—*Our Relationship with God and Others*, for ages 10 and 11
Series Number 3—*Living Out Our Faith*, for ages 12 and 13
Series Number 4—*The Book of Proverbs*, for ages 14 and 15
Series Number 5—*Promise Keepers*, for ages 16 and 17
This is an overview of the Bible, tying Old Testament and the New Testament truths together. This series can be purchased in workbook form from the author. Churches can also save money by purchasing the rights to duplicate their own copies from PDF files that the author can email the church. Contact Jan VanDyke at Camp Beechpoint, 1-800-991-2267, or contact her by email at jvandyke@beechpoint.com.

The Story of Jesus for Children DVD, published by the Jesus Film Project, Inspirational Films 2005. This sixty-seven-minute video teaches the life of Christ through the eyes of children and is available in many foreign languages. Book 1, *Beginning the Christian Adventure* from the Children's Discipleship Series above recommends you use the video as part of the first lesson.

Passing the Baton: Guide Your Child to Follow Jesus, by Grant Edwards. Loveland, CO: Group Publishing. This is a ten-week, forty-five-minute, elementary discipleship series for parents as they help their children to grow spiritually. This material is not comprehensive but provides good material with hands-on lessons and many extras that can provide ideas for parents as they make disciples at home. This material can be purchased from Group Publishing online at http://search.group.com/search?p=Q&w=passing+the+baton, or call 1-800-447-1070.

VeggieTales DVD Series, Franklin, TN: Big Idea Entertainment. This is an excellent series to teach basic concepts to children from four to fourteen years old.

Wonder Devotional Books, published by Child Evangelism Fellowship. The series includes numerous books designed to help the child grow spiritually. Call toll free at 1-800-748-7710, or order online at http://cefpress.com.

Appendix II

Discipleship Topics

For the New Believer

(Taken from chapter headings in the NavPress book *Growing in Christ*)
Assurance of Salvation
Assurance of Answered Prayer
Assurance of Victory
Assurance of Forgiveness
Assurance of Guidance
Putting Christ First
His Strength
God's Word
Love
Giving
The Church
Good Works
Witnessing

For the Growing and More Mature Disciple

(Taken from Gary Kuhne's book *The Dynamics of Personal Follow-up.*)
The Biblical Focus
1. Bible Doctrine
   - Doctrine of the Bible
   - Doctrine of God
   - Deity of Christ
   - Doctrine of the Holy Spirit
   - Doctrine of Man
   - Doctrine of Satan/Demons
   - Doctrine of Future Events
   - Bible Knowledge
   - Old and New Testament Survey
3. Apologetics
4. Biblical Counseling
   - Dealing with Anger

- Dealing with Worry and Anxiety
- Dealing with Depression
- Dealing with Jealousy
- Dealing with our Thought Life
- Dealing with Moral Issues
- Salvation
- Assurance of Salvation
- Confession of Sin
- Dealing with Temptations

The Devotional Focus (Christian disciplines)

- Personal Devotions
- Prayer
- Memorizing Scriptures
- Bible Study Methods
- The Spirit-Filled Life
- Obedience
- God's Discipline
- Godly Habits of Living
- Knowing God's Will
- Stewardship including: Stewardship of Our Time, Temple, Talents (including spiritual gifts), Treasure, and Truth of God's Word
- Church Involvement

The Outreach Focus (The disciple's involvement in service)

- Evangelism
- Writing and Sharing One's Personal Testimony
- Follow-up with New Converts
- Learning to Disciple Others
- Time Management

APPENDIX III

COVENANTS

THE DISCIPLE'S COVENANT FOR LIFE-ON-LIFE DISCIPLESHIP

The purpose is to guide your growth as you practice the Word of God. With the Holy Spirit's transformation you will experience great growth during the discipleship process as you seek to be a mature disciple of Jesus Christ. I will meet weekly, except for excused absences, for a period of one and a half years.

To participate in dedicated growth, I will dedicate myself to God by making the following commitment. As a disciple of Jesus Christ:

- I will devote myself to the process of spiritual growth.
- I will attend all meetings with my disciple maker, unless excused, to dialogue over the content of the assignments and other subjects as the Holy Spirit leads.
- Understanding that my disciple maker's time is valuable, I will arrive at all meetings on time.
- I will complete all assignments prior to my discipleship appointment in order to contribute fully.
- I will participate in social activity and/or ministry experience with my disciple maker as time and schedule allows.
- I will develop a quiet time with God five days a week, including a study of God's Word and prayer.
- I will faithfully attend Sunday morning worship, Sunday Bible study, and midweek prayer service.
- I will place myself under the spiritual authority of my disciple maker participating in a spirit of honesty, trust and personal vulnerability.
- I will listen and follow the biblical directions of my disciple maker to the best of my ability.
- I will give serious consideration to continuing the discipling chain once I am ready, by seeking to share my faith with others and by discipling another person.

With God's help, I will keep this covenant to the best of my ability.

Signature _____ Date _____

THE DISCIPLE MAKER'S SMALL-GROUP COVENANT

The purpose is to guide your growth as you practice the Word of God. With the Holy Spirit's transformation you will experience great growth during the life of the group as you seek to be a mature disciple of Jesus Christ.

The disciple making group will meet each week on _____ evening, from 7:00–8:30 p.m. Each meeting will be held at the home of _____ located at _____.
The duration of the group will be for a period of one and a half years.

To participate in dedicated growth, I will dedicate myself to God by making the following commitment. As a disciple of Jesus Christ:

- I will devote myself to the process of spiritual growth.
- I will attend all meetings with my group unless excused, to dialogue over the content of the assignments and other subjects as the Holy Spirit leads.
- To make the most of our meeting, I will arrive at all meetings on time.
- I will complete all assignments prior to my group meeting in order to contribute fully.
- I will participate in social activity and/or ministry experience with my group as time and schedule allows.
- I will develop a quiet time with God five days a week including a study of God's Word and prayer.
- I will faithfully attend Sunday morning worship, Sunday Bible study, and midweek prayer service.
- I will place myself under the spiritual authority of my group leader, participating in a spirit of honesty, trust, and personal vulnerability.
- I will be honest and transparent with my agreed-upon accountability partner.
- I will listen and follow the biblical directions of my group leader to the best of my ability.
- Once trained, I will seek to share my faith with others and give serious consideration to discipling another person one-on-one once I am trained.

With God's help, I will keep this covenant to the best of my ability.

Signature _____ Date _____

APPENDIX IV

Topical Scripture Passages for Counseling

Adultery

Ex. 20:14
II Sam. 11:2
Prov. 2:16–18; 5:1-23; 6:23–35; 7:5–27; 9:13–16
Mal. 2:13–16
Matt. 5:28; 15:19; 19:9
1 Cor. 6:9–11

Alcoholism

(See Drunkenness)

Anger

Gen. 4:5–7
Ps. 7:11
Prov. 14:17, 29; 15:1, 18; 19:11, 19; 20:3, 22; 22:24; 24:29; 25: 15, 28: 29:11, 22
Mark 3:5
Eph. 4:26–32
James 1:19, 20

Anxiety

(See Worry)

Association (bad/good)

Prov. 9:6; 13:20; 14:9; 22:24; 23:20, 21; 29:24
Rom. 16:17, 18
1 Cor. 5:9-13
2 Cor. 6:14-18
2 Tim. 3:5

ASSURANCE

> John 3:36; 6:37; 10:27–29
> Eph. 1:13, 14
> Heb. 6:11; 13:5
> 1 Pet. 1:3-5
> 1 John 5:13

AVOIDANCE

> Gen. 3:8
> Prov. 18:1
> Eph. 4:25–32
> 1 Tim. 6:11
> 2 Tim. 2:22

BITTERNESS

> (See Resentment)

BLAME-SHIFTING

> Gen. 3:12–13
> Prov. 19:3

BODY

> Rom. 12:1, 2
> 1 Cor. 3:16, 17; 6:18–20
> 2 Cor. 5:1-4

CHANGE

> Ezek. 36:25–27
> Matt. 16:24
> Eph. 4:17–32
> Col. 3:1–14
> 1 Thess. 1:9
> 2 Tim. 3:17
> Heb. 10:25
> James 1:14–15
> 1 Pet. 3:9

CHILDREN

(See Family)

CHURCH

Eph. 4:1–16
Heb. 10:25
Rev. 2, 3

COMMANDMENT

Ex. 20
Prov. 13:13
Luke 17:3–10
John 13:34; 15:12
1 John 5:2–3

COMMUNICATION

Eph. 4:25–32

CONFESSION

Prov. 28:13
James 5:16
1 John 1:9

CONSCIENCE

Mark 6:19
Acts 24:16
Rom. 2:15
1 Cor. 8:10, 12
1 Tim. 1:5, 19; 3:9
2 Tim. 1:3
Heb. 13:18
1 Pet. 3:16, 21

CONVICTION

John 16:7–11
2 Tim. 3:17

Jude 15

DEATH

Ps. 23:6
Prov. 3:21—26; 14:32
1 Cor. 15:54–58
Phil. 1:21, 24
Heb. 2:14–15

DECISION-MAKING

2 Tim. 3:15–18
Heb. 11:23–27

DEPRESSION

Gen. 4:6–7
Ps. 32:38, 51
Prov. 18:14
2 Cor. 4:8–9

DESIRE

Gen. 3:6; Ex. 20:17
Prov. 10:3, 24; 11:6; 28:25
Matt. 6:21
Luke 12:31–34
Rom. 13:14
Gal. 5:16
Eph. 2:3
Titus 2:12; 3:3
James 1:13–16; 4:2–3
1 John 2:16
Jude 18
1 Peter 1:14; 4:2–3

DISCIPLINE

Prov. 3:11–12; 13:24; 19:18; 22:6, 15; 23:13; 29:15
1 Cor. 5:1–13; 11:29–34
2 Cor. 2:1–11

Eph. 6:1–4
1 Tim. 4:7
Heb. 12:7–11

DIVORCE

Gen. 2:24
Deut. 24:1–4
Isa. 50:1
Jer. 3:1
Mal. 2:16
Matt. 5:31–32; 19:3–8
Mark 10:3–5
1 Cor. 7:10–24, 33–34, 39–40

DOUBT

James 1:6–8

DRUNKENNESS

Prov. 20:1, 23:20, 29–35; 31:4–6
Eph. 5:18
1 Pet. 4:4

ENVY

Titus 3:3
James 3:14–16
1 Pet. 2:1

FAMILY

Gen. 2:18, 24
Ex. 20:12

FAMILY— HUSBAND/WIFE

Gen. 2:18, 24
Eph. 5:22–33
Col. 3:18–21
1 Pet. 3:1–17
1 Tim. 2:11–15

FAMILY—PARENT/CHILD

> Gen. 2:24
> 2 Cor. 12:14
> Eph. 6:1–4
> 1 Tim. 3:4–5

FEAR

> Gen. 3:10
> Prov. 10:24; 29:25
> Matt. 10:26–31
> 2 Tim. 1:7
> Heb. 2:14–15
> 1 Pet. 3:6, 13–14
> 1 John 4:18

FORGIVENESS

> Prov. 17:9
> Matt. 6:14–15; 18:15–17
> Mark 11:25;
> Luke 17:3–10
> Eph. 4:32
> Col. 3:13
> James 5:15
> 1 John 1:8-10

FRIENDSHIP

> Prov. 27:6, 10; 17:9, 17
> John 15:13–15

GIFTS

> Rom. 12:3–8
> 1 Cor. 12–14
> 1 Peter 4:1, 11

GOSSIP

> Prov. 10:18, 11:13; 18:8; 20:19; 26:20–22

James 4:11

GRIEF

Prov. 14:13; 15:13
Eph. 4:30
1 Thess. 4:13–18

HABIT

Prov. 19:19
Isaiah 1:10–17
Jer. 13:23; 22:21
Rom. 6–7
Gal. 5:16–21
Heb. 5:13
1 Pet. 2:14, 19

HOMOSEXUALITY

Gen. 19
Lev. 18:22, 20:13
Rom. 1:26-32
1 Cor. 6:9–11
1 Tim. 1:10

HOPE

Prov. 10:28, 13:12
1 Thess. 1:3, 4:13–18
Rom. 15:4– 5
Heb. 6:11, 18–19

HUMILITY

Prov. 13:34; 15:33; 16:19; 22:4; 29:23
Gal. 6:1–2
Phil. 2:1–11
James 4:6, 10
1 Pet. 5:6–7

LAZINESS

Prov. 12:24, 27; 13:4; 15:19; 18:9; 26:13–16
Matt. 25:26

Living

Ex. 20:16
Prov. 12:19, 22
Eph. 4:25
Col. 3:9

Life-dominating Sins

1 Cor. 6:9–12; 21:8
Eph. 5:18
Rev. 21:8; 22:15

Listening

Prov. 5:1–2, 13; 13:18; 15:31; 18:13

Love

Prov. 10:12; 17:19
Matt. 5:44; 22:30, 40
Rom. 13:10
1I Cor. 13
1 Pet. 1:22
1 John 4:10, 19; 5:2–3
2 John 5–6

Obedience

1 Sam. 15:22
Luke 17:9–10
Acts 4:19; 5:29
Eph. 6:1
Heb. 5:8; 13:17
1 Pet. 1:22

Peace

Prov. 3:1–2; 16:7

John 14:27
Rom. 5:1; 12:18; 14:19
Phil. 4:6–9
Col. 3:14
Heb. 12:14

PRIDE

Pr. 8:13; 11:2; 13:10; 16:18; 18:12; 21:24; 27:1; 29:23

RECONCILIATION

Matt. 5:23–24; 18:15–17
Luke 17:3–10

REPENTANCE

Luke 3:8–14; 24:47
Acts 3:19; 5:31; 17:30; 26:20
2 Cor. 7:10; 12:21

RESENTMENT

Prov. 26:24–26
Heb. 12:15

REWARD/PUNISHMENT

Prov. 13:24; 22:15; 29:15
2 Cor. 2:6; 10:6
Heb. 10:35; 11:26
2 John 8

SEXUALITY

Gen. 2:25
1 Cor. 7:1–5

SHAME

Gen. 2:25
Prov. 11:2; 13:18
1 Cor. 4:14
1 Pet. 3:16

STEALING

Ex. 20:15
Eph. 4:28
Prov. 20:10, 22; 29:24; 30:7–9

WORK

Gen. 2:5, 15; 3:17–19
Prov. 14:23; 18:9; 21:4; 22:29; 24:27; 31:10–31
1 Cor. 15:58
Col. 3:22–24
1 Thess. 4:11
2 Thess. 3:6–15

WORRY

Matt. 6:24–34
Prov. 12:25; 14:30; 7:22
Phil. 4:6–9
Pet. 5:6– 7

APPENDIX V

ACCOUNTABILITY QUESTIONS

It is not recommended that these questions all be used at one setting; rather pick two or three to be used at each meeting. Remember, these questions are only as helpful as you are honest.

QUESTIONS FOR MEN:

1. How many days have you spent time in the Scriptures and prayer this past week?
2. When was the last time you had a spiritual discussion with a nonbeliever? Have you shared the gospel with a nonbeliever recently?
3. Have you been giving to God in proportion to how he has blessed you financially?
4. Have you been guilty of viewing pornographic images this past week?
5. When was the last time you participated in a flirtatious experience?
6. Has your speech been damaging to another person's reputation through slander or gossip this past week?
7. Have you done your best at your job or at school this week?
8. Are you angry at another person?
9. Have you given in to a personal addiction this past week? Explain:
10. Have you taken care of your body through proper eating and exercise this past week?
11. Have you told any half-truths or outright lies this past week?
12. Have you practiced honesty in your financial dealings this past week? Have you been a wise steward in your spending?
13. Have you made it a priority this past week to spend quality time with your family?
14. Have you tried to practice agape love with your wife this past week?

QUESTIONS FOR WOMEN:

1. How many days have you spent time in the Scriptures and prayer this past week?
2. When was the last time you had a spiritual discussion with a nonbeliever? Have you shared the gospel with a nonbeliever recently?

3. Have you been giving to God in proportion to how he has blessed you financially?

4. Have you read or watched any sexually alluring books, magazines, or videos this past week?

5. Have you allowed your mind to fantasize with a romantic relationship with someone this past week?

6. When was the last time you participated in a flirtatious experience?

7. Has your speech been damaging to another person's reputation through slander or gossip this past week?

8. Have you done your best at your job, school, or at home this week?

9. Are you angry at another person?

10. Have you given in to a personal addiction this past week? Explain:

11. Have you taken care of your body through proper eating and exercise this past week?

12. Have you told any half-truths or outright lies this past week?

13. Have you practiced honesty in your financial dealings this past week? Have you been a wise steward in your spending?

14. Have you shown respect and have you practiced submission toward your husband this past week?

ENDNOTES

INTRODUCTION

1. Barna, George, *Growing True Disciples* (Colorado Springs: WaterBrook Press, 2001), 8.
2. Ibid., 20.

CHAPTER 1
CALIBRATING OUR COMPASS: BULL'S-EYE—BUT WRONG TARGET

1. Adherents.com (2005), http://www.adherents.com/Na/Na_173.html#955 (accessed 9/10/13).
2. Frontier Harvest Ministries, http://frontierharvestministries.net/WorldMissionStatistics.dsp.
3. Latourette, Kenneth Scott, *A History of Christianity* (New York: Harper and Row Publishers, 1953), 1476.
4. Schaff, Philip, *History of the Christian Church, vol. 1* (Peabody, MA: Hendrickson Publishers, 1985), 198.
5. Kittel, Gerhard, ed., *Theological Dictionary of the New Testament*, trans. and ed. Geoffrey W. Bromiley, vol. 4 (Grand Rapids, MI: Eerdmans, 1967), 441.
6. Wilkins, Michael J., *Following the Master, A Biblical Theology of Discipleship* (Grand Rapids, MI: Zondervan, 1992), 38–39, 41.
7. Willard, Dallas, *The Spirit of the Disciplines* (San Francisco: HarperOne, 1991), 258.
8. Hadidian, Allen, *Successful Discipling* (Chicago: Moody, 1979), 31–32.
9. Hodges, Herb, *Fox Fever* (Chelsea, MI: Sharidan Books, 2006), 120.

CHAPTER 2
TURN THE WORLD UPSIDE-DOWN: GREAT IMPACT MULTIPLIED

1. Schaff, *History of the Christian Church, vol. 1*, 198.
2. Jackson, Thomas, *Centenary of Wesleyan Methodism* (New York: T. Mason & G. Lane, 1839), 69.
3. Henrichsen, Walter, *Disciples Are Made Not Born* (Colorado Springs: Cook Communications, 1988), 142.

CHAPTER 3

THE CONTEXT OF BIBLICAL DISCIPLESHIP:

HOW DISCIPLESHIP WAS VIEWED IN THE FIRST CENTURY

1. Hewett, James S., *Illustrations Unlimited* (Wheaton, IL: Tyndale House Publishers, Inc., 1988), 165–166.
2. Wilkins, *Following the Master*, 62.
3. Wilson, Robert R., *Prophecy and Society in Ancient Israel* (Philadelphia: Fortress, 1980), 202; 300-301; E. J. Young, *My Servants the Prophets* (Grand Rapids, MI: Eerdmans, 1955), 92–94; Hengel, Martin, *The Charismatic Leader and His Followers* (Eugene, OR: Wipf & Stock, 2005), 17–18.
4. Wilkins, *Following the Master*, 72.
5. Wilkins, Michael, *The Concept of Disciple in Matthew's Gospel: As Reflected in the Use of the Term "Mathetes,"* Novum Testamentum Supplements, vol. 59 (Leiden, The Netherlands: E.J. Brill, 1988), 12, 15–41.
6. Wilkins, *Following the Master*, 76–78.
7. Ibid., 84.
8. Ibid., 86.
9. Ibid., 88, 90.
10. Coleman, Robert E., *The Master Plan of Evangelism* (Grand Rapids, MI: Fleming H. Revell, 2001), 28–29.
11. Hodges, Herb, *Tally Ho the Fox* (Memphis, TN: Spiritual Life Ministries, 2001), 152.
12. Wilkins, *Following the Master*, 128.
13. Hodges, Herb, *Jesus the Greatest Disciple-Maker of Christian History* (Germantown, TN: Spiritual Life Ministries), 4.
14. Coleman, *The Master Plan of Evangelism*, 49.
15. Horne, Herman H., *Jesus the Master Teacher* (New York: Association Press, 1920), 93–106.
16. Coleman, *The Master Plan of Evangelism*, 80.
17. Ibid., 86.
18. Quoted in Hodges, *Jesus the Greatest Disciple-Maker of Christian History*, 7.
19. Hodges, *Fox Fever*, 174–175.
20. Hodges, Herb, *The Bible and Disciple-Making*, a paper (Germantown, TN: Spiritual Life Ministries), 2–3.
21. Coleman, *The Master Plan of Discipleship*, 30.
22. Wilkins, *Following the Master*, 314.

23. Hull, Bill, *The Complete Book of Discipleship* (Colorado Springs: NavPress, 2006), 76–77.

24. Corwin, Virginia, *St. Ignatius and Christianity in Antioch*, Yale Publications in Religion 1 (New Haven: Yale University Press, 1960), 228, n. 9.

25. Wilkins, *Following the Master*, 318.

26. Hull, *The Complete Book of Discipleship*, 63–64.

CHAPTER 4

THE GREAT COMMISSION REVISITED:

THE GREAT OMISSION OF THE GREAT COMMISSION

1. Carroll, Lewis, *Alice in Wonderland*, John Berseth, ed. (Mineola, NY: Dover Publications, 2001), 49.

2. Willard, Dallas, *The Great Omission: Reclaiming Jesus's Central Teaching on Discipleship* (San Francisco: HarperSanFrancisco, 2006), 5–6.

3. Lucado, Max, *In the Eye of the Storm* (Waco, TX: Word Publishing, 1991), 153.

4. Adsit, Christopher B., *Personal Disciplemaking* (Orlando, FL: Campus Crusade for Christ, 1996), 72.

5. Coleman, *The Master Plan of Discipleship*, 99.

6. Quoted by Hendricks, Howard and William, *As Iron Sharpens Iron* (Chicago: Moody Press, 1995), 132.

7. Barna, *Growing True Disciples*, 20.

8. Ibid., 19.

9. Hodges, *Fox Fever*, 195.

10. Ibid., 194–195.

CHAPTER 5—JESUS' REQUIREMENTS: ARE YOU A TRUE DISCIPLE?

1. Barna, *Growing True Disciples*, 7–8.

2. Ogden, Greg, *Transforming Discipleship* (Downers Grove, IL: InterVarsity Press, 2003), 49–50.

3. Barnes, Albert, *Barnes' Notes on the New Testament* (Cedar Rapids, IA: Parsons Technology, Inc.), Reference Matthew 16:24–28.

4. Tozer, A.W., *The Pursuit of God*, chapter 2, "The Blessedness of Possessing Nothing," http://www.ntslibrary.com/PDF%20Books/Tozer_Pursuit_of_God.pdf (accessed 9/10/13).

CHAPTER 6—THE RIGHT CHOICE: SELECTING A DISCIPLE WHO WILL FLOURISH

1. Quoted by Bennett, Ron and Purvis, John, *The Adventure of Discipling Others* (Colorado Springs: NavPress, 2003), 95.
2. Coleman, *The Master Plan of Evangelism*, 28.

CHAPTER 7—BASICS OF A DISCIPLESHIP MINISTRY: FOLLOWING THE EXPERT

1. Twain, Mark, *Letter to an Unidentified Person* (1908), quoted in John Bartlett, *Familiar Quotations*, chief ed., Emily Morison Beck (Boston: Little, Brown and Co., 1980), 626.
2. Ogden, *Transforming Discipleship* 135.
3. McDonald, Gordon, *Restoring Your Spiritual Passion* (Nashville: Thomas Nelson, 1985), 191.
4. Ogden, *Transforming Discipleship*, 126.
5. Hodges, *"Jesus the Greatest Disciple-maker of Christian History*, 4–5.
6. Coleman, *The Master Plan of Evangelism*, 74.
7. Ibid., 76.
8. Ogden, *Transforming Discipleship*, 145–149
9. Moore, *New Testament Follow-up*, 68.

CHAPTER 8—GOING TO THE NEXT LEVEL:
A DEEPER UNDERSTANDING OF DISCIPLESHIP

1. Kravetz, Andy, "Sargent Gets 100 Years in Prison," *Peoria Journal Star*, June 25, 2009, http://www.pjstar.com/homepage/x135726492/Peoria-man-sentenced-to-100-years-in-prison-for-death-of-son; Kravetz, "Mother Receives 50 Years for Baby's Death, *Peoria Journal Star*, Sept. 14, 2009, http://www.pjstar.com/news/x1808445687/Peoria-woman-sentenced-to-50-years-for-death-of-son (accessed 9/7/13).
2. Moore, *New Testament Follow-up*), 19.
3. Hodges, *Fox Fever*, 184.
4. Quoted by Bennet and Parvis, *The Adventure of Discipling*, 98.

CHAPTER 9—THE OBSTACLES TO GROWTH:
PROBLEMS AND SOLUTIONS IN DISCIPLESHIP

1. *The Visitor Magazine*, Columbia Union Conference, 5427 Twin Knolls Road, Columbus, MD, 21045, April 1984.

2. *D. L. Moody's Anecdotes, Incidents and Illustrations* (Chicago: Fleming H. Revell Company, 1898), 101–102.
3. Briscoe, Stuart, message presented at Moody Bible Institute, Founder's Week, 1986.

CHAPTER 11—THE PROCEDURE OF DISCIPLE MAKING:
A STEP-BY-STEP APPROACH

1. Hadidian, *Successful Discipling*, 31–32.
2. Hodges, *Fox Fever*, 101.

CHAPTER 12—SMALL-GROUP DISCIPLE MAKING:
A COMPANION TO THE LIFE-ON-LIFE APPROACH

1. Atkinson, Harley, *The Power of Small Groups in Christian Education* (Naperville, IL: Evangel Publishing House, 2002), 10.

CHAPTER 13—DISCIPLESHIP AT HOME:
PARENTS—THE PREMIER DISCIPLERS OF CHILDREN

1. Grigg, Viv, *Companion to the Poor* (Monrovia, CA: MARC, 1990), 29.
2. Morehouse Conference on African American Fathers, *Turning the Corner on Father Absence in Black America* (Morehouse Research Institute, 830 Westview Dr. SW Atlanta, GA 30314 (404) 215-2676); Institute for American Values 1841 Broadway, Suite 211, New York, NY 10023 (212) 541-6665), 6.
3. Tripp, Tedd, *Shepherding a Child's Heart* (Wapwallopen, PA: Shepherd Press, 1995), 80.
4. Ibid., 84.
5. Ibid., 113–114.
6. Lloyd, Janice, "Home Schooling Grows," *USA Today*, January, 5, 2009, http://www.usatoday.com/news/education/2009-01-04-home schooling_N.htm (accessed 9/10/13).
7. Barnes, Albert, *Barnes' Notes on the Old Testament*, reference Proverbs 22:6.
8. Lewis, Robert, *Raising a Modern-Day Knight* (Colorado Springs: Focus on the Family Publishing, 1997), 75.
9. Walvoord, John F. and Zuck, Roy B., *The Bible Knowledge Commentary: An Exposition of the Scriptures by Dallas Seminary Faculty* (Wheaton, IL: Victor Books, 1985), reference Prov. 22:6.
10. Ibid.

CHAPTER 14—DISCIPLING CHILDREN THROUGH THE CHURCH:
WHEN PARENTAL DISCIPLESHIP IS NOT AVAILABLE

1. Kinnaman, David, *You Lost Me: Why Young Christians Are Leaving Church*, (Grand Rapids, MI, Baker Books, 2011), 24.
2. Barna Group, "Evangelism Is Most Effective Among Kids," October 11, 2004, http://www.barna.org/barna-update/article/5-barna-update/196-evangelism-is-most-effective-among-kids? (accessed 9/10/13).

CHAPTER 15—WHY HAVE WE FAILED?
A COURSE CORRECTION FOR REVOLUTIONARY IMPACT

1. Quoted in Ogden, *Transforming Discipleship*, 22.
2. Ibid., 43.
3. Koessler, *True Discipleship*, 176.
4. Ogden, loc. cit., 43.
5. Barna, *Growing True Disciples*, 46.
6. Coleman, *The Master Plan of Discipleship* 15.
7. Barna, *Growing True Disciples* 94–96.
8. Groeschel, Craig, *IT: How Churches and Leaders can Get IT and Keep IT*, (Grand Rapids, MI: Zondervan, 2008), 62.
9. Quoted in Watson, David, *Called and Committed* (Wheaton, IL, Harold Shaw, 1982), 53.
10. Coleman, *The Master Plan of Evangelism*, 21.

Also by John Thompson

After thirty years of urban ministry, John Thompson writes *Urban Impact: Reaching the World through Effective Urban Ministry:*

Half the world's population lives in cities of one million or more. If we don't reach and disciple from these masses, our future missionary and pastoral force will be diminished.

Urban Impact: Reaching the World Through Effective Urban Ministry (Wipf & Stock, 2010) is a trumpet call to muster our forces, and deals with the philosophy and practical principles that make any urban ministry successful. Brandishing a practical writing style coupled with real-life experiences, John Thompson helps the reader understand the problems, burdens, joys, and powerful impact cities have on the rest of society.

Thompson elaborates on seven principles that will help any city pastor or missionary develop an effective urban ministry. The book then turns to two of the leading challenges of great cities: The first, how to reach the disenfranchised: those from minority groups, people who have substance abuse problems, and the homeless, to name but a few. The second challenge deals with one of the foundational problems in our cities and in all of society: the plight of the absent father. Other chapters address urban discipleship as the most effective approach to promote life transformation; planting churches in a difficult urban environment; and a topic rarely discussed in urban books, raising a family in the city.

For more information please visit: www.urbanimpactbooks.com.

Contact the Author

After many years in pastoral ministry, John currently serves on staff with The Navigators, an international, interdenominational Christian ministry, where he coaches pastors and works with churches on making disciples.

Visit John's blog and further develop your disciple-making ministry:

www.making-disciples.com

- Read practical articles on disciple making
- Participate in discussions
- Enjoy podcasts: Training seminars with handouts, along with video presentations